The Future of Marketing

The Future of Marketing

Strategies from 15 Leading Brands
on How Authenticity, Relevance, and
Transparency Will Help You Survive
the Age of the Customer

Nick Johnson

Publisher: Paul Boger

Editor-in-Chief: Amy Neidlinger

Operations Specialist: Jodi Kemper

Cover Designer: Chuti Prasertsith

Managing Editor: Kristy Hart

Senior Project Editor: Lori Lyons

Copy Editor: Krista Hansing Editorial

Proofreader: Debbie Williams

Senior Indexer: Cheryl Lenser

Compositor: Patricia Ratcliff

Manufacturing Buyer: Dan Uhrig

© 2015 by Nicholas Johnson

Pearson Education, Inc.

Old Tappan, New Jersey 07675

For information about buying this title in bulk quantities, or for special sales opportunities (which may include electronic versions; custom cover designs; and content particular to your business, training goals, marketing focus, or branding interests), please contact our corporate sales department at corpsales@pearsoned.com or (800) 382-3419.

For government sales inquiries, please contact governmentsales@pearsoned.com.

For questions about sales outside the U.S., please contact international@pearsoned.com.

Company and product names mentioned herein are the trademarks or registered trademarks of their respective owners.

Printed in the United States of America

First Printing: June 2015

ISBN-10: 0-13-408450-0

ISBN-13: 978-0-13-408450-3

Pearson Education LTD.

Pearson Education Australia PTY, Limited.

Pearson Education Singapore, Pte. Ltd.

Pearson Education Asia, Ltd.

Pearson Education Canada, Ltd.

Pearson Educación de Mexico, S.A. de C.V.

Pearson Education—Japan

Pearson Education Malaysia, Pte. Ltd.

Library of Congress Control Number: 2015935956

Contents

Introduction 1

    Who Is It For? 2

    Research and Development 4

    A Note on Contributors 5

PART I   **WHAT'S CHANGED?** 9

Chapter 1   The 4 P's Are Passé 11

    Power Has Changed Hands 12

    How Has the Brand/Customer Relationship
       Changed? 15

        A Brief History of Online Marketing 15

        A Free Loudspeaker for All! 17

    New Competitors + More Noise = Need for
       Relevance 18

        Noise Levels Are Increasing 19

        Digital Has Changed the Game Marketers and
          Consumers Are Playing 20

        How Has the Changing Media Landscape
          Changed the Marketer's Role? 21

        How Media Disruption Has Impacted
          Marketers 23

        A Fragmented, "Transmedia" Landscape 25

        Things Are a Lot Harder Than They Were Back
          in the 1990s 28

        It's Not All Bad... 29

    How Does the "Flood" of Customer Data Impact the
       Marketer's Role? 29

        From Art to Science 30

        More Data = More Accountability 31

    The Democratization of Your Brand 32

        Your Customers Have More Choice and Power . . . 33

        Backstory Is More Important Than Tagline 34

        The Impact of the Global Financial Crisis 34

        Brand Is a Conversation Between Companies
          and Their Customers 35

Not Everything Has Changed: The Fundamentals
Remain the Same. 37

    ART Means Major Changes Must Be Made 41

The New Customer Contract: Authenticity, Relevance,
and Transparency. 41

    The New Customer Contract: Authenticity. 42

    The New Customer Contract: Relevance 44

    The New Customer Contract: Transparency 45

How ART Will Impact the Future of Marketing 46

Endnotes 48

Chapter 2 **What Is a Customer Journey, and Why Does
It Matter?** 53

The Customer Journey Means Expanded Roles 56

Endnotes 56

PART II   **HOW ARE COMPANIES COPING?**. **59**

Chapter 3 **How Are Companies Doing Right Now?** 61

The Marketer's Expanding Role: Confusion on
Next Steps 62

Internal Structures Are Beginning to Change. 62

Collaboration Is Key. 63

    Departure Lounge 66

Marketing Is Under Pressure to Increase Speed 68

    1. Customers Expect Responses to Queries Far
    More Quickly. 68

    2. Customers Reward Marketing Campaigns That
    Are Closely Linked to Developments in the
    World Around Them 70

    3. New Platforms Reach Maturity (and Huge
    User Bases) More Quickly Than Ever 70

    4. Data and New Measurement Methodologies
    Quickly Give Marketers Usable Insight into
    Campaign Success 72

How Are Marketers Beginning to Increase the Speed? . . 73

Media Fragmentation Is Tough to Deal With. 74

    Things Are Changing Fast 76

Marketers Must Mix Paid, Earned, and Owned
Channels. 76

Delivering a Consistent Brand Message Is
Increasingly Challenging 77

The Speed with Which Channel Fragmentation
Is Taking Place Is a Challenge All Its Own 79

Most Companies Are Not Fully Leveraging Customer
Data for Better Customer Insight 80

A Long Way to Go—But There's Increasing Clarity
on the Route to Take 82

Next Steps 83

Endnotes 84

PART III   BUILDING FOR THE FUTURE 85

Chapter 4   Brand Management and Storytelling 87

Managing a Brand in Collaboration with Customers 87

Experience Supersedes Logo 87

Brand Is How a Company Acts As a
Corporate Citizen 88

How Can Brand Storytelling Help? 89

This Isn't a New Coat of Paint—It's Deeper
Than That 92

How Can You Build Storytelling into Your Marketing
Campaign? 93

The Battle Between Art and Science Isn't Over Yet 94

Endnotes 94

Chapter 5   Getting Your House in Order: How Internal Buy-In
Impacts External Marketing 95

Consistent Experience Across Multiple Channels Is
Hard but Essential 96

Transparency Makes Consistency Essential 98

Build Your Corporate Onion 98

Internal Is Where This All Begins 99

Step 1: Build from the Ground Up, Not the
Top Down 100

Step 2: Build a Clear Role for the Individual and
Highlight the Benefits of That Role 100

Step 3: Immerse Your Employees in the Journey
to Reassure Them 101

Step 4: Focus on the Long Term, Not the "Year
of Customer Experience" 103
Endnotes 103
Molson Coors Case Study 104

Chapter 6   **How an Evolved Internal Structure Drives Authentic,
Relevant, and Transparent Marketing** **119**
The Chief Marketing Officer's Evolution 120
From Part of the Matrix to a Leadership Role . . . 121
Why a Centralized Marketing Community
Is Critical 122
Should Marketing Expand Itself Out of
Existence? 124
Splitting the Marketing Department 124
New Roles and Responsibilities 126
Focus on Agility 127
Why IT, Data, and Marketing Departments
Need to Work Together 128
Breaking Down Silos for a More Comprehensive
Customer Picture 130
Unification of Information 131
Internal Data 132
Uniformity of Response 133
Randstad Case Study 134
Endnotes 137

Chapter 7   **Data for Relevance and Agility** **139**
Importance of Data and Science 139
1: The Scale Is Incredible 139
2: The Opportunity Is Enormous—and the
Imperative Is Unavoidable 140
3: You're Now Competing with
Digital Natives 141
4: Data Helps You Spot Problems 142
Setting Up for Data 143
1: Hiring the Right People and Evolving the
Marketer's Role 144
2: Build the Right Organizational Model 144
3: Set Clear Goals Aligned to Overall
Corporate Goals 145
4: Find the Signal in the Noise 146

The Benefits One Can Expect from a Comprehensive,
Forward-Looking Approach to Data Management
and Analysis 147

Better Understanding for More Relevance 150

Finally, a Replacement for Focus Groups 151

Enhanced Relevance: Building Better Campaigns—
and Better Products. 152

Examples of Brands Using Data for Better
Marketing. 153

Data for More Agility: Insight at Speed for
On-the-Fly Campaign Evolution 156

Data is not a miracle cure. There are limits to
its utility. 157

Allowing Data to Replace Creativity 158

Are we headed for a data drought? 158

Avoiding Creepiness. 160

Conclusions 161

Endnotes 162

One Medical Group Case Study. 164

KidZania Case Study 170

Land O'Lakes Case Study 180

Chapter 8   **Why Multichannel Matters** **183**

You've Got to Spread Yourself Thin. 185

Work out Which Channels Are Worth the
Money to You. 186

Define How to Use Channels Appropriately. 187

You've Got to Make Sure That Channels
Work in Some Form of Harmony 188

Multichannel As a Foundation. 190

Endnotes 190

Hiscox Case Study. 180

Chapter 9   **Content Marketing to Drive Engagement** **197**

Create Content of the Requisite Quality. 200

Relevance: Appealing Directly and Engagingly to
Your Customers 201

Content That Is Useful. 201

Content That Is Entertaining. 202

Disseminate Content in the Right Way 203

Measure Impact and Track Success. 204

Endnotes 205

Chapter 10   The Imperative—and Opportunity—
of Conversation 207

How Conversation Drives Authenticity 210

Conversation Isn't Optional 211

Set Up for Social 213

7 Elements of Successful Conversational Marketing
from Brands Who've Done It Well 214

1: Strike a Chord That Appeals 214

2: Be Ready to Listen 215

3: Get Everyone Singing from the Same
Hymn Sheet 216

4: Ensure That Data Has Been Shared and
Silos Have Been Eradicated 216

5: Expose the "Latently Happy" 217

6: Don't Just Talk about Your Products 217

7: Don't Cause a Scene 218

Endnotes 226

PART IV   A PROPOSED NEW DEPARTMENT 229

Chapter 11   The Marketing Department of the Future 231

How Will Companies Deliver on Art? 233

1: The Marketing Department Will Put Customer
Experience at the Center of Its Operations . . . 233

2: A Simple Structure to Enhance Agility 236

3: New Skill Sets for a New World 239

4: The Walls between Employees and Customers
Come Down 241

Final Conclusions 243

Endnotes 244

Index 245

To my parents, who taught me that what you do
is more important than what you say.

About the Author

Nick Johnson is founder and CEO of the Incite Group, a leading business intelligence firm that provides highly relevant, research-based insights on customer experience for the marketing, communications, and advertising communities. He has worked closely with chief marketing officers and other senior executives from major brands since founding his first company, Useful Social Media, in 2009.

Introduction

I'll let you in on a secret. I'm a bit of a skeptic. I've worked in marketing for close to ten years now and founded two companies focused closely on the business of marketing for large corporations.

And gosh, there are a whole lot of snake oil salesmen, aren't there?

It's the names that give it away. Who, apart from 8-year-old boys and highly trained martial artists, calls himself a ninja? Why are there so many "gurus" nowadays? Why so many "rock stars" and so few guitar solos?"

My day job is to run a business intelligence company called the Incite Group. I founded it based on the observation that I wasn't the only one getting a bit tired of the big promises and buzzwords spouted all across the marketing "community." The gurus, the ninjas, and the rock stars talked a big game, but weren't giving much in the way of real-world, stress-tested, practical advice.

Marketers kept telling me that what they wanted, really, was to talk to each other. To people "at the coalface," people with real-world experience—not people with a couple big ideas and a slick Power-Point deck.

So that's what we facilitate with Incite—bringing together executives to have a robust, skeptical debate about the future of marketing. And that's how I've written this book: Ask the right people the right questions, and then get out of the way.

The book in your hands isn't my "'manifesto," nor am I attempting to foist a "Big Idea" on you. I do, however, introduce a new acronym (I know. Sorry): *ART* stands for Authenticity, Relevance, and Transparency. It has become increasingly clear to me that these three words should be the pillars of any marketing strategy moving forward.

The decision as to whether to use the three-letter acronym that arose as a result of my research was not one taken lightly (marketing is blessed with hundreds of these things), but I felt it would have been obtuse to ignore it.

Fundamentally though? I'm a delivery mechanism. This book is the result of years of conversations with senior marketers from major brands around the world. My job has been to listen and learn—spot common threads, identify trends, and turn their wisdom into eleven chapters of marketing analysis and best practice.

Who Is It For?

This book is designed for marketers who want to understand why their role is changing so quickly and how that evolution will continue.

As you can probably tell from the title, it is a pretty broad work. I've attempted to give you not only a clear look into the future of marketing (as anticipated by the people leading the charge into that future), but a grounding in the past—and how we've come to find ourselves in this situation in the first place.

Don't worry—there's depth too, and the book contains numerous practical guidelines and ideas, as well as case studies (from brand building in a multi-channel world to driving internal alignment), charts, and statistics you can use to benchmark your own activities and map your own path into our somewhat turbulent future.

The book is split into four parts:

1. Part I, "What's Changed?" investigates how we've gotten to where we are right now. It looks at the history of marketing (briefly) and the influences on the changing relationship between corporations and their customers. It also delves into why authenticity, relevance, and transparency should be the three pillars of any forward-looking marketing approach.

2. Part II, "How Are Companies Coping?" lays out where companies are right now. Filled with statistics, charts, and benchmarks, this part gives marketing executives clarity on the current corporate response to changing customer expectations. Armed

with this information, you can create benchmarks to ascertain whether you're ahead or behind.

3. Part III, "Building for the Future," highlights some of the core elements in a future-proof approach to marketing and investigates the following areas in depth:

   • **Brand building and storytelling:** Rising customer power has changed what "brand" means and how it is defined. Chapter 4, "Brand Management and Storytelling," looks at why storytelling is so popular and how it can help companies build an authentic brand. You'll find examples of how companies at the cutting edge have made storytelling the crux of their marketing strategy and find guidance on how you can do so as well.

   • **Internal buy-in and structure:** Delivering authenticity, relevance, and transparency requires not only a pretty fundamental restructuring of corporate organizational models, but strong buy-in from both the C-suite and the employee base. Chapter 5, "Getting Your House in Order: Internal Buy-In Impacts External Marketing," and Chapter 6, "How an Evolved Internal Structure Drives Authentic, Relevant, and Transparent Marketing," highlight how leading companies are getting their own houses in order to match up to new customer expectations, with case studies from Molson Coors on encouraging employee buy-in and Randstad on eradicating silos.

   • **Data for relevance and personalization:** Marketing has always been a mix of art and science. Chapter 7, "Data for Relevance and Agility," investigates the extent to which it should be dominated by science, given the flood of data available nowadays. You'll find examples of how successful companies have incorporated data-driven approaches into their marketing organization and see why relevance matters—and how data can help you achieve it. Two case studies spotlight One Medical Group, on using social listening to inform future strategy, and KidZania, on crafting a loyalty scheme to deliver exceptional customer experience through enhanced relevance.

- **Multichannel campaign management:** Chapter 8, "Why Multichannel Matters," looks at how successful marketers are able to deliver success on a rapidly fragmenting marketing landscape. It includes a case study on a multichannel brand launch from insurance company Hiscox.

- **Content:** Look here for examples of exceptional content marketing, currently a popular term in the marketing community. Chapter 9, "Content Marketing to Drive Engagement," explores why relevance is so critical to engaging content, looks at how to disseminate content in the right way, and covers ways to measure impact and track success.

- **Conversations and social media:** Part III also investigates the conversational approach to marketing in a world of social media—particularly in Chapter 10, "The Imperative—and Opportunity—of Conversation." It looks at how brands can build authenticity through conversation and examines the six core elements of conversational marketing taken from brands that have done it well.

4. Finally, Part IV, "A Proposed New Department," lays out one vision for what the future of marketing could look like. This part attempts to provide a framework for success in the years ahead, based on feedback from chief marketing officers (CMOs) from around the world.

Research and Development

The fundamental basis of this book is the primary research I conduct daily in my role as founder of the Incite Group. I am lucky enough to spend my time working with senior marketers from major brands around the world. Those conversations began to coalesce around a few key ideas back in early 2014.

I spent the latter part of 2014 deep in research, talking in particular with 18 CMOs from major global brands. You'll see detailed submissions, opinions, and predictions from them littered throughout the book, and I owe them a major debt of thanks.

I also conducted a major survey with 426 global marketers, based in-house at large corporations, not at agencies or consultancies. These experts contributed to four in-depth surveys on all elements of marketing's evolution. Charts based on their insight appear throughout the book to provide guidance on where the marketing world is right now, and where they expect to be moving forward. The results of that survey are also interspersed into the text and referred to as "Future of Marketing Survey" in the footnotes.

The full survey results can be accessed at www.nickjohnson.co. Given that responses from our 426 corporate marketers were spread over several surveys, the numbers make a somewhat small foundation on which to build a persuasive argument—so, they have been augmented by research, charts, and statistics from other sources wherever possible.

The result is a book based not on impressions, gut feeling, or guesswork, but, appropriately in an ever more data-focused marketing world, on research, numbers, and insight from those "at the coalface."

A Note on Contributors

I am particularly indebted to several executives whose insight and opinion I reference throughout the book. These senior marketers gave me several hours of their time as part of my research. Although several asked to remain anonymous, the 16 chief marketing and communications officers you'll hear from directly in this work are listed here, in alphabetical order:

1. Victoria Burwell, CMO of educational publisher McGraw-Hill Education. Burwell previously held marketing positions with JP Morgan Chase, Nextel, Gallo Winery, and Headsprout.

2. Dominic Collins, CMO of British multinational financial services company Legal & General. Collins was previously the director of digital for British telecommunications firm EE and also held roles with Orange, Unanimis, Sky, and Autotrader.

3. Frans Cornelis, CMO of Dutch multinational human resources consulting firm Randstad. In addition to serving as vice chairman

of the Dutch Association of Advertisers, Cornelis held marketing roles with KPN, Hillshire Brands, and AT&T.

4. Cammie Dunaway, global CMO and U.S. president for KidZania, the global chain of edutainment centers, and a member of the board of directors for both Nordstrom FSB and Red Robin. Previously, Dunaway was the CMO of Nintendo and Yahoo! She began her sales and marketing career at Frito Lay.

5. Russ Findlay, head of marketing for Hiscox USA, the American arm of the U.K. insurance firm. Previously, Findlay held senior marketing roles with Major League Soccer, Town Sports International, IHOP, and PepsiCo.

6. Andy Gibson, who when I spoke to him was CMO and president of Bacardi, the largest privately held, family-owned spirits company in the world. Previously, Gibson held senior marketing roles with Carlton United Breweries, Diageo, McDonald's, and Masterfoods.

7. John Kennedy, CMO of Xerox Corporation, the American multinational document management corporation. Previously, Kennedy held roles with IBM, Procter & Gamble, and Bank of America.

8. Jean-Claude Larreche, the Alfred H. Heineken Chaired Professor of Marketing at graduate business school INSEAD, and the founder and chairman of international management development firm StratX. He previously held non-executive directorships at both Reckitt Benckiser and Smart Pool. He is also the author of several books, including *The Momentum Effect: How to Ignite Unlimited Growth*.

9. Dan Lewis, chief public affairs officer of Molson Coors Brewing Company, a major global brewer. Lewis previously held communications and public relations roles with Delta Air Lines and Lufthansa.

10. Chris Linder, the president of Keds, the American shoe brand. Linder was previously the CMO for Sperry Top-Sider and Saucony, and he held marketing roles with Nike, Converse, and Electronic Arts.

11. Cavin Pietzsch, the general manager of General Electric Energy Management in Germany. He was previously the CMO of General Electric Germany, and he held sales and marketing roles with Súwag Energie AG and enviaM.

12. Marco Ryan, chief digital officer at Thomas Cook Group, the global travel company. He previously held roles with CapGemini, Accenture, and Premier Farnell. He is the author of the forthcoming book *The Digital Onion*.

13. Jason West, who when I spoke with him was CMO of North America for the food processing company H.J. Heinz. He previously held roles with Procter & Gamble and Bank of America.

14. Barry Wolfish, CMO and senior vice president of corporate strategy for Land O'Lakes, Inc., the member-owned agricultural cooperative focused on the dairy industry. Wolfish is a board member at Egglands Best, Moark, and Aseptic Food Products. He was previously a board member of the Dairy Marketing Alliance and he held marketing roles at General Mills.

15. Arra Yerganian, CMO of One Medical Group, the fast-growing American primary care medical practice. Yerganian was previously the CMO of the University of Phoenix, and he held roles at Lennar, Pulte Group, and Switchouse.

16. Michael Zuna, CMO and senior vice president of American insurance company Aflac. Zuna previously held roles at Arnold and Saatchi & Saatchi, where he was managing director.

The chapters in this book are the result of feedback from those executives and many of their peers—all of whom I've been lucky enough to learn from and work with over the years.

The result, I hope, is an insightful, cutting edge look at the future of marketing—coming straight from the people taking us there.

PART I
WHAT'S CHANGED?

1 The 4 Ps Are Passé 11

2 What Is a Customer Journey, and Why Does It Matter? . . . 53

1

The 4 P's Are Passé

"When I first became a marketer, we really believed that we could understand the environment, design products and services to address needs in the marketplace, and communicate directly to consumers using some fairly well-defined channels—and things would magically happen."

—Barry Wolfish, Chief Marketing Officer, Land O'Lakes

One can detect an air of wistfulness when talking with chief marketing officers (CMOs) nowadays.

If you glance at conference agendas, white papers, or the marketing trade press, you are welcomed with a plethora of new buzzwords and acronyms almost daily. *Digital* and *social*, en vogue just a few years ago, have been swiftly superseded by terms such as *omnichannel*, *native advertising*, and *programmatic*.

The applicability of these topics to the upper echelons of large corporations is still very much up for debate. But the fact that marketing departments around the world are facing a shifting, increasingly complex, and challenging new landscape is not.

In the course of conducting research for this book, I spent many hours talking with some of the most respected chief marketing officers from some of the most successful companies in the world. Their products and services span a wide range, from energy to entertainment, beer to ketchup, and electronics to education. I collected plenty of different insights, challenges, and opportunities. But one observation brings everyone into agreement:

Things are an awful lot more complicated than they've ever been.

Cammie Dunaway was one of the first CMOs I spoke with. During her more than 30 years in marketing, she has worked for companies that include Frito Lay, Nintendo, and Yahoo!; she served as CMO for the latter two companies. Now CMO at KidZania, a global chain of "edutainment" centers, Cammie is well-placed to reflect on the evolutions and revolutions in the marketing space during the last 30 years.

Previously, the formula for success was somewhat less complicated, Cammie says: "You learned your 4 P's of marketing, and provided you applied your particular brand challenges to that known framework, and had good products and good advertising, success was fairly predictable."

That's no longer the case. Over the last decade, a plethora of new influences—with digital and social technology to the fore—have increased the complexity of the marketer's role. Senior marketing leaders from a range of industries have made clear that the framework Cammie mentions has been dismantled. The rules of marketing—the famous 4 P's of Product, Price, Place, and Promotion—have been disrupted, and relying on that old framework is simply not sufficient in the face of unprecedented change.

"You still have the same goals, but all of a sudden, all the traditional wisdom that you've relied on isn't serving you anymore," Cammie says.

Power Has Changed Hands

The past ten years have seen a change in relationship between corporations and their customers. Essentially, the power has shifted away from the company and toward the consumer.

Customers can kill brand redesigns. Just ask Gap, who was forced to roll back a logo redesign in the face of social media uproar. Customers can kill entire brand strategies. Look at the Netflix decision to abort the Quikster brand when separating out that company's DVD and streaming business components. Customers also can demote incumbents in favor of disruptive newcomers with better customer experience. Look at the fortunes of taxi firms since Uber and Lyft came on the scene.

Previously successful marketing campaigns no longer pass muster, either. Look at the famous Modoc Oil Test, highlighted by the team at Marketing Experiments in the white paper *Transparent Marketing*. In 1885, an advertisement appeared in the *Altoona Tribune* in Blair County, Pennsylvania, promoting a new miracle cure, Modoc Oil. It certainly wasn't shy about highlighting the benefits of this new wonderstuff:

> Modoc Oil—the greatest medicine on earth. It has no equal. It relieves all pain instantly: Toothache in one minute—Headache in one minute—Earache in ten minutes—Sore throat in one night—Neuralgia in from three to five minutes...Modoc Oil is a sure and speedy cure. Every family should have a bottle within reach. It's a doctor in the house.[1]

The response was so explosive, and the demand so high, that the company producing this frankly incredible substance had to build an enormous new factory in Corry, Pennsylvania. It was still firing on all cylinders in 1912.

Nowadays, that approach simply doesn't work. The Marketing Experiments team put that exact same advertisement in a similar paper with a circulation of 35,000. They got no sales.

Of course, this is a rather simplistic example, but it speaks to a broader truth. What customers expect has changed. They're wary of "marketing." They're skeptical. And gaining their trust requires a lot more than overblown claims of instantaneous pain relief.

This shift is forcing global companies to reevaluate the fundamentals of how they do business, from product development right through to marketing campaigns. They must reflect this new reality in which the customer is in control, as the vast majority of marketing executives realize:

"73% of marketers now realize that competitive advantage will come from a singular focus on the customer."[2]

In-house, companies are beginning to transition their business models and their organizational structures to reflect the primacy of the customer. This often is known as a "customer-centric" strategy.

Yet although many will tell you that being customer-centric is an old precept masquerading as a new buzzword (after all, haven't companies always focused on the customer?), that thinking is somewhat disingenuous.

For many years now, companies have organized themselves around geographies and product lines. Only since customer power increased have forward-looking companies begun to focus on organizing around customer groups and understanding those groups—and even individual customers—in as much detail as possible.

On the external side, marketing is beginning to create more value for the customer, and striving to be more relevant to their target audiences. The increasing primacy of content as part of a marketing strategy is related to this recognition: Ninety-three percent of brand marketers are planning to create more content in 2015 and beyond[3]— and that's because content marketing can deliver relevance and value, both critical in this new world.

The rules of the game have changed. The rulebook is now written by the customer, not the corporation. Fundamentally, four tectonic shifts have contributed to the transfer of power between brand and customer:

1. **The move online:** Communication, content consumption, and customer touchpoints have all increasingly begun to move online.

2. **An explosion in transparency:** Customers can now see and understand their options far more clearly. Likewise, they are increasingly able to ascertain when someone is trying to make a silk purse out of a sow's ear, regardless of the marketing budget.

3. **A media landscape that is fragmenting quickly:** It's far more difficult for marketers to find their customers and talk to them where they are—and it's also difficult to follow the inherent rules and expectations of new channels and platforms.

4. **Customer data that is more readily available than ever:** Although this means companies have an opportunity to deliver more targeted, relevant campaigns, it also means that competitors are already doing so. Customers increasingly expect an equivalent—relevant and valuable—experience from companies in the same market.

How Has the Brand/Customer Relationship Changed?

"Digital disruption has driven much of this shift. Digitally enabled tools and processes have altered what and how a business sells, flipped the tables on the typical customer relationship, introduced a glut of new channels and competitors, and made it harder for organizations to break through 'the noise.'"[4]

—"The Rebirth of the CMO"

A Brief History of Online Marketing

The first "host-to-host" connection of the ARPANET, the precursor to today's Internet, took place October 29, 1969. Teams of researchers at Stanford University and University of California–Los Angeles shared a single message: "Login".

Two years later, Ray Tomlinson sent the first email—to himself. As far as he recollects, "Most likely the first message was QWERTYUIOP or something similar."[5]

From such inspirational beginnings, digital marketing was born. It took another six years for the first email marketing campaign (DEC Systems 2020's message about the "world's cheapest mainframe computer"[6]) to come to fruition. A full 25 years later, in 1994, the first-ever banner ad went online. It was part of AT&T's "You Will" campaign and featured the proto-clickbait headline "Have you ever clicked your mouse right HERE? YOU WILL."

Three months' worth of space on *Hotwired*, the first commercial web magazine, cost $30,000. In a powerful display of first-mover advantage, the banner achieved a clickthrough rate of 44%. How times change.

The Potential of the Internet Begins to Be Realized

For the first couple decades of its existence, the Internet (and digital technology more broadly) were little more than an academic curiosity. But over time, the world's population began to associate the clicks and whistles of a dial-up modem with a gate opening onto a new "information superhighway." And as customers lead, so companies follow. Customers began to spend more time online, and brands began to invite themselves to the party.

The banner ads ushered in by AT&T were quickly superseded by more sophisticated—and expensive—campaigns. Microsoft paid $200,000 to sponsor the 1996 Super Bowl website, and major nontech brands such as Toyota and Douglas began to spend money on online ads from this point on.[7]

In 2000, Google launched the "pay per click" element of AdWords, the first sighting of what's now known as programmatic advertising. The product brought in $85 million in 2001 and became the bedrock of one of the world's biggest companies.

Transparency Rising

But as the power of the digital world grew, the first rumblings of another fundamental shift were beginning to make themselves felt. Digital technology made it incredibly easy for customers to access information. Importantly, that information was often created and distributed by peers, not the traditional media or advertisers.

The sheer amount of information at a customer's fingertips facilitated a growing discernment in purchasing choice. Customers could compare and contrast price, investigate functionality, check out reviews, and more at the click of a mouse. More than that, they could educate themselves on companies in a way that was impossible previously.

According to Cammie Dunaway, it became thrillingly easy for customers to "find out pretty much anything about your company."

The Internet heralded a new age of transparency in the previously murky relationship between brands, their products, and their customers. This transparency began to shift power from the brand to the customer.

And then in 2005, "social media" was born.

A Free Loudspeaker for All!

In 2005, MySpace and LinkedIn launched, with Facebook following the next year. Web 2.0 and its more sophisticated younger sister, social media, gave customers the ability not only to hear more and understand more, but also to talk more. This development only accelerated the transition of power between brand and customer.

The Internet always had places for online discussion and debate. We've moved from early message boards such as the Well (launched in 1985[8]), through the now-desolate wastelands of Geocities and Tripod, past Friends Reunited and MySpace, through a period of dominance for undisputed leader Facebook. We've now arrived at a fragmented, more privacy-conscious environment populated by one-to-one and small group communications channels such as Snapchat, WhatsApp, and YikYak. That's a considerable departure from the "town square," public approach of Facebook and other social media networks.

Until social media became a societal norm, only companies with significant advertising budgets had the capacity to reach out to many people at one time to get a particular message across. With the advent of a social web, every individual with an Internet connection and something to say was given an industrial-grade loudspeaker powerful enough to be heard around the world.

Nowadays, that means the opinion of a single customer can hold as much weight as reviews from the *New York Times* or *Consumer Reports*. Ninety percent of people say that online reviews influence their purchasing decisions.[9] That development completely changes the customer's journey—and thus the marketer's role. Previously, brand communication played a fundamental part in defining how a brand was seen and determining the viability of products for purchase. These days, however, your customers, empowered by social media, hold that power.

Customers are no longer at the mercy of what a brand is telling them, no longer a prisoner of the marketing budget. Social media has contributed meaningfully to the growth of transparency in the relationship between brands and their customers, handing power to the customer.

New Competitors + More Noise = Need for Relevance

The growing power of digital communications has presented two other challenges to marketers. First, it has lowered the barrier to entry for smaller, more focused competitors. Those companies have begun to compete with established brands through an elevated customer experience in all sorts of industries.

Just look at Marc Speichert, who was the CMO at beauty giant L'Oreal when I spoke with him:

"You have lots of little brands that are appearing, and that are, in aggregation, becoming a pretty big chunk of the overall market."[10]

That means L'Oreal and their ilk are facing competition not only from the big brands they've historically been competing with—and with whom they have a well-established playbook for that competition—but also with smaller, more nimble competitors who bring with them a whole new set of challenges. It's a process that's not going away any time soon.

Thanks to digital distribution and promotion mechanics, a company can start in someone's bedroom and quickly begin to eat into the market share of companies that have boardrooms in the world's major cities.

Those small competitors don't have shareholders. They don't have diversified product lines. And they certainly don't have any of the internal challenges inherent in a company with hundreds of thousands of employees and marketing teams spread around the globe.

What these companies do tend to have is focus on one, or a small number of, products. They also have the ability to ensure that those products are exceptional. In a world increasingly drawn to the artisanal, to craftsmanship and locally sourced goods, the keywords are *authenticity* and *experience* (concepts more fully introduced in the later section "The New Customer Contract: Authenticity, Relevance, and Transparency").

Social media, or "word of mouth on steroids," can help these companies quickly build passionate, engaged audiences. No longer, then, does a company need scale or a multimillion-dollar marketing budget to make a dent in the bottom line of the biggest companies, the biggest advertisers in the world.

These smaller companies tend to be closer to their target audience, with less barriers between employees and customers. That knowledge is put to work to develop products that are more focused, relevant, and attractive to that user base.

When competing with a plethora of small brands like this, the challenge for the multinational company is clear. Where digital marketing has begun to neuter the built-in advantages of scale that previously gave large brands an edge, that large brand must now beat the smaller company at its own game: The larger entity must become as nimble, relevant, and focused on the customer as its competition.

Companies must build processes and systems to be as close to their customers as the brands that live next door to them, regardless of whether they're even on the same continent. They must build products—and marketing campaigns—with the same level of authenticity, focus, and relevance that these smaller companies have as inherent facets of their existence.

Noise Levels Are Increasing

So a legion of smaller competitors is beginning to crowd into already busy marketplaces. At the same time, the marketing landscape is expanding.

The fragmentation of that landscape (first adding channels such as banner ads, pop-ups, and email lists, and now adding social ads, PPC, native, and even programmatic advertising options), not to mention the plethora of platforms springing up in the space between media company and technology provider (Facebook, Twitter, Snapchat, Pinterest, and so on), results in many more opportunities for engaging a customer.

Customers no longer rely on four TV channels; they have access to hundreds. They no longer visit one social network; they split their time across several social and, increasingly, private messaging platforms. That means the places where a brand can contact a consumer are growing.

Marketers are grabbing this opportunity with both hands. Unfortunately, they're grabbing a little too tightly, and they're beginning to throttle their subjects. Customers are now exposed to 577 marketing messages per day. They retain less than 1% of them.[11] And they can increasingly pick and choose what to watch—and what to skip.

This phenomenon puts increasing weight on the importance of relevance. If a brand is to stand out in an ever-more crowded landscape, it must convince customers that it's worth listening to. It must speak to them in the right place, at the right time, with the right message. Otherwise, the brand is just adding to the background noise.

Digital Has Changed the Game Marketers and Consumers Are Playing

Perhaps more than anything else, the rise of digital technologies has led to a redistribution of power from brands to consumers. The Internet, social media, and digital platforms have ushered in a new era of dialogue, information, and transparency. Customers can easily understand both companies and their competitors. Customers have become more discerning as a result.

Thanks to social media, online reviews, and the resulting increased power of word of mouth, the size of your marketing budget will never again make up for poor products and services.

The shift of content distribution to an increasingly digital landscape gives customers more power to choose what to watch—as well as what ads to skip.

The capability of smaller brands (with built-in advantages of customer understanding and relevance) to reach large numbers of people has eradicated the benefits of scale to a significant extent. The exponential growth of locations in which one can market has increased the noise to a deafening degree. If your message isn't valuable or relevant, it will be drowned out.

Customer attention is indeed becoming increasingly scarce. The power is definitely in their hands. This redistribution of power has led to heightened expectations from customers and a change in what they expect from their relationships with major corporations.

But we're not done. Customers aren't the only factors that have fundamentally changed the marketer's role over the last decade or so. Digital models have heralded two other major shifts in the customer–corporate relationship:

1. The media landscape has begun to fragment at great speed.
2. Digital footprints are everywhere. The savvy marketer can use them to hunt their prey more effectively than ever.

How Has the Changing Media Landscape Changed the Marketer's Role?

Unless you've been living under a rock somewhere on the dark side of the moon for the last decade, you'll know that the media landscape has been deeply affected by the changes that a new digital world has wrought.

The impact of digital distribution models, in which content can be transmitted effectively for free to screens as small as new Apple Watches, has shaken up the media industry. Like their peers in marketing departments across the world, media pros have been forced to cede power to their customers.

Digital distribution has led to an explosion of user-generated content and given consumers an unprecedented ability to choose what media they consume, where they do so, and how they do it. This, in turn, has led to an "unpackaging" of subscriptions, an increasing preference for online viewing, and a series of platforms that allow customers to watch what they want, when they want to, and in a location that's convenient for them, whether on the sofa or on the subway.

What does this mean for the marketer? Well, all the traditional marketing channels are undergoing massive disruption, and it's impacting the role those channels play in marketing strategies for companies large and small.

TV

Look at the rise of Internet TV viewing. By the end of 2014, 34% of Millennials[12] said they were watching more TV online than via their television set; 24% of the U.S. population reported watching TV online at least once a day[13], with 19% going without cable subscriptions entirely.[14] In mid-2014, total TV viewing over the Internet grew by 388% versus the same time a year earlier, with the number of unique viewers growing 146% year over year.[15]

Typically, TV provided online gives customers more choice. Not only can they choose when they watch a show (witness the slow decline of the phrase *water cooler TV*), but in many cases, they can choose to do so without ad breaks—or they can at least skip through them. Advertising in a primetime slot during NBC's *The Voice* currently costs about $275,000[16]—that money could buy a whole lot of YouTube, or Facebook, or Google ads.

Print Media

TV's troubles are somewhat dwarfed by the obvious problems we see in print media. Local papers are shuttering every week; the *Boston Globe* sold itself for $70 million to Amazon founder Jeff Bezos in the same month Pierre Omidyar pledged three times as much to found a new digital-only venture titled First Look Media.

Magazine circulation is decreasing, and even the venerable *New York Times* is finding it hard to move as quickly as the Buzzfeeds and Huffington Posts of this world. Those competitors are growing faster than the *New York Times* itself, according to the company's own leaked *Innovation Report*.[17] (The report also highlights the Gray Lady's declining website performance, from 140 million visitors in 2011 down to 80 million in 2013.)

The print advertising industry has revenues of $36.8 billion forecast for 2015, down 9.9% since 2014[18] and representing about 20% of all U.S. ad spend for 2015. Yet according to eMarketer, the average time a U.S. adult spends using print media is falling off a cliff. In 2008, the average U.S. adult spent 63 minutes per day on print media. By 2014, that had dropped to 26 minutes, down nearly 59%.[19] The problems for print aren't over yet.

Radio

At the tail end of 2014, even radio had begun to feel the impact. Digital radio has been around for more than a decade, but by the end of the year, the media press was abuzz with commentary on the renaissance of the podcast. Consider breakout series *Serial*, which garnered 1.5 million listeners per episode.

Podcasting, which incorporates "listen when you want" elements mimicking the core USP of TV delivered over the Internet, has grown 25% year on year from 2013 to 2014.[20] Almost 40 million people currently listen to some form of podcast. Thirty-six percent of all Americans age 12 and older (94 million people) listen to some form of online radio.[21]

How Media Disruption Has Impacted Marketers

These developments have certainly impacted the media industry, and they've had an effect on the marketer's operating environment, too.

Look at Super Bowl advertising costs. A 30-second spot during the Super Bowl cost $4.5 million in February 2015,[22] up 50% from $3 million in 2012. At first, this seems counterintuitive. Surely this proves that TV advertising is in rude health? No—scarcity costs money, and that's the mechanism at play here.

Live sports are one of the last bastions of the age in which families, friends, and communities gather around the television to watch programming communally. They do so at a set time—live viewing is inherent in watching big sporting events (a fact that anyone who has watched a recorded sporting event and felt the peculiar lack of intensity will attest to).

Hence the skyrocketing Super Bowl prices.

It's a reflection of the fact that consumers can skip advertising with the click of a button. Indeed, they can (and do) skip regular scheduled programming altogether. In most cases, a marketer can no longer be sure when or where a particular advert will be viewed. And remember, given the sheer amount of marketing a person is now exposed to, this is a consumer base primed for skipping advertisements.

The explosion of new content distribution channels, coupled with an Internet business model based on free services supported by advertising means, as we've seen, that consumers are hit with an average of 577 individual marketing messages per day. Somewhat unsurprisingly, only 1% of those messages are retained, and consumer appetite for advertising continues to shrink.[23]

An Increasing Need for Relevance

Not only does this shift show that it's somewhat harder to make sensible decisions about ad buying, but it also highlights, again, the need for marketing to be relevant in two ways:

A. It needs to be valuable to the customer: useful, engaging, or entertaining—whatever it takes to encourage people not to skip it.

B. It needs to be visible in places where customers now spend their time. You've got to know the right platforms and channels to put your marketing on, ensuring that the ad is placed in one of those fragmented channels and platforms that customers are actually using.

Forward-looking marketers know that their world has changed irrevocably. In the course of researching this book, I not only spoke with many CMOs personally, but I also surveyed many hundreds of other executives for their views on how marketing has changed, how they're responding, and what the future holds. (Any statistics drawn from the results of this survey will be referenced in the footnotes as "Future of Marketing Survey." The full survey results are available online at www.nickjohnson.co.)

When I asked those executives about their views on traditional channels, the responses were striking: 54% of respondents said that traditional marketing channels (TV, radio, billboards) have *definitely* become less important even over the last five years; another 29% said that's *probably* the case.[24]

The process isn't over, either: 63% of respondents were relatively confident that traditional channels would continue to diminish in importance over the next five years.[25]

The Rise of the Second Screen

Remember the rising cost of those Super Bowl advertising slots? Well, imagine that you're peering in on a family of Seahawks fans at 4:30 p.m. on February 1, 2015. What do you see?

You see the Millennials in the room watching the TV but also trash-talking their Patriots-supporting friends over Twitter. During the 2014 Oscars, 5 million people sent 19 million tweets, seen by 37 million people—considerably more than the viewership of the ceremony itself.[26] Twitter itself has made a great play of wanting to be the "synchronized social soundtrack for whatever is happening in the moment, as a shared experience."

And that's why even with this last bastion of traditional ad models, the 30-second Super Bowl spot, you can see the change that's afoot. Increasingly, Super Bowl advertisements serve as a tent pole for a broader, omnichannel, "transmedia" campaign. In 2015, 50% of all media[27] is now a multiplatform affair: 66% of Americans and 61% of the global population use a "second screen"[28] (typically a phone or tablet) while watching TV. Also, 72% of Twitter users tweet during a live broadcast.[29] The new episode of the British iteration of *X Factor* is accompanied by tweets from more than 1.2 million viewers.[30]

All this brings us to the second great shift in how media is consumed in the twenty-first century: fragmentation.

A Fragmented, "Transmedia" Landscape

From the embers of the traditional marketing landscape has arisen a new type of phoenix—new channels, platforms, and other services that consumers now frequent to get their media of choice. This has led to two fundamental shifts for marketers.

The first is the fact that, as outlined earlier, for a campaign to be truly pervasive, it must increasingly spread itself across multiple platforms and services to engage customers where they are, not where a business would like them to be.

Second, the sheer number of new platforms and services on which your customers spend time is fragmenting every few days. The challenge, as later chapters discuss, is to assess which of these options you could and should use for your next campaign.

New Platforms Grow Fast

On Valentine's Day 2005, YouTube launched into an unsuspecting world. By July 2006, users were viewing 100 million YouTube video clips daily, with 65,000 new videos uploaded in that same time frame.[31]

YouTube (and other user-generated content sites like it) got so popular that the 2006 *Time* Person of the Year was "you": The magazine's cover featured a YouTube screen with a large mirror, highlighting the rapid growth of user-generated content.

At the time of this writing, more than one billion unique users visit YouTube each month, and almost 6 billion hours of video are watched in that period. That's almost an hour for every person on earth, according to official YouTube figures.[32]

In April 2014, Google (which bought YouTube in 2006) launched a marketing campaign to promote the service, with ads placed on Google services, TV, print, and billboards. The transport network in London, New York, and similar cities was filled with advertisements, and TV networks from ABC to the CW ran ads highlighting the network's roster of stars.

When you look closely at the ads, you might wonder why Google bothered. There, in relatively small type, was a number—a big number. It denoted the number of subscribers the profiled personality had on YouTube itself.

Three personalities initially were chosen for the campaign. Michelle Phan, a beauty "vlogger," had 7 million subscribers in late 2014 and secured a recent cosmetic partnership with L'Oreal as a result of her success. Bethany Mota, a stylist, had more than 8 million subscribers in late 2014 and boasted a clothing line co-designed with Aeropostale. The third star profiled was Rosanna Pansino, who had a comparatively paltry 3 million subscribers to her online cookery show.

Given those numbers, it's unsurprising that YouTube is now an established location for brands to allocate their marketing budgets: A hefty $5.6 billion was spent on advertising on the platform in 2013.[33]

New platforms and sites are springing up constantly. For many Millennials, the 30-minute TV program is an alien concept; they prefer the 4-minute clip. Indeed, even these short bursts of entertainment are being superseded. Consider Vines, capped at 6 seconds, or even the increasingly popular 1SecondEveryDay app (with the most backers ever for a Kickstarter campaign and a profile raised through placement in the recent Hollywood film "Chef"), which allows users to shoot and then share 1-second video clips.

In other areas, new platforms are springing up almost daily. Flipboard, a news aggregation app, has 90 million active users. By contrast, the newspaper with the highest circulation, the *Wall Street Journal*, has just 2.4 million subscribers. Online, the *New York Times* home page traffic has shrunk from 140 million in 2008 to less than 80 million by 2013.

The launch of a viable new advertising channel used to happen rarely. The launch of an entirely new advertising medium was even more infrequent. Yet in these early years of the twenty-first century, both phenomena are occurring fairly often.

The Millennial generation, of which I am a part, is nothing if not fickle. Check out MySpace, Bebo, or, further back, Geocities. They're almost quaint in how passé they now seem.

In August 2006, the 100 millionth MySpace account was opened; by 2007, MySpace was valued at $12 billion. Now it's a depressing procession of empty profiles, flashing text, and autoplaying pop songs. At the time of the latest site redesign in 2013, users there to see it had plummeted to 36 million.

But then check out the growth numbers of Ello, Snapchat, and WhatsApp. This is where customers are moving this year. Last year, it was Pinterest, Tumblr, and Vine. Next year, who knows?

Ninety-four percent of marketers think that the pace of change in their role has increased.[34] One of the most common comments I hear is that this pace of change is terrifying and almost unmanageable, certainly within current corporate structures and processes. Yet adjusting to this speed is a critical part of the marketing campaign of the future. According to a recent study by Rishi Bhandari, Marc Singer, and Hiek van der Scheer for McKinsey, the best-performing marketers reallocate up to 80% of their marketing spend while a campaign is in progress.[35]

There's no sign of things slowing down anytime soon.

Things Are a Lot Harder Than They Were Back in the 1990s

The relationship between marketing budget and marketing reach was once somewhat simple: Pay more money, get in front of more eyeballs (notwithstanding John Wanamaker's oft-repeated aphorism "Half the money I spend on advertising is wasted. The trouble is, I don't know which half"[36]). Nowadays, complexity reigns.

As Barry Wolfish, CMO at Land O'Lakes, told me, there's "an incredible fragmentation of ways to reach the end user."

Of course, another challenge is that whereas TV advertisements were relatively uninterrupted, nowadays every message is competing with many others—at the same time. This is largely due to the second screen phenomenon in TV and the multitude of other content (and ads) presented on the same page online.

The uninterrupted TV spots of old are no more. Your new video ad, playing in Facebook's news feed, is presented alongside messages and photos from your potential customer's friends and family. Your online banner ad is located on a page within an article your viewer has actually decided to read. Your Twitter campaign is surrounded by tweets from news organizations, celebrities, and friends that your customer has actually chosen to follow.

People have an unprecedented amount of "noise" blaring at them daily. For brands, becoming the signal in that noise is getting ever more challenging.

Michael Zuna, CMO of insurance giant Aflac, asked me some good questions: "How do I reach Nick Johnson? How do I engage with you and connect with you in the most effective way, given the proliferation of media opportunities you're engaged with on a daily basis? That challenge is multiplying at a significant rate."

His concerns add weight to the theory that, for marketing to be successful, it must be both valuable to consumers and relevant to their needs and interests.

It's Not All Bad...

Of course, this coin has another side. If marketers use this plethora of options well and coordinate campaigns across many channels with consistency, providing value and relevance, these changes become an opportunity. Victoria Burwell of McGraw-Hill put it best when alluding to Wanamaker's famous aphorism:

"Before, it was much more spray and pray. You put up one ad that you hope got folks across the nation. Now, I can send not only distinct messages to distinct people, but using a vehicle I know they'd prefer. While they're searching, I can catch them. I think we just have so much more data that we can actually personalize the message, because we understand the customer so much more."

For marketers to run successful campaigns, it's essential that they provide relevant, valuable creative material across a plethora of channels. Those channels change fast, so it's essential to pick the ones where your customers hang out. And people tend to be doing two things at once now—second screens are the new norm—so the campaign must be multifaceted and available across multiple channels.

Fundamentally, brands must understand customers—their habits, their needs, and their usual behaviors—better than ever if they want to flourish in this challenging and rapidly evolving space.

How Does the "Flood" of Customer Data Impact the Marketer's Role?

With the rise of the digital world, and with the concurrent growth of online media business models based on advertising-supported free services that track customer behavior, the world has been flooded with data.

According to a 2013 study, 90% of the sum total of the world's data had been created within the last two years. According to the U.K.'s *Daily Telegraph*, back in 2007, YouTube consumed the same amount of bandwidth as the entire Internet at the turn of the millennium.[37]

The explosion is still continuing. Later chapters cover how this data has been leveraged; this chapter moves on to investigate how this flood of data has changed the relationship between brand and customer.

From Art to Science

For as long as many in marketing can remember, the marketing function was acknowledged to be a delicate blend of art and science. To many of its critics in the boardroom, the needle often swung too far toward art.

Nowadays, science holds sway. Frans Cornelis, Chief Marketing Officer at global employment services provider Randstad, told me that:

"You're no longer going to become CMO if you don't know the numbers. [Marketing] has changed. It used to be—and there are still some places where this exists—that a beautiful campaign from the aesthetic point of view could conquer all evils. But in the vast majority of cases, marketers now must have an appreciation of the nitty gritty."

Marketing2020[38], an in-depth study initiated by Millward Brown and led by Keith Weed, CMO at Unilever, found some interesting results: "Companies that are sophisticated in their use of data grow faster."

Seventy-two percent of the marketing teams categorized by the study as "overperformers" were making their decisions based heavily on the back of data insights, versus 45% of those labelled "underperformers."

Why does data have such an impact on marketing success? In large part, it's because a marketer's customer base has grown used to data—or rather, to the benefits customer experience gains from data. Those customers expect the relevance, precision, and value that a data-led marketing department provides. As Dominic Collins, Chief Marketing Officer for UK insurer Legal & General, puts it:

"Digital homogenizes expectations. That means that if you're in a more heritage type business, or a legacy business, and you're competing with pure [digital] plays, you can't get away with not making the entire experience of your organization more digital and more modern."

When a customer has experienced marketing from a data-led company—enabled by that data to provide timely, relevant messaging—those customers begin to expect this level of experience from every company they interact with.

This can be a problem for legacy brands. Virtually every market has a number of "digital native" companies: Consider Uber in taxi service, Netflix in media, and Airbnb in hospitality, to name but three.

Perhaps the most famous, and one of the earliest examples, is Amazon, the retail behemoth. Amazon and its peers have educated customers to expect a level of personalized service in their interaction with brands. Customers logging in to Amazon's site see a personalized list of products. These customers see this not as an exceptional level of personalized service, but as the norm. "If the place where I buy my books can deliver personalized, relevant products and experiences, why can't my bank? Why can't the place where I buy my sneakers?"

For "predigital" companies competing with Amazon, not matching up to this new normal is a serious problem. It's increasingly hard for these "heritage" companies to be able to get away with not offering an entire customer experience that's more modern, relevant, and personalized. Data has driven a deep shift in customer expectation of their relationship with your brand.

More Data = More Accountability

Data also has had significant impacts on the marketer's role internally. Close to 75% of CEOs agree with the statement that marketers "are always asking for more money, but can rarely explain how much incremental business this money will generate."[39] Marketers themselves seem aware of their weakness in tracking impact: Just over one-third say they can quantitatively prove the impact of their marketing outlay.

The increased availability of data has only added pressure on marketers to prove that impact. The belt-tightening engendered by the Financial Crisis of 2008 has prompted boardrooms to expect marketers to tie their activity to corporate KPIs. What's more, marketers are being asked to do more with less. As Cornelis from Randstad points out, "The fat has been squeezed out of the industry."

Marketers are under increasing pressure to stretch their budget a little further, of course—but it also means they're expected to show real, tangible results for any campaign they produce.

The increasing capacity to track success and understand the more granular impacts of marketing decisions and strategies means the three-martini lunch, with ad space bought over drinks and a steak dinner, is a thing of the past. Were a marketer to repeat the tired old Wanamaker adage about not knowing which half of his budget was working, he wouldn't be greeted with wry laughter and backslapping—he'd get a box containing his personal items and a request for his security pass.

Ten years ago, most marketing departments weren't asked to show much in the way of return on investment (ROI). Nowadays, in this data-rich age, ROI is a huge focus. In fact, new three-letter acronyms have sprung up to keep consultants' pockets lined and CMOs' headaches consistent: return on engagement, return on relationship, and so on. As insightful metrics, they may all have limited utility—but one purpose they certainly do serve is to throw into sharp relief the pressure on marketers to show results.

The Democratization of Your Brand

"Brand is what you do."
—Dominic Collins, Chief Marketing Officer of Legal and General

In days gone by, a *brand* was a shortcut to quality and a particular set of attributes for customers.

People bought Coca-Cola because they knew what Coca-Cola was, they knew it was likely to be safe, they knew it would taste broadly the same in Brazil as it would in Belgium, and they knew it would contain broadly the same ingredients.

Those people didn't have much of a say in how Coca-Cola was perceived by the general population. If the people marketing the brand decided they would make a somewhat counterintuitive move into promoting a make-believe old man who gives children presents in a red suit, a consumer could do little other than either accept it or switch to Pepsi.

That gave companies power to define their brands rather more easily than they do nowadays. To simplify radically, if Anheuser-Busch wanted Budweiser to be seen as a premium product, they started calling it premium. Sooner or later, it stuck.

Not anymore. Brand management as we knew it is dead. The increasing power of the customer has killed it.

The changing definition of *brand* is both an effect and an example of the rising power of customers in their relationships with businesses.

The overarching message companies want to disseminate—the way they want to look, how they act and feel, and how they deal with customers—is changing. There's a deep, penetrating, and permanent change in what brand is, how it is built, and how it is maintained—and the power a marketer has to influence it.

Essentially, the marketer has significantly less of that power. Fortunately, marketers can still have a meaningful impact—and end up with a stronger, more engaging brand than they started with.

Your Customers Have More Choice and Power

"Brands don't belong to companies any more—they belong to the people who choose to buy them."

Dan Lewis, Chief Public Affairs Officer for beer company Molson Coors, told me this while we were working on the Molson Coors case study that's included in Chapter 5. Customers no longer need your brand as much as they once did. Now they have a choice. Indeed, they have more choice than they've ever had.

As we've seen, hundreds of new marketing messages and new competitors are vying daily for your customers' attention. And those new companies aren't backward about coming forward. Your competitors are doing all they can to engage with your target audience as quickly, meaningfully, and efficiently as possible.

The brand with the biggest marketing budget will not win. The brand with the best customer experience will. And for you to be that brand, you must build the customer into every element of your business. You must avoid the lazy confidence of many large corporations the world over in thinking that your priorities matter to anyone outside your company, that people will see the value in your product, and that your quippy little piece of marketing copy will be as fascinating for your customers to read as it was for you to write.

Backstory Is More Important Than Tagline

Increasing customer power means increasing customer expectations. And nowadays, customers expect an awful lot more from their engagement with brands than that which results from an exclusive focus on Product, Place, Price, and Promotion.

This newfound power means customers feel entitled to look behind the curtain, investigating the inner workings of a company and holding them to the high standards they now expect. Their increased ability to choose means that they look beyond simple product benefits to find a brand they can buy into, a way of working that appeals, and an authenticity to communication and marketing.

In short, they look for a story they can believe in.

Brand is not about communications strategy. It's no longer appropriate to simply "have a message." You have to live up to that message in a far more extensive and deep-seated way than ever before. An authentic brand story isn't a confection manufactured by the PR team—it's a representation of everything about how a company works, its position in the world, its goals, and its relationships with customers. In short, branding just got a whole lot more complicated.

The Impact of the Global Financial Crisis

I had the opportunity to speak with Andy Gibson when he was still Chief Marketing Officer for Bacardi. He said that: "There's been a huge mental shift, toward a more truth-seeking, discerning, authentic experience for consumers than there has been in many generations."

Many feel that the advent of the global financial crisis precipitated a shift in consumer approaches to corporations. Customers began to be aware of the repercussions of mistakes they made and began to strive for something more grounded, real, and authentic. Andy Gibson also commented that customers were now seeking products and companies that "have a heart, a soul, and a truth, as opposed to something that's made up and created."

That shift in what customers are looking for has a significant knock-on effect on marketers. It changes how you must approach every element of your role. Customers are demanding that your brand story stacks up, and they demand to be let behind that velvet rope. It's your responsibility to ensure that they like what they see when they get there.

Brand Is a Conversation Between Companies and Their Customers

"Your brand is always going to be a conversation between what your customers view it as, and where you're trying to take your brand."
—Victoria Burwell, CMO, McGraw-Hill

Customers still care about brand—perhaps now more than ever——but what they care about has changed.

In a post-financial crisis world, customers want to buy into a company that means something. They want to buy a product that does what they want as well as they want it to. They care considerably less about the size of your marketing campaign, the fact you're a market leader, or the fact that you advertise at the Super Bowl. As a marketing executive, it's up to you to ensure that this message gets into the heads of a corporate boardroom laboring under the misapprehension that the world hasn't changed.

The process of building and maintaining a brand is now collaborative. Customers have more power, and more of a contribution to make, in defining what your brand is. This process isn't a new one, as Russ Findlay, Chief Marketing Officer for Hiscox Insurance, points out: "When I read your overview for the book, it reminded me of a project I worked on back in the mid-'90s where we tried to predict the future of consumers. We did a big global trawl through a number of countries and came back with a number of observations [regarding] global megatrends. And one of those trends was 'Consumers in Control.'"

So customer power has been increasing for decades. But the process reached critical mass in recent years, with 88% of marketers saying that customers have had more ability to influence and define their brand over the last five years.[40]

In large part, that's due to the growing power of social media. The rise of social networking has meant that corporations no longer have the whip hand in defining a brand. Fundamentally, your brand is now a conversation between your company and your customers.

I've been somewhat dismissive of the "4 P's" thus far. It's worth pointing out that it's still incredibly important for a company to choose what it's going to stand for and what it wants to talk about. However, the 4 P's of Product, Place, Price, and Promotion now simply define the subject and parameters of a conversation. Not the conversation itself, which is controlled to a great extent by your customers—and importantly is happening whether or not your brand is involved. As Jason West, former Chief Marketing Officer of food giant Heinz told me, "We used to control the conversation. And now we sometimes do, sometimes don't, sometimes never."

Companies must therefore not only initially set out what they hope their brand comes to be, but also listen to the response from customers and act accordingly. Barry Wolfish, Chief Marketing Officer for dairy brand Land O'Lakes, said:

"There's a recognition that brand has been democratized. So it's not just us pushing messages at consumers and hoping that we get it right. We get very real-time feedback about what resonates and what doesn't, and we also get feedback on what's missing."

The challenge is for companies to set up in such a way that they can engage meaningfully in that dialogue. It's a risk not to, as Arra Yerganian, Chief Marketing Officer for One Medical Group, told me:

"If you've had a great experience, you're encouraged to talk about it. A lot of people do. If you've had a terrible experience, you do so as well. And any company that's not listening in to that is at a huge disadvantage."

When you ask marketers about their budgets, you can see that they have already begun to take action. Currently, 9.4% of marketing budgets go toward "social" activities, according to The CMO Survey.[41] This is expected to increase to 13.2% in 2015 and accelerate to 21.4% by 2020.

Victoria Burwell, CMO at McGraw-Hill Education, puts it best: "I think the era of 50 years ago, when marketing happened at you, is dead. Now consumers expect and demand a conversation. It's something they want to be privy to."

Conclusions: Your brand is your story, and it's told in collaboration with your customers.

That means that the definition of your brand changes whenever your customers want it to. And that definition is based not on your marketing messages, but on your customer experience, your operations, and how those customers see you.

It's a broad and confusing area. But two things we do know:

1. **The backstory is as important as the tagline.** Your consumers are searching for something more. If they scratch at the truth and find there's no substance under it, they'll leave your brand and find something more aligned to their needs and values.

2. **Brand is driven by conversation.** In a world of social media and customer power, brand is no longer defined by a company and consumed by the customer. It's the product of an organic, ever-shifting discussion between those two parties. The company can influence that discussion, of course, but the owner of the brand is now, in Dan Lewis's words, your customers.

Not Everything Has Changed: The Fundamentals Remain the Same

This book is on the future of marketing. It's set in the context of a shifting landscape. In writing it, I've attempted to cover the fundamental changes to the marketer's ability to do their job, as well as the rapidly evolving customer expectations that have added complexity and challenge to what was once a simpler role. It talks about how authenticity, relevance, and transparency have become ever more critical elements of the function.

In short, the book focuses on change.

Yet it's important to note that many elements of marketing have remained the same, and will continue to do so. Certain priorities and foci have remained consistent—and always will.

Take a look at the following list pulled from a McKinsey article on broad trends that impact on the role of the marketer:

1. **The dominance of the customer:** "The need to understand and anticipate future customers is bound to become even more essential than in the past...the company that is not alert to the customers' needs and the changing complexities of marketplaces is inviting disaster."

2. **The impact of digital and the need for companies to quickly turn customer data into actionable insight:** "Generally speaking, I think it must be conceded that companies have dragged their feet in taking advantage of electronic data-processing analyses, online communications, and information-retrieval systems as tools to help make marketing more efficient."

3. **The challenges of marketing to a global audience:** "Top management must think through how best to coordinate a multinational selling effort to [ensure] adequate corporate control over a worldwide marketing plan—yet without unduly restricting initiative and responsibility within each national segment."

The author ends with a warning that the face of marketing is changing radically, and that it's essential for brands to make significant changes to stay in the game:

"To keep pace with these changes, and to play the strong role in the future that I believe to be the key challenge to marketing executives, the face of the marketing function will have to change accordingly."

To "keep pace," then, marketers must focus on customer-centric business practices, use data to become more agile, and be cognizant of their place in an increasingly global marketplace. That's a sensible set of goals for the marketer in 2015, and each is highlighted as a core focus in the research I've been doing for this book.

Yet this article was written in 1966.[42]

When considering changes and evolution within the marketing function, it's important to draw a distinction between what has changed and what will (and should) remain the same. As Jason West, formerly Chief Marketing Officer of Heinz, told me:

"I feel like two thirds of marketing is unchanged. And one third is dramatically changed."

The two thirds that stay the same? Those pieces involve three important elements:

1. Finding something that matters to your customer
2. Finding something you can deliver against
3. Finding something that differentiates you from your competition

Most of marketing is about figuring out who you are and what you want to say. Fundamentally, marketing will always come down to finding what matters to the customer, working out how to deliver against that, and then differentiating against your competition. The 4 P's then, while a little passé, are still important.

Jason West also had this to say about it: "If you can consistently figure out a way to answer those three questions, you can succeed as a marketer, regardless of what's happening in the different channels, or in the different ways of marketing in 2015, 2020, 2025."

So what part changes? According to many, that's only the delivery mechanism—Channels. Those mechanisms are constantly changing and evolving, and in this digital age, the pace of that change has increased.

Changes in the delivery mechanism are essentially a surface, tactical concern. Yet many snake oil salesmen in the space promise a new platform or channel that offers untold benefits. Many breathless trade press pieces laud the benefits of new channel X. And plenty of fads come and go. Indeed, an increasing challenge for savvy marketers is spotting the channels and platforms worth their time and, likewise, identifying those that are a waste.

It seems to me, however, that something broader and more fundamental has happened over the last ten years. That more than one third of marketing has changed. Attempting to shoehorn these broad shifts into a discussion of new channels and platforms would be doing it a disservice. This is far bigger than a discussion on the rise of Facebook or Twitter. Perhaps it's more sensible to separate three distinct elements of marketing:

1. **Unchanging: the consistent goals of the marketer:** Executives must always keep in mind that their ultimate goals (surrounding both marketing and the delivery of customer experience) will require answers to the same questions they always did. Concerns surrounding customer need, consumer behavior, who you are and what you want to say will remain, regardless of other shifts. The 4 P's will continue to matter.

2. **Always changing: delivery mechanisms:** This is where the majority of consultancies and other vendors make their money. This is also where most buzzwords and fads creep into marketing. New channels and platforms will always crop up. Marketers have been coping with new channels and platforms since Gutenberg invented the printing press.

3. **Slowly changing: the shifting changes to consumer expectations:** This is the area I feel is worthy of more attention, and it's the area this book focuses on. In the last decade, customers' expectations of corporations have changed significantly.

A plethora of influences have led to a marked shift in what customers expect from marketing and their interactions with businesses. These are loosely summed up in the acronym 'ART' (for Authenticity, Relevance, and Transparency).

Marketers must now be in a position to deliver authenticity, relevance, and transparency in all their dealings with their customer base if they plan to flourish in the years ahead. The turbulence from new channels and platforms and the fundamental need to get the message across is sure to continue unabated.

ART Means Major Changes Must Be Made

It's simply impossible to focus on delivering authenticity, relevance, and transparency without a significant amount of groundwork done by marketers, CMOs, and the entire C-suite.

To deliver nimble, targeted marketing that cuts through the noise and engages a target audience (all now expectations of your customer base), brands must make more extensive changes than shaking up the channels on which they disseminate their marketing messages.

After all, channels and platforms are always changing. Technological advancements will always happen; new startups will always offer shiny new apps and tools for people to communicate. The speed with which marketing now develops is inextricable from the speed at which technology progresses. The "incredible speed" and "fearful pace of change" that many CMOs have highlighted to me isn't going to slow.

But no recent shift will be as big as the one we've experienced with the rise of social and digital marketing. Marketers have seen a tremendous impact on customer expectations and must focus on the customer more than ever.

The New Customer Contract: Authenticity, Relevance, and Transparency

All the changes highlighted in this chapter (the rise of digital and social marketing, a media landscape that's quickly fragmenting, and an influx of new data sources) have led to a fundamental shift in the consumer/brand relationship.

Customers are demanding a new contract with the corporations they do business with. This contract includes a commitment from businesses that the marketing they produce will have these characteristics:

1. Authentic
2. Relevant
3. Transparent

Every one of these elements is interlinked; every one influences the others. Separating them into individual foci for your business is unrealistic and simply doesn't work. You take all three, or you take none of them.

Although each element has been an important part of a comprehensive marketing strategy for decades, each one has grown meaningfully in importance over the last decade. The most successful marketing departments of the next decade will be those that make each element work in concert, prioritize them at the top of their strategic goals, and design marketing strategies with them as the key pillars.

The New Customer Contract: Authenticity

"The backstory is as important as the tagline."
—Andy Gibson, formerly of Bacardi

On September 15, 2008, Lehman Brothers filed for bankruptcy. So began a global financial crisis whose aftereffects still course through the world nearly a decade later.

As significant elements of the global economy were revealed to have been built on sand, many marketers identified a fundamental shift in customer sentiment. Customers seemed increasingly aware that the good times (funded on credit and often focused on conspicuous consumption and "bling") were impermanent and could not continue. They seemed to realize that a settling of accounts had begun. The crisis was a shock to the system. It encouraged consumers to become far more discerning in their brand choices and consumption habits.

Authenticity hasn't been a discrete part of the history I've laid out thus far because it works on somewhat of a "deeper" level. Authentic communications and authenticity in the brand is something all companies have recognized to be important since the first company started promoting the date at which they were "established." Authenticity is a powerful motivator—the customer is buying something real, something established, something with a backstory. This isn't a faceless corporation selling you a mass-produced, high-priced but low-cost item; you're buying into a company that stands for something, that is built on craft, and, again, that is real.

In my conversations with CMOs of companies in industries as varied as insurance, medical care, entertainment, and alcohol, the growing importance of authenticity became obvious. Senior global marketing leaders told me that they noticed that their customers were becoming more discerning, very aware of artifice and hungry for something more authentic.

The growing popularity of the Hipster subculture (defined and sometimes mocked for love of artisanal olive oil, craft beer, locally woven hair shirts, and fixed-gear bikes handmade of iron from a local Brooklyn foundry) seems perhaps the most obvious example of this growing drive for authentic goods and services. As Andy Gibson told me:

"I think there's been a huge mental shift, towards a more truth-seeking, discerning, authentic experience for consumers than there has been in many generations....Consumers are searching and if they scratch at the truth, and there's no substance under it, they quickly walk away."

Authenticity is inextricably linked to transparency, one of the other three elements of marketing as ART. Fundamental to an authentic brand and authentic communications is the ability for customers to "look behind the curtain" and understand how products are made, what ingredients are used, and exactly where that Brooklyn foundry owner sources his iron ore.

Authenticity is about scratching the surface of a bracelet and seeing that it's gold the whole way through, not plated nickel. Transparency is both a driver and a result of this authenticity.

Dan Lewis, Chief Public Affairs Officer for beer company Molson Coors, is confident in the rising importance of authenticity to his customers:

> "So critical now to the beer experience for any beer drinker is authenticity, a story behind the brand. There's a lot more interest in what the ingredients are, where they come from. Beer has gone from being a pretty straightforward consumer purchase to a much deeper, richer, fuller engagement—not only with a liquid, but also with the story behind that liquid. In my own category, there has been a dramatic shift just in the last five years I would say."

In a world where brands reach potential customers when they're in bed, when they're commuting, and when they're at work, where brands reach customers on the same networks that those customers use to interact with their friends and family, it is perhaps unsurprising that there's an increasing expectation for brands to behave as good friends would. Tell the truth. Don't be fake.

The New Customer Contract: Relevance

Delivering relevance is increasingly becoming an essential part of doing business. Relevance, as we've seen, was facilitated by and expanded through a mass shift to digital interaction. "Digital native" companies, with customer data at the core of their operations, were able to provide exceptional, tailored customer experiences from their foundation.

And as customers grew to appreciate the level of service and experience that the Amazons and Ubers of this world could deliver, they began to expect the same level from legacy companies that existed well before the Internet did.

Exacerbating this need was the explosion of ways in which brands could communicate with those customers. Multiple screens means multiple advertising opportunities. The fragmentation of media consumption has led to many more places brands can show advertising— and customers are showing signs of being overwhelmed.

In terms of attracting and keeping customer attention, the bar has been raised. It is increasingly essential that marketers reach out to specific, targeted groups of people with messages that are informed by their previous relationships, their needs, and their interests. It's equally important to reach out in the right place (the right network, channel, or platform) at the right time (waking up in the morning, watching sports on a Sunday, or commuting to work on Monday morning).

Fortunately, brands have opportunities to improve. The fragmentation of the media landscape not only gives companies the chance to identify niches and communicate with them, but also results in an explosion of customer data available to forward-looking brands. The picture of the customer has gotten considerably more defined and detailed.

The New Customer Contract: Transparency

"The expectation of transparency—the ability to get the information one needs to address one's concerns—has skyrocketed just in my lifetime."
—Dan Lewis, Chief Public Affairs Officer, Molson Coors

It's easier now for your customers to find out about your products, operations, and brand story than at any point in history. What happened to give customers all this power? The biggest and most impactful answer is the transparency of information. Within a second, I can open my web browser and find pricing for products in any store. I can find reviews. I'm no longer at the mercy of what brands choose to tell me.

Customers no longer rely on packaging or advertising to define their view of a brand. Previously, any conversation about a brand or product was based largely on the brand's own communications, traditional media reviews, or slow-moving word of mouth restricted by smaller social groupings before the advent of social media. Nowadays, however, customers can access a rich trove of feedback, discussion, and conversation around brands—and it's all powered by customers themselves. Brands have significantly less control over this conversation than customers do.

Therefore, it's increasingly hard for marketing to act as a shield—brands can't use clever marketing to pull the wool over the eyes of the customer. Customers can 'see through' marketing now. As Cammie Dunaway, CMO at KidZania, points out:

> "Even back in the 90s, or perhaps even the early 00s, you could take a suboptimal experience, a suboptimal product, and if you had really, really clever communications and enough money, you could still grow a brand. Today, it's like brands are defrocked of all of that. It's like the *Emperor's New Clothes* might be a good metaphor. Consumers just aren't going to be tricked."

This has wide-ranging and fundamental effects on the role of the marketer within a business. For instance, if marketers cannot be successful when marketing a weak product, they have additional incentive (and need) to take a broader role in the production and design of that product—to make it stronger.

Transparency has also contributed significantly to the general increase in speed inherent in marketing. Previously, a global company's audiences around the world were rarely in contact with each other. A problem in one market wouldn't likely influence brand perception in others. That's not the case now. As Dunkin Donuts found[43], a controversial ad in Thailand is absolutely visible to, and influential on, the U.S. market. In a world where marketing departments are still primarily split over geographies, with different cultures and communities having different expectations, that causes significant challenges.

So transparency is not simply about communication externally. Brands also need to become transparent in their internal operations. It's increasingly important for brands to speak with a consistent voice across multiple channels and platforms as well as across geographies. Finally, and as we'll cover in some depth in later chapters, it's vital that the walls on data silos internally become transparent so that marketing, customer service, and other customer facing departments can build a full and clear picture of customers that would be impossible otherwise.

How ART Will Impact the Future of Marketing

"We're in an era where all internal corporate functions are changing as a consequence of technology—but none as fast or as greatly as marketing."
—John Kennedy, CMO, Xerox

Customer expectations are increasing. As we've touched on, marketing must have three characteristics to succeed in this new environment:

1. **Authentic:** Customers can see behind the curtain. They respond better to humans than to international conglomerates. And they're looking for an engaging story to get behind, not

another product pitch. Marketers must expand their role across business units to ensure that all elements of a corporation are living up to the brand promise and purpose they were so integral in building. That means marketers must spend far more time collaborating, cajoling, and coordinating. Messages to the outside world used to come only from marketing and communications departments; now they come from everywhere. Those messengers must all be on the same page. Equally, corporate strategy and development must be part of a consistent whole.

2. **Relevant:** In an age when your marketing message is one of more than 500 your target audience gets per day, you've got to ensure that you stand out. Customers are getting choosy and expect you to get in touch only when you're saying something they want to hear. You must have the capacity to understand as much as possible about your customer and the agility to tailor and target campaigns to individuals.

3. **Transparent:** Transparency in marketing has both internal and external elements. Internally, transparency means understanding among departments, with data shared effectively and greater collaboration and communication taking place. Externally, it refers to the fact that the corporate iron curtain no longer exists and that your customers have almost as many opportunities as you do to learn about the inner workings of your company.

Marketers can build a personal connection with customers now. They can use their insight to design messages and products that better fit customer needs and priorities. They can reach out to customers at the times customers want to be spoken to, cutting through the noise of a thousand branded messages through the delivery of relevance and value.

Clearly, the marketer's role and responsibilities must expand to cover these areas:

1. **Experience:** This is the most recognizable responsibility for "old school" marketers. The marketer must be responsible for how a customer experiences their brand. Every time a brand reaches out to the customer, and every time the customer

reaches out to the brand, the experience and interaction should be governed by the marketing department. Of course, nowadays, customers can get in touch with brands in far more places. Likewise, brands have far more ways to get in touch with customers, leading to an exponential rise in complexity.

2. **Insight:** Tied to the data explosion, marketers must become adept number crunchers. Marketers must be able to understand data and translate it into actionable insight for peers within and beyond the marketing department. They must be able to find where data is, choose the right data to take note of, gather it quickly enough, and, importantly, work with other departments to ensure the accessibility of data gathered in touchpoints not directly under the marketers' control.

3. **Agility:** From the speed with which marketers can gauge a campaign's success, to the speed at which a mistaken or ill-judged tweet goes viral, to the speed at which new channels and platforms spring up, to the speed with which customers expect responses, to the success of "real-time" marketing campaigns, everything seems to be getting faster. Marketers are under pressure to ensure that the departments they work in, the customer touchpoints they're responsible for, and the whole company that employs them is equipped with the systems, processes, and culture to be agile enough to flourish in this rapidly changing world.

By focusing on authenticity, relevance, transparency, and taking responsibility for experience, insight, and agility, marketers not only can survive in an era of radically heightened customer expectation, but also thrive. Now more than ever, marketing is about customer relationships, customer understanding, and ways to deliver customer value.

Endnotes

1. Marketing Experiments, *Transparent Marketing: How to Earn the Trust of a Skeptical Consumer* www.marketingexperiments.com/ whitepapers/MEx-Transparent-Marketing.pdf.

2. Sheryl Pattek, with David M. Cooperstein and Alexandra Hayes, "The Evolved CMO in 2014" (Whitepaper, Forrester Research and Heidrick & Struggles, March 2014).

3. Future of Marketing Survey.

4. Peter Dahlstrom, Chris Davis, Fabian Hieronimus, and Marco Singer, "The Rebirth of the CMO," *Harvard Business Review* (August 2014). https://hbr.org/2014/08/the-rebirth-of-the-cmo/.

5. Mario Aguilar, "The Inventor of Email Did Not Invent Email?", Gizmodo (22 February 2012). http://gizmodo.com/5887480/the-inventor-of-email-did-not-invent-email.

6. Dayna Rothman, "Ten Fantastic Facts About the History of Internet Marketing," Marketo (24 April 2013). (http://blog.marketo.com/2013/04/ten-fantastic-facts-about-the-history-of-internet-marketing.html).

7. Ankit Oberoi, "The History of Online Advertising," AdPushup. www.adpushup.com/blog/the-history-of-online-advertising/.

8. http://en.wikipedia.org/wiki/The_WELL.

9. Amy Gesenhues, "Survey: 90% of Customers Say Buying Decisions Are Influenced by Online Reviews," MarketingLand (19 April 2013). http://marketingland.com/survey-customers-more-frustrated-by-how-long-it-takes-to-resolve-a-customer-service-issue-than-the-resolution-38756.

10. Nick Johnson, "How Marc Speichert has evolved L'Oreal's marketing focus," (Incite Marketing and Communications, 14 June 2013). http://incitemc.com/marc-speichert-on-how-he-has-evolved-loreals-marketing-focus/.

11. "Transparent Marketing: How to Earn the Trust of a Skeptical Consumer," Marketing Experiments. www.marketingexperiments.com/whitepapers/MEx-Transparent-Marketing.pdf.

12. Meg Wagner, "34% of Millennials Watch More Online Video Than TV," Mashable (11 October 2013). http://mashable.com/2013/10/11/millennials-online-videos/.

13. Sonali Kohli, "Chart: How Much of the World Watches TV vs. Internet Video," Quartz (14 July 2014). http://qz.com/233451/chart-how-much-of-the-world-watches-tv-vs-internet-video/.

14. Geoffrey A. Fowler, "Getting Rid of Cable TV: The Smartest Way to Cut the Cord," *The Wall Street Journal* (15 July 2014). www.wsj.com/articles/getting-rid-of-cable-tv-the-smartest-ways-to-cut-the-cord-1405472757.

15. Marcus Wohlsen, "As Online TV Viewing Soars, Internet TV Will Soon Be the Only TV," *Wired* (20 October 2014). www.wired.com/2014/10/online-viewing-soars-internet-tv-will-tv/.

16. *Advertising Age* and Crain Communications, "Marketing Fact Pack: 2015 Edition." http://brandedcontent.adage.com/mic/regform/index.php.

17. Joshua Benton, "The Leaked *New York Times* Innovation Report Is One of the Key Documents of This Media Age," Nieman Lab (15 May 2014).

18. *Advertising Age* and Crain Communications, "Marketing Fact Pack: 2015 Edition."

19. *Advertising Age* and Crain Communications, "Marketing Fact Pack: 2015 Edition."

20. Tom Webster, "The Infinite Dial 2014," Edison Research (5 March 2014). www.edisonresearch.com/the-infinite-dial-2014/.

21. Tom Webster, "The Infinite Dial 2014."

22. John McDermott, "What the Cost of a Super Bowl Ad Can Buy Online," Digiday (30 January 2015). http://digiday.com/platforms/cost-super-bowl-ad-can-buy-online/.

23. Marketing Experiments, "Transparent Marketing: How to Earn the Trust of a Skeptical Consumer" (www.marketingexperiments.com/whitepapers/MEx-Transparent-Marketing.pdf).

24. Future of Marketing Survey.

25. Future of Marketing Survey.

26. Stuart Dredge, "From YouTube to Vice: 10 Trends That Are Changing How We Watch TV," The Guardian (18 April 2014). www.theguardian.com/tv-and-radio/2014/apr/12/10-viewing-trends-for-2014-future-tv-twitter-youtube-amazon.

27. David Goldman, "Half of Super Bowl Ads Had Hashtags," CNN Money (2 February 2015). http://money.cnn.com/2015/02/02/technology/social/super-bowl-ad-hashtags/.

28. Statista, "Second Screen Usage Among Mobile Internet Users in Selected Countries as of January 2014." www.statista.com/statistics/301187/second-screen-usage-worldwide/.

29. Lauren Dugan, "Twitter Is Dominating the Second Screen," AdWeek (25 March 2014). www.adweek.com/socialtimes/twitter-second-screen/497438.

30. Stuart Dredge, "From YouTube to Vice: 10 Trends That Are Changing How We Watch TV."

31. "YouTube Serves up 100 Million Videos a Day Online," USA Today (16 July 2006). http://usatoday30.usatoday.com/tech/news/2006-07-16-youtube-views_x.htm.

32. YouTube's own statistics. www.youtube.com/yt/press/statistics.html.

33. "Advertisers to Spend $5.60 Billion on YouTube in 2013 World-wide," eMarketer (11 December 2013). www.emarketer.com/Article/Advertisers-Spend-560-Billion-on-YouTube-2013-Worldwide/1010446.

34. Future of Marketing Survey.

35. Rishi Bhandari, Marc Singer, and Hiek van der Scheer, "Using Marketing Analytics to Drive Superior Growth," McKinsey (June 2014). www.mckinsey.com/insights/marketing_sales/using_marketing_analytics_to_drive_superior_growth.

36. http://en.wikipedia.org/wiki/John_Wanamaker.

37. Lewis Carter, "Web Could Collapse As Video Demand Soars," *The Telegraph* (7 April 2008).

38. Millward Brown Vermeer, "Marketing 2020: Key Study Findings." http://mbvermeer.com/wp-content/uploads/2014/08/Millward-Brown-Vermeer-Marketing2020-Brochure.pdf.

39. Jonathan Gordon and Jesko Perrey, "The Dawn of Marketing's New Golden Age." McKinsey Quarterly, Feb 2015.

40. Future of Marketing Survey.

41. The CMO Survey, "Survey Results—August 2014." http://cmosurvey.org/results/survey-results-august-2014/.

42. John D Louth, "The Changing Face of Marketing," McKinsey Quarterly (Autumn 1966). www.mckinsey.com/Insights/Marketing_Sales/The_changing_face_of_marketing?cid=other-eml-cls-mip-mck-oth-1407.

43. Adam Gabbatt, "Dunkin Donuts apologises for 'bizarre and racist' Thai advert." *The Guardian*, 30 August 2013. http://www.theguardian.com/world/2013/aug/30/dunkin-donuts-racist-thai-advert-blackface.

2

What Is a Customer Journey, and Why Does It Matter?

"The funnel—the classic linear progression in which customers narrow their buying options as they advance from product awareness to purchase—is becoming a lot less relevant because customers are engaging in a much more iterative and dynamic decision journey."[1]

—"Marketing's Age of Relevance," McKinsey on Marketing and Sales

Until recently, customer relationships with brands tended to be described using a "funnel" metaphor, in which people's various touchpoints with a brand were designed to push them farther down a funnel until they popped out of the bottom as customers.

Over the course of the last decade, that analogy has been superseded by the "customer journey." A customer journey is a more complex beast than the elementary funnel that preceded it. It's also more lucrative:

"Delivering excellent customer journeys can increase revenues up to 15% and cut costs by up to 20%."[2]

With a customer journey lifecycle, marketers concede some key points:

1. Customers are influenced by more than the touchpoints a brand has to offer them. According to David Court at McKinsey, reviews and feedback from peers has rather more impact than marketing from brands:

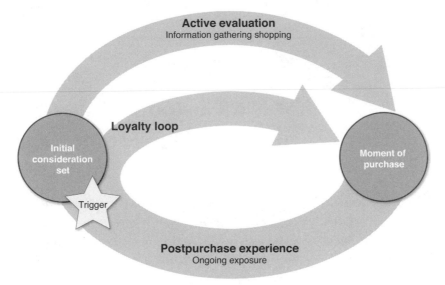

Source: David Court, Dave Elzinga, Susan Mulder, and Ole Jørgen Vetvik; "The Consumer Decision Journey", *The McKinsey Quarterly*, June 2009. http://www.mckinsey.com/insights/marketing_sales/the_consumer_decision_journey

Figure 2.1 From funnel to circle

"Two thirds of touchpoints during the active evaluation phase involve consumer-driven marketing activities, such as Internet reviews and word of mouth...[and only] one third involve company-driven marketing.... Marketers must move aggressively beyond purely push-style communication and learn to influence consumer-driven touchpoints and internet information sites."[3]

2. The experience of the entire journey has a significant impact on purchase decisions. According to an article on the increasing digitization of the customer journey, "two thirds of the decisions customers make are informed by the quality of their experiences all along their journey."[4]

3. The data and insight one can glean from customer journey behavioral metrics is significantly more relevant than demographic and other segmentation-based data. In recent research published in "McKinsey on Marketing and Sales,"

"Event trigger data (e.g. customer purchase in a related product category of clicking on a display banner for your product) has been shown to be five to ten times more predictive and powerful than externally appended demographic data."[5]

The lifecycle metaphor, proposed by David Court and associates of McKinsey, includes four stages: "initial consideration; active evaluation, or the process of researching potential purchases; closure, when consumers buy brands; and post-purchase, when consumers experience them."[6] The lifecycle metaphor has influenced some of the most successful marketers of the last decade, and using it illuminates other core questions you and your peers must ask in your own business.

Marc Speichert, who was Chief Marketing Officer at L'Oreal when we spoke, had this to say: "[Making] sure I select the right channels in the area of evaluation is critical. How do I do the same [in] the consideration phase, making sure I've ROI-optimized my selections in terms of awareness building? What are the best, most efficient print books, TV channels, display banners—and how do I optimize that so I can redistribute some of those savings into other areas, like evaluation?"[7]

Essentially, once we have clarity on the lifecycle and where a customer is along that lifecycle, we can ask better questions. Hopefully, we also can find better answers regarding resource allocation, copy, and campaign goals for that individual customer at any given time.

4. A marketer's job is not done just because the customer passes the point of purchase.

The "funnel" has become a circle. Product and experience are far more important now than they were when the funnel analogy was coined, when the purchase itself was an implied endpoint. This is supported by the fact that 60% of facial skin care products conduct more post-purchase research online.[8]

The Customer Journey Means Expanded Roles

A deeper understanding of the customer will lead to a clearer, better, more relevant, and more efficient marketing outreach strategy in both the short and long terms.

Customer journeys currently cover several different departments across a business, as Dahlstrom et al make clear in their article for *Harvard Business Review*, "The Rebirth of the CMO": "Customer journeys are complex and crisscross the organization. Even simple-seeming tasks, such as browsing or buying, often involve several steps, each touching a different part of the business."[9]

The increasing importance for corporations to focus on the customer journey holistically, not simply to manage individual customer touchpoints, increases the pressure to organize responsibilities and internal structures differently. It's critical to understand the full consumer journey and all the ways that consumers are interacting with your brand—if it's a point of retail, if it's the experience they're having on the web, if it's the experience they have when they have a problem and they call customer care. The marketing department itself doesn't necessarily have to *own all* of that, but should play the role of a champion for the consumer. Equally, a marketer must act as an advocate and a voice within the organization [for] how all those touch points add up to the brand experience.

As you'll see throughout the book, this changing role and responsibility adds an extra challenge for the CMO and his or her department: to evolve and expand to manage the entire customer journey. They must refashion and reorganize not simply their own department, but the entire company.

Endnotes

1. Brian Gregg, Wouter Maes, and Andrew Pickersgill, "Marketing's Age of Relevance," McKinsey on Marketing and Sales (August 2014).

2. Peter Dahlstrom, et al., "The Rebirth of the CMO," *Harvard Business Review* (5 August 2014).

3. David Court, et al., "Winning the Consumer Decision Journey," McKinsey on Marketing and Sales (December 2011).

4. Edwin van Bommel, David Edelman, and Kelly Ungerman, "Digitizing the consumer decision journey" (McKinsey, June 2014).

5. Brian Gregg, Wouter Maes, Andrew Pickersgill, "Marketing's Age of Relevance: How to read and react to customer signals" (McKinsey on Marketing and Sales, August 2014).

6. Court, et al., "Winning the Consumer Decision Journey."

7. Nick Johnson, "Peacekeeper, Navigator, Student: The Marketer to 2015," Incite Marketing and Communications. http://incitemc.com/publications/.

8. Court, et al., "Winning the Consumer Decision Journey."

9. Peter Dahlstrom, et al. "The Rebirth of the CMO."

PART II

HOW ARE COMPANIES COPING?

3   How Are Companies Doing Right Now? 61

3

How Are Companies Doing Right Now?

"[Marketers have to] work far harder than we ever have in the past."
—Andy Gibson, formerly CMO at Bacardi

The environment in which marketers operate has changed fundamentally. The last decade brought new platforms, new channels, new customer expectations, new challenges and, lest we forget, new opportunities.

Large companies have begun to recognize challenges and form a response, their disparate strategies coalescing around a few key points of consensus. There is an increasing recognition that marketing—and business as a whole—must deliver authenticity, relevance, and transparency if a company is to thrive in the next decade and beyond.

Although there are indeed constants in the field of marketing, change has been significant and deeper than simply a shift in the message delivery mechanism. Companies are still scrambling to catch up to those changing customer expectations. In this chapter, we investigate the core pain points companies have found and the progress they've made in adapting to this new and challenging landscape.

At first glance, the fact that companies are struggling to catch up is somewhat surprising. After all, the changes laid out in previous chapters have been developing for over a decade or more. Yet their struggle is perhaps testament to the sheer size of the change. The last decade heralded what can reasonably be called a fundamental restructuring of the relationship between business and customer.

The Marketer's Expanding Role: Confusion on Next Steps

One of the fundamental tenets of an "ARTful" approach to marketing is that the marketer is intricately involved in overarching business strategy and must adapt to a role as customer representative at every level of a business.

- Increased transparency means that marketing can no longer hide poor products. A marketer could and should be more involved in product development.
- Given the need to deliver relevant messaging, a marketer must be the leading expert on (and the voice of) the customer in much corporate decision making.
- Given the importance of authenticity, the marketer must ensure that all levels of the company are unified behind an authentic brand story and are truly living up to the brand promise.

These three elements of the new marketing role suggest a position of fundamental importance in almost every element of a business's practices. It follows, then, that a marketing executive with this broader responsibility would have a fundamental role in driving business growth.

Yet, according to the Marketing2020 study—run in collaboration between the ANA, ISBA, Spencer Stuart, Forbes, Adobe, and others—only 40% of industries currently see the marketing function "as a strategic partner for driving business growth."[1] There is evidently a disconnect between where marketers need to be, and where they are in the corporate hierarchy right now.

Internal Structures Are Beginning to Change

Eighty eight percent of marketers say that customer expectations have increased, with 56% saying they're "a lot higher" than they were five years ago.[2] What's more, 63% of marketers find it hard to match these increased expectations.

And we can begin to make out the first semblance of a response from the marketing community. The vast majority (80%) of executives say that changing customer expectations have already impacted internal organizational models. Many of them point out that a "customer-centric" approach to business operations is the end goal.

While only 11% of marketers can say they have a customer-centric business now, a majority are confident that their companies will become more customer-centric over the next five years.

Collaboration Is Key

It seems clear that the increasing customer power laid out in Chapters 1 and 2 is encouraging companies to evolve internal organizational models to become more customer-centric.

But how is this change manifesting? What changes are companies actually making?

First, there seems to be a drive to build more transparency into internal operations. As companies struggle to become more agile and relevant to an increasingly demanding customer base, the marketing department is working increasingly closely with product development, IT, customer service, communications, and multiple other internal teams (see Figure 3.1). They're making this change to ensure that the business builds a full picture of their customer and uses it to not only disseminate consistent, relevant messaging—but also engaging, useful products.

That's why 62% percent of marketers say the dividing lines between internal departments responsible for different customer touchpoints are blurring—it's the result of an increased need to focus on the customer and deliver a superior customer experience (see Figure 3.2).

Companies also seem to be starting to address the need to provide a consistent, smooth, holistic customer journey—a response to the findings outlined in Chapter 2. Many companies have begun to pull all customer touchpoints and relationship management systems under one department—the marketing department.

Is the dividing line between marketing, communications, IT, data, customer service departments blurring?

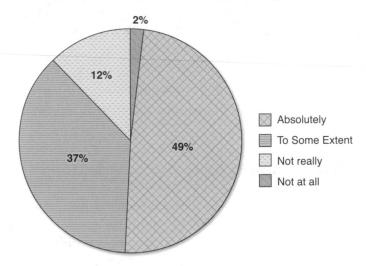

Figure 3.1 Previous departmental separation is being eradicated

Is blurring of dividing lines down to increased focus on better customer experience?

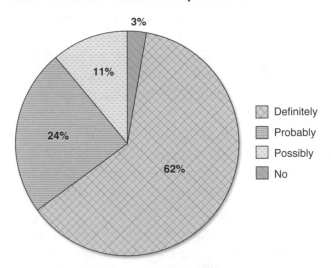

Figure 3.2 A focus on customer experience is changing internal organisational models

Over half (51%) of the marketers at work today feel that this is already happening; and that the currently existing dividing lines between those departments with a direct relationship with customers will "definitely" or "probably" disappear completely.

This eradication of previously important dividing lines is significant. For decades, companies have organized themselves into separate departments responsible for different elements of the customer experience. Communications teams were responsible for branding and public relations. Marketers were responsible for the 4 P's: Product, Price, Placement, and Promotion. Customer service was responsible for solving customer issues. And latterly, social media teams were responsible for doing pretty much all of these things over Facebook and Twitter.

More than this, although product development teams were influenced by marketing, they were often working in separate worlds. Equally, those people working on processing and analyzing customer data were set in different parts of the business—with different responsibilities—to marketing teams.

Teams were incentivized as such. Roles were clarified based on this paradigm of separate departments with separate responsibilities. Career progression was dictated by it. And an often fragmented customer experience was a product of it.

Yet in a more fluid, fast-moving, and complicated world, these neat internal barriers and guidelines are fast becoming unsuitable. Customers will no longer accept the slow-moving, flawed, inefficient customer experience that's a result—nor the irrelevant, untargeted, and unengaging marketing and products that are a corollary. That's why 86% of marketers nowadays can see that a transition to a more collaborative, agile, and flexible internal organizational model is either imminent or already happening.[3]

Most marketers point out that their departments get reorganized at least once every couple years (see Figure 3.3). But for the reorganization that we're discussing, the scale is somewhat expanded. This isn't simply a reorganization of a marketing department—it's the reorganization of an entire business. The change concerns every aspect of the delivery of customer experience, from product development to after-sales service.

How often does your marketing department undergo some sort of reorganization?

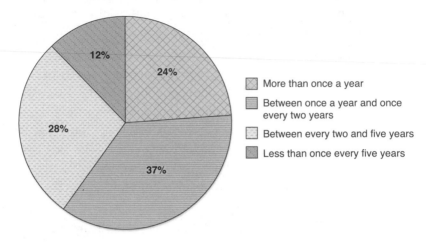

Figure 3.3 Departmental re-organizations happen pretty frequently

A fundamental refashioning of how companies organize themselves is beginning to take place. Although 60% of executives are certain that their company will become more customer-centric over the next five years, only 50% expect the process of transition to go smoothly.[4]

Departure Lounge

Companies have a long way to go, but this new internal model is beginning to take shape.

Marketing departments are beginning to take a senior role in an increasing number of internal relationships—communications, data analytics, and customer service, all departments with a significant impact on the delivery of customer experience.

The majority of communications, data analysis, and customer service departments now report to the marketing department, which tends to be the more senior partner in any collaboration (see Figure 3.4).[5]

Who reports into the marketing department?

Figure 3.4 The relationship between marketing and other departments

Eighty-two percent of all communications executives report to the marketing department (63% directly and 19% with a "dotted line" responsibility). The two departments are (and have always been) closely linked, if not indistinguishable, with the Head of Communications often reporting to the Chief Marketing Officer. Even so, the extent of the collaboration (82%) seems to belie a concerted effort to bring the two teams into even closer alignment.

In the customer data analysis team, the collaboration is nearly as marked. Data analysis departments have sprung up rapidly since the potential for data to guide corporate decision making became clear. Understandably, a key internal client for these departments' insights has always been the marketing team. Still, an 83% reporting rate suggests a very close link between the two teams.

For customer service, the numbers are lower but still significant (24% direct reports and 35% dotted line reporting). This department is a little more removed from the level of collaboration between marketing and communications, although most customer service teams do report to marketing these days, to some extent. As one of the main customer touchpoints, this figure likely will increase rapidly during the next five years.

Although significant collaboration is taking place, more work needs to be done. For instance, we have not looked at one of the most obvious relationships needed to deliver ARTful marketing: marketing and IT. As has often been pointed out the last couple years, marketers now spend more on IT than IT departments do.[6] In some ways, this reflects the increasing primacy of customer data collation and the increasing reliance on this data by the marketing department—as the transition between art and science continues.

Yet only 41% of current marketers feel that executives in their business "share a common vision of how marketing and IT should work together."[7]

So although signs suggest that companies have begun to take note of the scale of the challenge ahead of them, work remains to be done. Meaningful change has taken place in internal organizational structures, and companies seem to be serious about building a model in which customer-centricity is the guiding principle.

Marketing Is Under Pressure to Increase Speed

To a great extent, the internal organizational refashioning that marketing departments around the world are experiencing is intended to ensure that companies are able to *quickly* deliver relevant customer experiences (and, on a more basic level, marketing campaigns).

This is a clearly defined and acknowledged challenge for global marketers: A full 94% have stated that the pace of change in marketing has increased (see Figure 3.5). This increasing pace of change is impacting marketing in the following four main ways:

1. Customers Expect Responses to Queries Far More Quickly

We've already looked at the rise of social media and its role in the fragmentation of the marketing landscape during the last decade. As a result, marketing is now increasingly focused on dialogue and conversation. Given the need for marketers to convey an authentic, human face to their customers, a company must be able to respond to customers as quickly as it would in a real-life one-to-one conversation (see Figure 3.6).

Has the pace of change increased?

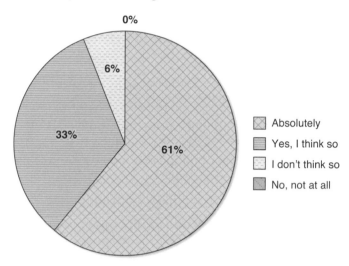

Figure 3.5 The speed at which marketers must operate is increasing

Can you engage customers at the speed they expect?

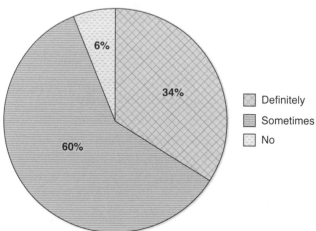

Figure 3.6 Only a third of companies are moving as quickly as their customers want

Yet only 34% of marketers currently feel confident that they are able to engage with their customers at the speed the customer base expects. Also, 60% said that they were able to do so in some instances, whereas 6% lagged behind, under the impression that they were never able to talk to customers at the pace expected.

2. Customers Reward Marketing Campaigns That Are Closely Linked to Developments in the World Around Them

Real-time marketing is the relevant term here, to denote marketing campaigns that are able to react in real time to real-world developments. Brands need to insert themselves into the communal conversation taking place over social media. The Oreo "You Can Still Dunk in the Dark" tweet in reaction to the power outage at the 2013 Super Bowl is still the most famous example.

Well-executed real-world campaigns deliver both relevance (hitting customers at a time and place that works for them) and authenticity (brands legitimately involving themselves in conversations on topics that matter to their customers).

3. New Platforms Reach Maturity (and Huge User Bases) More Quickly Than Ever

As discussed in the previous chapter, new marketing platforms are springing up frequently and quickly proving worthy of consideration by marketing departments.

About ten years ago, marketing was awash with warnings about the speed with which individuals were adopting profiles on new-fangled social networks such as Friendster and MySpace.

Then, Facebook's dominance gave the impression that things were about to get simpler. With one clear winner in the social user race, marketers could begin to trim back on other, less vibrant and less pervasive platforms. They could afford to focus a bigger chunk of time and resource on this one social channel.

Yet the last three years have seen an additional fragmentation—and, importantly, an increase in the speed with which this fragmentation has occurred. You can see this in the growth rates of Instagram, Snapchat, Vine, and WhatsApp (see Figure 3.7a-c).

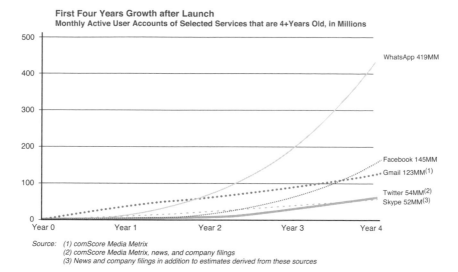

Source: (1) comScore Media Metrix
(2) comScore Media Metrix, news, and company filings
(3) News and company filings in addition to estimates derived from these sources

Figure 3.7a Growth of WhatsApp *(oyagroup.com/2014/02/facebooks-expensive-acquisition-whatsapp-takes-social-media/)*

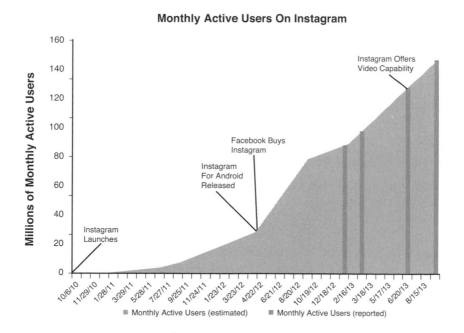

Source: BI Analyst Estimates, Instagram Statements

Figure 3.7b Growth of Instagram *(www.businessinsider.com.au/instagram-grows-maus-to-150-million-2013-9)*

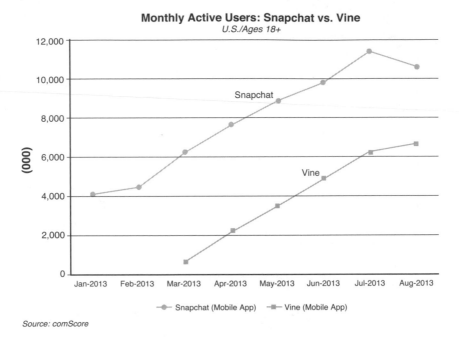

Source: comScore

Figure 3.7c Activity of Snapchat versus Vine *(www.bullfax.com/?q=node-snapchat-and-vine-show-first-signs-decelerating-user-gr)*

As new channels rise up, older ones crumble. Marketers need to deal with the speed at which their landscape is changing. Many stories suggest that younger audiences, wary of Facebook's somewhat questionable approach to privacy, are moving to more anonymous social platforms. They may even be shunning social platforms altogether, explaining the rapid ascent of one-on-one messaging apps like WhatsApp and Snapchat, and even anonymized versions like Secret and YikYak.

4. Data and New Measurement Methodologies Quickly Give Marketers Usable Insight into Campaign Success

As we've seen, increasingly the best marketing departments are those that can analyze campaign success midway through execution and make meaningful changes based on that analysis.[8]

Understandably, companies are struggling to do so right now. Forty-six percent of marketers are not confident that their department is equipped with the skills and structures needed to function at this increased pace. Thirty-four percent had begun to take action to "work at pace"; another 7% were not confident that they had the skills and tools necessary to make the changes we've discussed.[9]

How Are Marketers Beginning to Increase the Speed?

We asked hundreds of marketers how they've gone about dealing with this issue. When we asked them about specific tasks they've completed in an effort to increase the speed at which marketing takes place, they highlighted three core areas—given in priority order (see Figure 3.8):

How have you increased the speed?

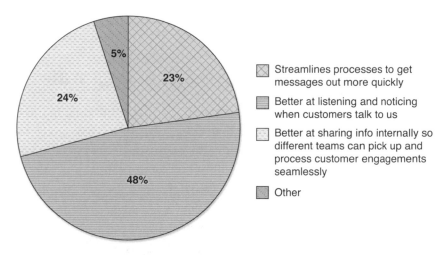

Figure 3.8 Increasing marketing speed

1. **Get better at listening and noticing when customers talk to you:** 48% of executives say that good listening is essential to a fast, responsive marketing department. More than that, companies must have the ability to know, fast, *what* to listen to. A whole lot of conversation happens on Twitter, and it's a waste of resources to listen to it all (be sure to check out the case study

with One Medical Group on this topic in Part III, "Building for the Future").

2. **Get better at sharing information internally so different teams can pick up and process customer engagements seamlessly:** 24% of survey respondents said that to be a quicker, more agile marketing department many distinct departments must work closely together. A key focus involves the ability to share customer insight and data accurately and quickly with the right people.

3. **Get better at streamlining processes to get messages out more quickly:** Too often in laggard marketing departments, the systems and processes required to disseminate a message or share a piece of content are too onerous for today's standards and requirements. The third area—highlighted by 23% of executives—for any company looking to increase its speed is to work out ways to sensibly cut through bureaucracy without increasing risk to an unacceptable level.

Media Fragmentation Is Tough to Deal With

Eighty-three percent of marketers think that traditional marketing channels are less dominant than they were five years ago.[10] TV ads, billboards, and newspaper advertisements have all become less useful to marketing executives than in the recent past.

And they have been replaced with not one or two alternative channels, but a plethora of new, smaller, more niche opportunities, each with its own code of conduct. Each channel must be dealt with differently, and marketers must deliver campaigns based on the relative strengths and weaknesses of these new channels.

Yet within corporate marketing departments around the world, email and websites are clearly still the most popular and useful channels available (see Figures 3.9 and 3.10).

This makes the challenge for marketers right now clear. The issue is not simply that a new channel has replaced a traditional channel; it is that new channels are being *added* to the workload of already stressed and overworked marketing executives.

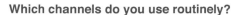

Which channels do you use routinely?

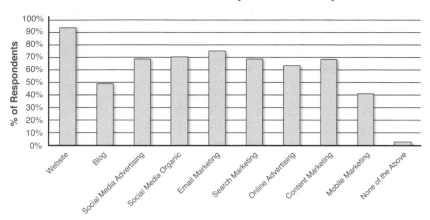

Figure 3.9 Channels regularly used

Which channel delivers the best ROI?

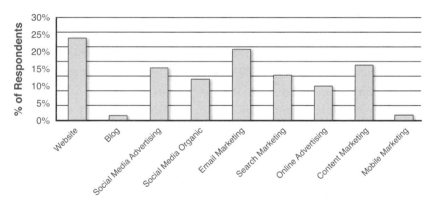

Figure 3.10 Best ROI delivery

As you can see in Figure 3.9, most brands now use eight distinct marketing channels on a regular basis.

Yet in the medium term, the influence of those more traditional channels is expected to dissipate. Only 14% of our respondents predicted that traditional channels will maintain their current level of usefulness over the next five years. This explains the fact that 77% of those marketers will spend less money on more established channels during that period.[11]

So traditional channels are on the decline. But it would be wrong to say that they are already redundant. If you ordered this list based on buzzwords, consultancy whitepapers, and LinkedIn opinion pieces, email marketing and corporate websites would fall somewhere below carrier pigeon and semaphore.

Evidently, orchestrating a multichannel campaign to reach customers in the changing locations where they spend time is more complex than ever.

Things Are Changing Fast

As a topic, content marketing reached common parlance toward the end of 2013. For in-house marketers, it became a valid element of a comprehensive marketing approach somewhere over the last 24 months.

"And over a very short period of time, content marketing has gone from something that marketers should think about to a core element of the majority of companies' marketing strategy." 65% of our respondents call content marketing a strategy that's working very well, with 73% of companies going so far as to do the content creation and development work in-house. What's more, programmatic advertising, an even newer marketing opportunity, has already been built into in-house operations at 21% of companies.

In a world where the most senior marketers at large brands are those who 'came of age' in a world before social media, this is a terrifyingly quick race to maturity.

Marketers Must Mix Paid, Earned, and Owned Channels

The old-school marketing model of allocating a budget to a series of media buys—TV, radio, and print ads—no longer works. Yes, of course "advertising" has a place in a marketing campaign. According to Figure 3.9, 69% of marketers are paying for social media advertisements, and 64% are spending on online ads. While TV, radio, and print spend is anticipated to decline, it still dominates spending patterns for many major brand marketers.

The big change is that currently, a marketer must combine this paid spend with more complex, and newer, channel types. "Paid" media is one of three pillars of a marketing campaign. The others are "Owned"—one's website, CRM database, and the like—and "Earned" channels, which denote the attention one garners through social media activity.

Unsurprisingly, 94% of companies still rely on their corporate website, 76% on email campaigns, and 49% on a company-owned blog.

Earned channels have come into their own, and without them one would have a campaign with some pretty big holes in it. 70% of our respondents use "organic" social media activity to drive marketing campaigns, whereas 69% are reliant on increasing their presence in organic search results—based on Google's algorithms.

Delivering a Consistent Brand Message Is Increasingly Challenging

Only 32% of marketing executives say they're as consistent as they would like to be across multiple marketing channels.[12] What do they mean?

Often you'll find that a major corporation has several distinct teams running different customer touchpoints. One team is working on Facebook, another "owns" the email database, and a third runs the brand website.

Having these three teams be effectively one and the same would be ideal, and lend itself far better to consistent messaging and tone. However, the inevitable small-minded "little-kingdom" mentality bedevils such idealistic organizational modeling, and this scenario rarely occurs in the real world.

Consider a company we'll call Acme Toiletries. At Acme, Rodrigo Santoro runs the Facebook and Twitter accounts and is desperate to "bring the company into the twenty-first century." He's been retweeted several times by the "Brands That Say Bae" Twitter account,[13] and rather than be offended, he wears it as a badge of pride. Rodrigo is big on "talking like the customer." His Facebook messages are conspicuously youthful, are littered with slang terms, and involve a lot of unbelievably positive responses to the customers who've chosen to like the Acme Facebook page. Rodrigo wants to show that he's up on current affairs, so he took the step of making that Facebook page rainbow striped during Gay Pride.

Jane Doe, who runs the email database, has been at the company for 20 years. During that time, she's been responsible for building the structures and processes dictating when and how email should be used as part of a broader marketing strategy. The legal team is very clear with her (because the government is very clear with them) on what is and isn't acceptable as part of a marketing campaign conducted over email. That means Jane has rather less leeway to be either a) obsequiously youthful or b) self-consciously "real time."

The email campaigns Jane crafts take longer to plan and execute than the latest Facebook status update, and they require approval from many different executives across the multinational corporation. So this year the team missed the Gay Pride memo and made no mention of it in their weekly email. At the same time, the legal team's input means that street slang does not make much of an appearance, and messages are more obviously "corporate."

Jeroen Flink, who works on the website, spends a lot of his time working with the in-house IT department, figuring out what is and isn't possible to do with the site. The team also has a lot of meetings with legal, and because the CEO has set the company site as her personal homepage when she opens her web browser, they get a lot of input from her, too. The team did mention Gay Pride, but it was in a blog post from the CEO herself, halfway down the page and underneath the massive banner pushing the company's most recent sale and a cool social plug-in that Rodrigo had successfully lobbied IT to build.

This scenario is a somewhat tongue-in-cheek reflection of some of the challenges facing large marketing departments. Unfortunately, a structure like this causes problems. From a customer's point of view, the Acme Toiletries brand voice veers dangerously close to the schizophrenic. It is patently obvious that these messages all come from a massive conglomerate, not a group of human beings. It's obvious that this conglomerate doesn't have an authentic brand voice, making it harder for customers to build a relationship with the company. And once that customer gets on the phone with the customer service team, it becomes equally obvious that the teams don't do much talking to each other—the first complaint might have happened over Twitter, and the customer was then asked to repeat it both in a follow-up email and during the first two minutes of the phone call.

Wouldn't it be better if, instead of shouting over each other, Rodrigo, Jeroen, and Jane worked together better? What if they were pushing out a consistent message and the differing voices they used added depth and richness, not confusion?

That's the challenge marketers are highlighting when 68% of them say they're not as consistent as they'd like to be. And who can blame them? For consistent, harmonious approaches, you don't need just strong campaign planning; you need structure, collaboration, oversight, and agile processes. This struggle with consistency isn't the somewhat more basic question, "How do I make my online and offline presences work together?" (Fifty percent of marketers say they've solved that problem.) The issue at hand is the complexity inherent in the fragmentation and maturity of a plethora of new campaigns and those inherent in a fragmented internal customer experience approach.

That's why, even though they're struggling, only a tiny 2.1% of all marketers we spoke to said they didn't think being consistent in a multichannel approach was important.

Why?

For many marketers, this is an issue because the internal organization, the thought put into workflows and processes, just isn't there. Seventy-six percent of respondents in a recent research paper said that their multichannel strategy wasn't as developed as it should be.[14]

The Speed with Which Channel Fragmentation Is Taking Place Is a Challenge All Its Own

Only 35% of marketers are confident that their team is set up well to rapidly assess and integrate new marketing channels as they arise.

Social media is still a relatively new space, and the media reporting on it certainly reflects that. Every new channel/technology/platform that comes above the parapet, from Snapchat to Ello, is heralded as a game changer in a way the launch of a new magazine or TV channel never was.

That's because these new channels can often *do* things their predecessors never could. When a new TV channel launches, it doesn't offer viewers a whole new way to experience television. It's simply another catalog of content delivered in the same medium as before. But when the next Snapchat launches, marketers won't need to solely concern themselves with the reach and content disseminated on the channel, but the method by which that dissemination occurs. That exacerbates the challenge.

Facebook allowed companies to leverage a target audience's "social graph" and the approval of friends in an attempt to increase legitimacy and build engagement. Twitter's hashtags meant companies could begin to insert themselves into organic conversations in a way that hadn't been possible before. Snapchat's self-destructing messages present other new challenges and opportunities for brands.

Today, channel fragmentation isn't simply a problem of choosing which TV ad spot to pick. It's about discovering the capabilities that new technologies offer a marketing campaign, understanding how to leverage them effectively, and working out whether this activity will meaningfully "move the needle" on a company's overarching marketing goals.

It's essential, therefore, to pick the right channels and platforms. And because we're living in a post-recession world, where the "fat has been squeezed out of the industry,"[15] you've got to do it while keeping ROI and opportunity cost front and center. If spending is increasing on Snapchat, for many companies it will have to decrease on Google. Thus, there's a very real risk that jumping on the next shiny new platform will make you miss other opportunities and actively harm your existing marketing campaign.

Most Companies Are Not Fully Leveraging Customer Data for Better Customer Insight

According to Dahlstrom, et al., better analysis of customer insights can improve marketing return on investment by 10% to 20%

and drive an average profit growth of 14%.[16] Yet nearly 75% of companies think their customer insights budget is too low; only 6% say they understand customer needs extremely well (see Figure 3.11).

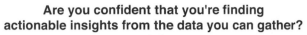

Are you confident that you're finding actionable insights from the data you can gather?

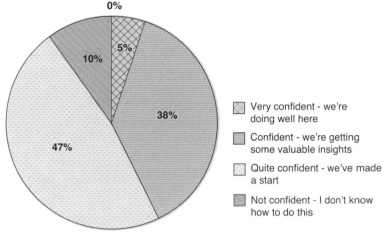

0%

5%

10%

38%

47%

Very confident - we're doing well here

Confident - we're getting some valuable insights

Quite confident - we've made a start

Not confident - I don't know how to do this

Figure 3.11 Confidence from actionable insights

Yet the flood of customer data generated by a wide-scale move "to a predominantly digital" world offers savvy brands a powerful weapon in the fight for customers' attention and trust.

It's essential to deliver relevance and make the right marketing decisions in the resource-constrained environment most companies still find themselves in post-2008. For the vast majority of companies, that only makes their underperformance more frustrating.

Fifty-nine percent of marketers feel that the influx of new data is making their job easier, but only 41% say they're confident in their ability to turn this data into actionable insights (see Figure 3.12).

Fifty three percent say they're able to segment marketing better than ever, but only 17% say they're closer than they were to being able to talk directly to individuals instead of merely broad demographic groups and other segments.

**Is the influx of data having an
impact on your ability to do your job?**

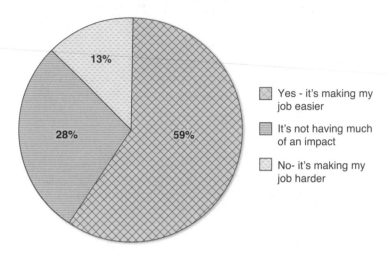

Figure 3.12 Influx of data impacting job

A Long Way to Go—But There's Increasing Clarity on the Route to Take

On their journey to becoming authentic, relevant, and transparent, companies are taking their first steps in three main areas.

The first deals with speed. Companies are finding it hard to work at the speed customers expect for dialogue, agility, and real-time campaigns.

Second, companies are struggling to keep pace with shifting marketing dollars and other resources quickly enough to be where the customer is. The customer is fickle and switches his attention to the hot new platform, channel, or technology with alarming frequency. Companies then must make wholesale changes to often complex and expensive campaigns midway through them.

Third, companies are struggling to build a comprehensive, multifaceted, 360-degree view of their customer base (and the individual customers within it), even though they have the technology and the desire to do so. "Silos" of data are still prevalent across the majority of companies, a result of the fact that different departments within the same company often seek to own their own data and don't share well with others.

The constant? Companies are struggling.

Marketers can see the potential for significantly increased performance, but have not realized that potential yet. Some outliers have found the key to open the door, but the vast majority are still outside in the cold staring through the window. The rest of this book is designed to help you fashion your own key to get through that door.

Next Steps

The next part of this book looks at how leading companies have begun to innovate to deliver the authentic, relevant, and transparent messaging that customers increasingly expect. You'll find input from 16 Chief Marketing Officers, survey results from more than 500 marketing executives, and in-depth case studies on loyalty, brand building, internal buy-in, internal organizational structures, and social listening. Part III, "Building for the Future," is designed to help you learn from these leaders and augment your own marketing campaigns.

Marketing campaigns themselves are only the tip of the iceberg, and although they are perhaps the most obvious element to a customer, they are the product of a marketing department's strategy, setup, organizational model, and more.

We will cover how leading companies are innovating to deliver "ART" (delivering authenticity through storytelling, conversation, and internal buy-in; implementing multichannel approaches to deliver pervasive, relevant campaigns where your customers spend time; and leveraging the opportunity that data presents). We will also cover marketers' increasing responsibility to contribute to the broader corporate strategy, given the expectation that the marketer is now best placed to understand customers and act as their voice.

The final part of the book proposes a new organizational framework for the future marketing department that focuses on insight, experience, and agility. It can help you restructure to deliver those three critical elements your customers will increasingly demand: authenticity, relevance, and transparency.

Endnotes

1. Millward Brown Vermeer, "Marketing 2020: Key Study Findings." http://mbvermeer.com/wp-content/uploads/2014/08/Millward-Brown-Vermeer-Marketing2020-Brochure.pdf.

2. Future of Marketing Survey.

3. Future of Marketing Survey.

4. Future of Marketing Survey.

5. Future of Marketing Survey.

6. Lisa Arthur, "Five Years from Now, CMOs Will Spend More on IT Than CIOs Do" *Forbes* (8 February 2012). http://www.forbes.com/sites/lisaarthur/2012/02/08/five-years-from-now-cmos-will-spend-more-on-it-than-cios-do/.

7. Sheryl Pattek, with David M. Cooperstein and Alexandra Hayes, "The Evolved CMO in 2014," *Forrester* (24 February 2014).

8. Rishi Bhandari, Marc Singer, and Hiek van der Scheer, "Using Marketing Analytics to drive superior growth," McKinsey (June 2014). www.mckinsey.com/insights/marketing_sales/using_marketing_analytics_to_drive_superior_growth

9. Future of Marketing Survey.

10. Ibid.

11. Ibid.

12. Ibid.

13. https://twitter.com/brandssayingbae.

14. Nick Johnson, "Peacekeeper, Navigator, Student: The Marketer to 2015," Incite Marketing and Communications. http://incitemc.com/publications/.

15. Frans Cornelis, Chief Marketing Officer, Randstad.

16. Peter Dahlstrom, et al., "The Rebirth of the CMO," *Harvard Business Review* (5 August 2014).

PART III
BUILDING FOR THE FUTURE

4   Brand Management and Storytelling 87

5   Getting Your House in Order: How Internal Buy-In
    Impacts External Marketing 95
    Molson Coors Case Study

6   How an Evolved Internal Structure Drives Authentic,
    Relevant, and Transparent Marketing 119
    Randstad Case Study

7   Data for Relevance and Agility 139
    One Medical Group Case Study
    KidZania Case Study
    Land O' Lakes Case Study

8   Why Multichannel Matters 183
    Hiscox Multichannel Case Study

9   Content Marketing to Drive Engagement 197

10 The Imperative—and Opportunity—of Conversation 207

4

Brand Management and Storytelling

"Transcendent purpose is effectively communicated through stories."[1]
—Paul J. Zak, "Why Your Brain Loves Good Storytelling"

Managing a Brand in Collaboration with Customers

As we've seen, what it takes to build and maintain a brand has changed extensively over the last decade. Changes will continue as marketers begin to build authenticity, relevance, and transparency into everything they do.

Experience Supersedes Logo

Experience now defines a brand more extensively than the public relations and communications team ever could. Every time someone picks up the phone to call your customer service department, every time someone clicks through to your Facebook page, and every time someone walks into your store—every one of those instances is far more powerful in supporting or breaking down your brand than any number of poster campaigns or TV advertisements.

Equally, the rise of social media has given every one of your customers a loudspeaker—a tool with which to influence how your brand is perceived on a large scale. As such, brand is now more than ever a conversation between company and customer. As Jason West, formerly Chief Marketing Officer for HJ Heinz, points out, it's absolutely critical for the company to listen to those customers, understand their perception of brand, and use this understanding to inform future decision-making. All too often, this simply doesn't happen:

"There's a temptation for brands when writing a brand positioning statement to assume they're writing down what their consumers say—like, 'Ah, this is what we mean to consumers.' Instead, those brands are actually making their own choice as to what they want to stand for."

That's a remarkably dangerous mistake. Brands can no longer lazily assume that they're taking on board customer feedback to define a brand. Dan Lewis of Molson Coors certainly thinks so: "I think the biggest mistake—and maybe it's the biggest shift for brands—is to set aside a lot of the arrogance of the past, of being more knowledgeable about this brand than the consumer." Instead, marketers must understand that customer feedback better than ever before (discussed in depth in Chapter 7, "Data for Relevance and Agility"). They must build this customer view into every decision that's made, and do so whether it tallies with previous strategy or not. This need to react and respond in a wide-ranging way to customer feedback and insight on what your brand means to them requires a fundamental restructuring of business to not only be closer to its customers, but more agile—and able to make the changes and react to the feedback that those customers provide.

Brand Is How a Company Acts As a Corporate Citizen

Customers are now more able to influence a company's brand themselves. As such, the marketer's role transitions from unilateral decision making on a brand's future, and becomes more about influencing and evolving existing customer perceptions.

Given their somewhat "weaker" position, a sensible marketer must take seriously every opportunity to successfully influence that perception. As such, factors like corporate responsibility loom ever larger—and become increasingly important to a marketer grasping for any tool possible to influence a customer's perception.

On a simple level, the perception of your brand is built by conversation with customers about what you *do*, not just what you *sell*.

Therefore, a company's wider actions as a corporate citizen have extra weight attached to them. It would be dangerous for the Corporate Responsibility department and marketing departments to collaborate too frequently and work too closely—that sort of relationship tends to engender greenwashing (where a company's actions as a corporate citizen are altered and polished to make them sound more impressive and wide-ranging by the marketing department). However, it *is* essential for the marketing team to understand that their remit is no longer limited to product messaging and customer engagement in the traditional sense. That remit must broaden quite considerably so that those marketing teams have an understanding—and maybe even oversight—of the many different influences that will impact on their role as steward of the company's brand.

This isn't all risk mitigation, of course. It means that there are now other differentiators available to the marketer—for instance, a company's role as a corporate citizen. As Cammie Dunaway, CMO at KidZania, points out:

"The brand means much more to consumers than the packaging and the advertising. So what the brand is doing in the world really matters. For example, the stance that Coca-Cola is taking on access to clean water for consumers and on sustainable packaging—those efforts are building their brand credibility. They become part of the information by which consumers decide whether the brand is something they want to associate with. So I think that the narrow, traditional view of brands as defined by their communications strategy is what no longer works."

How Can Brand Storytelling Help?

In a world where brands must move beyond marketing messages and strive to deliver authenticity and an engaging brand story, marketers tend to find themselves aiming somewhat higher than traditional marketing methods allow. Rather than engagingly communicating the benefits of a product or service, marketers are now tasked with communicating a loftier, broader purpose. Old methods don't work as well. Storytelling does.

The focus on telling stories rather than pushing messaging is scientifically proven, as Paul Zak discussed in *Harvard Business Review*. His work showed that "to motivate a desire to help others, a story must first sustain attention—a scarce resource in the brain—by developing tension during the narrative."

As companies respond to changing customer expectations, marketers are attempting to communicate their brand as rather more than simply logos and packaging—and in so doing, building a broader, more relatable picture of the brand's purpose and place in the world. Storytelling is an essential tool for this because, as Zak highlights: "transcendent purpose is effectively communicated through stories."

Equally, a focus on a *story* rather than specific messages works better in our fragmented landscape when searching for consistency and a pervasive message.

Brand storytelling represents a broadening of the original remit of marketers and communicators to communicate a brand's mission, goals, and positioning.

It's perhaps why 70% of marketers think storytelling is such an important element of their marketing strategy (see Figure 4.1).[2]

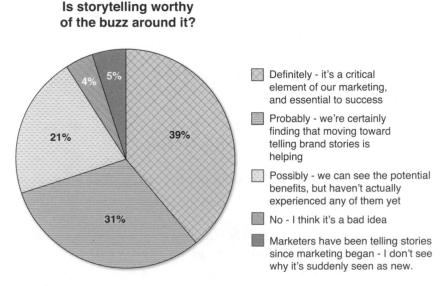

Figure 4.1 The vast majority of companies see storytelling as an important weapon in their arsenal.

Indeed, good storytelling has a meaningful impact on every aspect of "ART." It is a critical element in delivering authentic marketing and an authentic brand. The choice of story and how it's delivered speaks to relevance. And the extent to which that story pervades everything a company does helps brands strengthen in a more transparent age.

A drive from customers for a believable, consistent backstory for a brand has led to new tasks being added to the marketer's To Do list. According to Andy Gibson, former Chief Marketing Officer at Bacardi, marketers must ensure that the brand story is disseminated everywhere possible:

"[Your brand story must be] present in the current marketing story, all being present in the shop, on the phone, in the event, in the ads, in earned media."

It's incumbent upon you, as a marketer, to build on the brand story to add depth and richness and to propagate it both internally and externally.

It's about giving something for people to buy into and reasons to choose you over the competition. It's about showing how your product is superior in many more ways than your competition is even talking about. It's about adding differentiating factors. And it's about ensuring that when the "surface" inevitably gets scratched, the gold goes all the way through—it's not tin underneath.

Your brand story extends beyond your marketing campaign and defines your company holistically. People buy into that story, not your product. They are alienated when you don't live up to that story, and they are increasingly loyal and passionate when you do.

Customers have plenty of choice nowadays. Yours is not the only option. You want them to choose to associate with you, not the competition.

A leading example of brand storytelling success is Dove's campaign for real beauty. Dove, Unilever's brand, has one of the strongest and most clearly defined brand stories out there, centered on "real beauty" for women. Its advertising campaigns have abandoned the faux-science and aggressive catwalk strutting of their cosmetics rivals and replaced it with feel-good stories about women getting into showers to show off their natural glow.

Although it's easy to be dismissive of the slight change (after all, Dove and its rivals are in competition to sell an ever-increasing range of beauty products to people who probably don't need them all), it does work.

Dan Lewis, Chief Public Affairs Officer at Molson Coors, comments: "I look at things like Dove's campaign for real beauty and look at that as almost a CSR approach to engaging with consumers at an emotional level that no standard advertising model would provide."

Dove has done a great job of moving beyond product messaging and tapping into a broader, deeper, more emotional topic—what Andy Gibson called passion platforms. This is something more than a marketing message; the campaign focuses on a belief that the company stands for, something deeper and more profound than simply "Our shower gel leads to softer skin."

There has always been a need for this sort of thinking; it's just that nowadays that need has gotten much more prevalent—and in the future, it will continue to shoot up the marketer's to-do list.

This Isn't a New Coat of Paint—It's Deeper Than That

It's easy to build up a brand story and dismiss your audiences' capacity to find out that, once you scratch the surface, there's nothing there and you've simply added an artisanal skin to a mass-produced product.

And that would be a great mistake. Customers, as we know, are driven increasingly by a search for authenticity. Equally, transparency is putting more a pressure on corporations. These two facts in combination mean that marketers have less ability to pull the wool over the eyes of their target demographic.

You've got to live your brand story, not just say you do. Dan Lewis has certainly noticed this in his work at Molson Coors:

"I think [customer] expectations of seeing more of that kind of engagement with their brand is just going to grow and grow, and that's going to put a lot of pressure on those of us who develop content, do the storytelling, find ways to engage...to make the connection in a different way, as opposed to hitting them over the head with an ad."

That's why it's so essential that your whole company buy in. We cover this in depth in Chapter 5, "Getting Your House in Order: How Internal Buy-In Impacts External Marketing."

How Can You Build Storytelling into Your Marketing Campaign?

The benefits—even the requirement—of building storytelling into a broader marketing strategy seem obvious. I've put together your To Do list—based on feedback from 16 Chief Marketing Officers—if you'd like to begin to tell a story around your brand:

1. **Determine where your brand story will come from.** The main lesson here? Don't manufacture something from nothing. Pick something you're already doing. This can be aspirational (a "campaign for real beauty"), it can be a legacy point (the rich history of Coors Banquet Beer), it can be based on sustainability and corporate responsibility (Coca-Cola's work on clean water), or it can come from your employees (First Direct and customer service).

2. **Don't tell it yourself.** This is beyond marketing and communications. Your job is to accentuate a message that's already out there and already being communicated. Twenty percent of marketers say customers have more power to define your brand than anyone else. Your employees are a good bet, too.

3. **Make sure you can tell it persuasively.** If you're going to ascribe the responsibility to tell the story to employees instead of the marketing and communications departments, you'll need a different set of processes to sign off. You can't strangle a story by running it past legal every time you have an opportunity to propagate it. You'll need to do an internal communications job to ensure that your C-suite and legal departments are on board with employees—and customers—discussing this stuff freely.

4. **Ensure that this is for the long term.** A brand story is most emphatically not a campaign with an end date. It's far more wide-reaching than that. You need to plan further ahead and build foundations that last longer than any typical marketing

campaign planning process you've done before. That means getting employee buy-in (which is why we talk not about creating a story, but about accentuating an existing one). This isn't a paint job—it's something people sign up for.

5. **Use the story with more than just your customer base.** Your brand story will help engage and build morale with your workforce, too. Use it to do so.

The Battle Between Art and Science Isn't Over Yet

The growing importance of storytelling raises an interesting counterpoint to our data-obsessed age.

Yes, in many ways, marketing is moving along the continuum away from art and toward science, but there is still an important role for emotion, and human connection to play. After all, however precise and automated marketing campaigns become, the target will always be a human.

Campaigns like Dove's—broader, story based, and emotionally affecting—are the types of engagements customers will see a lot more of in the years ahead.

Consumers will respond better to them and, consequently, will expect more of the same. They will expect the brands they patronize to be able to deliver engagement like this.

And as Dan Lewis, Chief Public Affairs Officer at Molson Coors told us, "That puts pressure on those who develop content and do that storytelling to make the connection in a different way, as opposed to hitting them over the head with an ad."

Endnotes

1. Paul J. Zak, "Why Your Brain Loves Good Storytelling," *Harvard Business Review* (28 October 2014). https://hbr.org/2014/10/why-your-brain-loves-good-storytelling/

2. Future of Marketing Survey.

5

Getting Your House in Order: How Internal Buy-In Impacts External Marketing

"The ability to cross lines and connect the various parts of the organization (in a way we've never worried about histori-cally) is much more of an imperative—there's much more of a collaborative, matrixed way of thinking [needed]."

—Barry Wolfish, Chief Marketing Officer, Land O' Lakes

Internal engagement has a strong correlation to external engagement.

Why? Because your employees are increasingly important to any future customer experience delivery:

1. For a consistent, authentic, and engaging external brand story, it's essential that multiple departments communicate, collaborate, and innovate together—that they "sing from the same hymn sheet" in external communications.

2. It's going to be impossible to foment the collaborative, transparent internal approach necessary for "ART" in marketing without considerable buy-in from all levels and areas of the business.

3. Transparency and authenticity mean that your customers are increasingly able to "look behind the curtain" and will judge your company on its inner workings. Only by engaging other internal teams will you be able to ensure these inner workings are of the requisite standard.

This chapter covers how your company should engage employees so they're an asset when building authentic, relevant, and transparent marketing instead of a risk to be managed.

We look first at internal buy-in—how to engage, inspire, and encourage disparate internal groups to get behind the broader brand messaging and corporate "story" you want to present.

From there, we look at internal organizational models, including how they're evolving, why there's pressure to evolve, and how your company can take steps to deliver a more agile company through internal restructuring.

Consistent Experience Across Multiple Channels Is Hard but Essential

"To deliver a seamless experience, one informed by data and imbued with brand purpose, all employees in the company, from store clerks and phone center reps, to IT specialists and the marketing team itself, must share a common vision."[1]

—Arons et al., "The Ultimate Marketing Machine"

The focus on delivering a consistent customer experience across all channels and touchpoints has never been more important—and is continuing to grow in importance at an exponential rate.

Marketing channels are fragmenting, and the customer journey is changing markedly. As we saw in Chapter 2, "What is a Customer Journey and Why Does It Matter?" we've transitioned from a funnel to a circle in which far more elements impact on a customer's experience, both pre and post sale. Not only that, but customers now expect companies to be where they are and respond when they ask them something

Typical internal organizational models make this challenge more complex: Social media teams tended to be set up as discrete units separate from the rest of marketing. Customer service is only now becoming part of a broader marketing department. Communications and marketing are often still entirely separate departments. Within marketing departments, different people are responsible for managing different channels and platforms. There is a lot of fragmentation, so delivering a consistent voice to customers—wherever they are, for whatever they need, on whatever channel they use—is incredibly difficult.

Every marketing message must be part of a unified whole, and that required unification means internal departments must collaborate and CMOs must have a broader role than ever. Consistent internal buy-in is essential for future success in the new world of marketing. Andy Gibson, formerly Chief Marketing Officer at Bacardi, knew this challenge well:

"Everything needs to be linked up. An event that I run in Puerto Rico for Bacardi Triangle has to show up in shop, it has to show up in bar, it has to show up in social ecosystems, it has to show up in earned media and paid media. The consumer is now so demanding of everything being consistent, joined up and available wherever they go, that I don't think that the CMO can any longer be disconnected from the commercial customer end of the organization.

"The customer end is the consumer end, is the brand end. I think it's a circle these days—I don't think it's an end."

It's critical for us to move beyond a paradigm of different departmental responsibilities for different aspects of the customer journey. Your customers expect everything to be part of a unified, consistent process—a circle, not a funnel.

And that circle passes through many new and fragmenting channels. As Michael Zuna, Aflac's Chief Marketing Officer told me: "What we're trying to do at Aflac is ensure that, no matter what way you want to shop, no matter what level of service you want to receive and/or expect, no matter how you want to interact, we're trying to be there to provide you with the highest level of experience."

Therefore, internal organization and communication needs to reflect that change. There has been a huge expansion in customer touchpoints that a brand is forced to manage. You must ensure that, across that proliferation of touchpoints, you have an organization and an internal communications structure that allows for consistency.

Transparency Makes Consistency Essential

Of course, this consistency isn't just there as a carrot. There's a stick, too. And that's the result of transparency.

Social media means that customers are more able to communicate with one another than ever before. That means inconsistent treatment gets highlighted. That corporate *faux pas* get highlighted. And not just highlighted in a locality or particular market, but worldwide.

According to Frans Cornelis, Chief Marketing Officer at Randstad, "Everything is connected, and viral comments on social media travel from France to the U.S., to the U.K. fast. It's akin to us having woken up a very dangerous dragon, and we haven't found sleeping pills for the beast yet."

The main reason firms are forced to bleed the same color wherever they're sliced is that we live in an age of unrivaled transparency.

Build Your Corporate Onion

You've already seen that your brand must deliver consistent messaging whenever and wherever it is consumed. Beyond that, to deliver an authentic, engaging customer experience in an age of unparalleled transparency between brand and consumer, the company must look the same however it is sliced.

Every level and department in a company must exhibit the same traits as those proposed as fundamental tenets of the brand in external marketing and the brand story. Marco Ryan, chief digital officer at Thomas Cook, has been responsible for "digital transformation" across several companies in his career. He advocates the strengths of digital to help deliver this drive for internal consistency.

In his view, we should be imagining a "digital onion" (the title of his forthcoming book on the subject). At the core of the digital onion is the customer. The outer skin that gives the onion its shape is the customer lifecycle, representing all the different customer touchpoints, or places where the customer "touches" the brand. Ryan states:

"No two onions are the same, and there is an organic nature about them. But as you peel back the shell, you discover, layer by layer, the different capabilities that support the core. Closest to the core are factors such as user experience, content marketing, and CRM. Toward the top, you might find analytics and product innovation. Farther out, but enabling all the layers beneath, you might find technology, and so on."

Ryan's point is that brands must organize themselves and deliver experience so that whichever slice out of the onion you take, you see, top to bottom, the same capabilities and focus.

So regardless of where customers are along the journey—discover, purchase consideration, or post-sale—the experience they get is consistent, based on the same information and corporate capabilities.

Internal Is Where This All Begins

Being honest and transparent in one part of your business but not the other isn't going to work. The experience that the Customer Service department delivers can't be markedly different from that which the Marketing department promises. You can't communicate authentically if your internal workings don't match up to your external communications.

For a company to flourish, the coordination and alignment across a vast, complicated, multinational business must be more successful than it ever has been.

Everything starts with internal activation. When you get everyone singing from the same song sheet, progress can be made.

For that to happen, marketing leaders must persuade and encourage the rest of the organization to buy in. CMOs have constantly highlighted to me the necessity to spend increasing amounts of time on internal activation.

So how do you "activate" internal employees and help them help you?

Further Reading

Be sure to read the case study on page 104 at the end of the chapter on Molson Coors and "Our Brew." It's their tool for internal engagement, which has been enormously successful.

On a broader level, four steps are involved in getting your employees activated—passionate and committed to a brand story, tied to the broader corporate refocus you're promoting, and knowledgeable enough to act as brand ambassadors and corporate storytellers.

Step 1: Build from the Ground Up, Not the Top Down

"You have to get the team involved as the recipe [is] put together rather than just present them with the cake."

—Cammie Dunaway, Chief Marketing Officer, KidZania

This is Management 101. If you want people to invest in a project or task, you should give them the autonomy to help build it, and let them see that their input helps influence the project.

Cammie Dunaway realized this while she was the CMO at Yahoo!. Early in her time at the company, she ran a major brand repositioning exercise. Her big takeaway? Get the team "baking the cake" with you. No amount of icing, candles, or funny little models on top of it will make that cake as appealing to those team members.

It's essential that the teams you need to buy into a project are able to influence and understand that project from the ground up. If you need engineer buy-in, get engineers running the focus groups. Don't just reveal a finalized product and a pretty new brand video. Allow the team to build with you, and they're more likely to buy into the whole thing.

Step 2: Build a Clear Role for the Individual and Highlight the Benefits of That Role

Back to Marketing 101: To persuade anyone, you've got to talk about benefits to the individual.

You've also got to clarify the role that individual plays in what is often a broad, company-wide shift. It's essential that marketers render explicitly for different groups how they participate, what their role is, and what the value is in enhancing customer experience.

Your job is to draw the connections in what the company is trying to do, what the employee's active role is in doing that, and why that role matters.

That means a certain level of cheerleading and motivating. Exuberance ultimately helps you transform an organization so that employees are ready to focus on customer experience. As Arra Yerganian, CMO at One Medical Group told me:

"If everyone inside the organization has a mentality of service to the customer, because they understand, at its purest sense, the mission of the organization, I think there's great opportunity for the company to be successful."

As part of this internal communication, it's essential to have clarity not only on roles and benefits, but also on what it means to be successful in those specific roles you're outlining. You must be explicit in terms of the metrics you'll be using. If you're engaging your customer service team, you focus on metrics specific to customer service; if you're in product development, it's essential to look at what is being done with the design of the product to enhance usability, stickiness, and satisfaction.

Step 3: Immerse Your Employees in the Journey to Reassure Them

In any company-wide engagement, particular groups of employees matter more, and have a more important role to play. For these people, you should go further than with the rest of the employee base. Axel Springer, the German media company, did exactly that.

In 2012, the CEO of the company decided that the company wasn't well-equipped to deal with the enormous changes that digital was driving in their area of operations. He needed to effect a broad change across the whole organization, and he determined that several members of his top leadership team weren't engaged enough or comfortable enough with this mission.

He decided to immerse that top leadership in the "digital way of life," and he sent two of his top executives on a "Silicon Sabbatical" to Silicon Valley for six months. While there, those executives were expected to share a house, get rid of their corporate phones, and immerse themselves in the community and environment of Silicon Valley.

This represented a major risk for the company as a whole. These major executives weren't really staff that the company could afford to lose for any extended period of time. Kai Diekmann was the editor-in-chief and publisher at the BILD group; and Peter Wurtenberger was the chief marketing officer for Axel Springer Media Impact.

On their return, the executives were not only fully committed to the digital transformation the CEO was advocating, but they led the adoption themselves, setting and driving toward goals, cutting waste, and focusing correctly.

Indeed, the visit and process were so valuable that the first executives extended their stay by two months. A "Visiting Fellow" program also was established to ensure that other employees routinely got the benefits Wurtenberger and Diekmann experienced. As a write-up on the company's own blog stated,

"The personal contact to Silicon Valley and the proximity to developments for future digital businesses in the past months proved very valuable for Axel Springer."[2]

The engagement you're looking for from employees might or might not center on a digital transformation, but the general observation—to get important employees immersed in the project and focus on getting them to buy in—is important whatever that process is. As Marco Ryan, Chief Digital Officer for Thomas Cook, states:

"I think people underestimate the degree of stress digital change can have on the individual, some of whom don't know what they don't know, so often in their minds, you are asking the 'turkey to vote for Thanksgiving.'"

It's essential that you communicate clearly the role you're asking an employee to play—and how that role will benefit not only them, but the company as a whole. And you should repeat that message often. Many CMOs I spoke to told me they found themselves reiterating the same message, again and again—that to do so was necessary to ensure that the message got across.

Step 4: Focus on the Long Term, Not the "Year of Customer Experience"

One CMO talked with some frustration about phrases like the "year of customer experience" because it implies a temporary project—and a temporary mindset—that's somewhat unhelpful. After that year's done, it's often assumed that the strategy is over.

With the broad, deep changes this book is advocating—fundamentally changing a company to deliver authenticity, relevance, and transparency—it would be enormously dangerous to suggest that this change is a temporary one. Starting down a path as challenging as "ART" and then giving up would not only be a waste of resource, but actively damaging. It's akin to abandoning a corporate Twitter account a year after you start it. It's worse than never having started it in the first place.

Instead, companies must take a long-term approach. An approach where employees are involved from the start, have clarity on their roles and responsibilities, and are enthused to help take the company on this challenging journey.

Of course, all that is easier said than done. What follows is an in-depth case study with Dan Lewis, Chief Public Affairs Officer for Molson Coors, about how the beer giant did all this in the real world—and reaped the reward.

Endnotes

1. Marc de Swaan Arons, Frank van den Driest, and Keith Weed, "The Ultimate Marketing Machine," *Harvard Business Review* (July 2014). https://hbr.org/2014/07/the-ultimate-marketing-machine.

2. "Axel Springer extends its presence in Silicon Valley with new personnel." http://www.axelspringer.de/en/presse/Axel-Springer-extends-its-presence-in-Silicon-Valley-with-new-personnel_16674966.html.

CASE STUDY

How Molson Coors Achieved Deep Employee Engagement and Alignment Through "Our Brew"

"Our Brew has become our story internally. It's the story that people tell each other. It's the story that they tell others when they're asked about the company."

—Dan Lewis, Chief Public Affairs Officer, Molson Coors

In 2008, the top 100 executives at Molson Coors met up. That meeting's purpose was to build a plan to accomplish two goals:

1. To pull together employees from diverse cultures. Several markets had recently come together under one company, and they needed to be unified. The different areas had different understandings of what the company was and what it should mean. The executive team wanted to resolve that.
2. To convey the company's longer-term business strategy, to make the longer-term vision and direction of the company accessible to all employees.

Why? Those hundred executives had noticed that they weren't able to accelerate the way they would like to, nor get the benefits that should be accruing from this larger, new company. They'd identified a lack of common ground across the organization. According to Dan Lewis, Chief Public Affairs Officer at the company, they were looking to build:

"A common understanding of the business, but also a common vocabulary, shared values, a belief in ourselves, an understanding of the things that are important to us as a company, and a clear idea of what success looks like for Molson Coors."

The executives believed that building up that common ground across the organization, and up and down every level of the business, was fundamental to achieve this new acceleration into the future.

The strategy they used to make that acceleration? "Our Brew."

CASE STUDY

About Molson Coors

Molson Coors is a North American brewing company, formed in 2005 with the merger of the Molson and Coors beer companies. Those two companies have considerably longer histories: Molson was founded in 1786 and Coors in 1873.

Molson Coors is the world's seventh-largest brewer by volume, with revenues of $6.7 billion in 2011, and has more than 5,000 employees across operations in the United States, Canada, and Europe.

Dan Lewis has been the company's chief public affairs officer since 2006. He previously held management, public affairs, and corporate communications roles with airlines Lufthansa and Delta. In addition to being a contributor throughout the book, Dan allowed me to interview him for this more in-depth case study on the company's Our Brew internal communications work.

What Process Did You Use?

Working in collaboration with the consultancy ?What If! (www.whatifinnovation.com), the company began to reach out to its employees. "These guys were really good at this. They had done this for a number of companies, and they had a process. And I have to say, I had been a part of change efforts at a number of companies for a couple of decades at that point and had never encountered a process like this one.

"But they brought their process in for us, and walked us through it, and what was interesting about it was they didn't expect us to just adopt this process, or just allow them to come marching through the door to do it—they actually allowed us to customize it and evolve it to work in our company."

From the ground up, Our Brew revolved around eliciting feedback from existing employees at all levels of the company. From that first step of gathering feedback, through a process the company referred to as clue hunting, four other steps were taken to achieve the two goals stated at the outset.

This case study takes you through the five steps that Molson Coors took to build Our Brew. It looks at how the company disseminated its message internally to drive engagement and sustained interest over many years, including through the acquisition of a large business in Europe. It also covers the deliverables and assesses the success of the project.

CASE STUDY

Step 1: Clue Hunting

"What we found through the process was that we were actually able, in the Our Brew 'keg,' to actually bring together the company's culture, its values, its beliefs, in how it wanted to work, together with the business strategy and make it all feel very consistent and unified for people."

Clue hunting was a fundamental part of the process that the team at ?What If! proposed. Essentially, the goal was to gather as much feedback from the company as possible—to guide the definition of the company's culture, beliefs, and goals. The process was as follows:

1. Assign individuals around the company as "clue hunters." These were the "foot soldiers." Importantly, they were drawn from all levels of the company to engage their fellow employees—this wasn't a top-down approach.

2. Give them specific questions to ask—"a handful of really very direct but thoughtful questions...they would cause a person to pause in their daily routine and really ask themselves about the culture they work in." In addition, ensure that each clue hunter asked these questions of ten employees from around the company, working in different functions and at different levels. Some of the questions asked included:

   a. What's good about our culture?

   b. What is worth keeping?

   c. What do we need to improve on?

   d. What do we need to leave behind altogether?

   e. What's distinctive about our culture?

   f. What do you believe is somewhat bland and indistinct from everybody else?

Step 2: Collating Clues

The clue-hunting exercise elicited thousands of clues. From there, the team at ?What If! was responsible for pulling all this raw data into some sort of order and bundling bits of feedback into groups.

Importantly, *no editing took place*. Responses to the clue hunter questions were left exactly as given, with no changes made. They were simply organized under 50 to 60 different headings, put on yellow sticky notes, and placed on walls in one conference room (one would assume those walls were very yellow by the end).

CASE STUDY

Step 3: Consolidating Clues

The clue hunters were then invited back together to take a look at their efforts. Facilitators gathered the clue hunters into teams, whose job was to consolidate the thousands of individual bits of feedback into a handful of core messages.

Lewis characterizes the process thus far as "a funnel process that went very broadly out to the company, to gather up the feedback and then make it useful by pulling it down to a level where the most important themes would rise to the top."

Listening Only

All the way through to Step 3, a relatively advanced stage, company leaders did nothing but listen. They had no role in directing questions, editing answers, or suggesting changes.

Control was handed to the clue hunters, sourced from across the business, who themselves largely functioned as data gatherers.

Important here is the CEO's approach to the exercise. Instead of structuring the process to learn more about, for instance, three topics he'd already chosen as important, he allowed this to be a wider process, with no bias or premeditated points of view.

Step 4: Senior Leadership

At this stage, the process gathered up "maybe a couple of big themes, and lots and lots of reinforcing messaging that came directly in the voice of the people who offered it up." It was a process similar to the one many companies use to gather external consumer insights, of "really gathering up those nuggets of insights, reflections, beliefs that people had and, again, allowing the best to rise to the top."

That feedback then came before the most senior leadership in the company—a group of eight executives representing the biggest divisions across the entire business.

That leadership team met for a day and a half and, facilitated by the team at ?What If!, "carved through this stuff and decided what to do about it." At the end of that meeting, the CEO stood up and said, "I believe now I've

CASE STUDY

heard from everyone very clearly, and I think it's my job now to go back and sit down and draft what I believe to be the story of our company."

The CEO took responsibility from that point on to come up with a response to the company's feedback—surfaced through clue hunting—and use it to build the future.

Step 5: The CEO

Using feedback from the entire employee base, as well as from the leadership team specifically, the CEO drafted the first items to go on the first Our Brew "keg"—a visual aid for the dissemination of those first items (literally a keg of beer with words printed on it), which was released in 2009.

1. **What Will We Do?** This element aimed to define the company's overarching purpose. That purpose was initially defined as: "Challenge the expected to deliver extraordinary brands that delight the world's beer drinkers."
2. **Who Will We Be?** This element attempted to define the sort of people who work at Molson Coors—and those who would fit well with the company's culture and goals.
3. **How Will We Work?** This element proposed details on how employees would work—both together and individually—to fulfil their responsibilities and achieve their goals. As Lewis points out, this section clarified "a 'right way' and 'wrong way.'"
4. **What We Value:** The core values that the Our Brew process highlighted as important to employees were given pride of place in the center of the keg.
5. **Our Ambition:** This section clarified the fundamental vision that the company was attempting to achieve, while...
6. **What We Must Deliver:** ...this section helped define the more specific and practical long-term goals to 2012.

The CEO essentially "put [the feedback] into words that, to him, reflected where he believed the company was going."

At this point, that first keg went to the rest of the senior leadership team for review and then again to the entire body of clue hunters. Only afterward was the first keg of Our Brew ready for wider consumption.

The entire process took approximately six months, although, as Dan Lewis points out, they knew they had "enough" feedback only when things began to repeat themselves. Taking time to get this right was important. "It's

CASE STUDY

the tendency of organizations to want to short-circuit this process because it does feel cumbersome. It's uncomfortable. It's a period of transition and unpredictable outcomes, and you have to have a CEO and a leadership team who are willing to let go."

Dan also points out that Molson Coors was operating from a position of relative strength throughout the process: The company was under no real pressure to transform itself. Taking this amount of time to go through the process as comprehensively as Molson Coors would be considerably harder for a company under some form of duress, as is often the spark for a review process like this in the first place.

How Did You Disseminate That New Keg of Our Brew to Ensure Buy-in?

The Our Brew method had a built-in advantage when looking to secure buy-in for that first keg. Employees had been engaged, obviously and publicly, from the very beginning of the process. Employees from all levels of the company had even asked the questions, as clue hunters. As a result, they were confident that the end result was based on their own feedback and were more receptive to the findings than they would have otherwise been. They had built this.

Other steps were taken to build on that initial progress. First, the company felt it was important to build out "a lot of color" essentially, further details and nuance around the six headings on the keg, to ensure that people understood them as clearly and fully as possible. That additional color was important to "get people to get very comfortable using the keg in their daily lives, and make it a part of the conversation, the vocabulary of the company."

In attempting to achieve this goal, the team made a handbook. This wasn't the typical corporate value statement glossy brochure, though—it was more practical, usable, and relevant.

What Did the Handbook Look Like?

1. It provided a lot of simple description around each section of the keg, sometimes simply adding a couple comments or images per page.
2. It contained a series of exercises for group work, to encourage interactivity.
3. It contained stories reflecting what certain values meant.

CASE STUDY

4. It contained deeper definitions of some of the terminology used on the keg. "So what do we mean by an 'extraordinary brand'? We felt we should define that for people so that those conversations taking place around Our Brew could be deeper and richer than they would otherwise be."

5. It had an environment-specific format—wire bound, so it could lie flat and be used in the various different parts of the Molson Coors operation, from board room to brewery floor. This format was intentional, to avoid the risk of many corporate internal communications: "[A lot of times, the company's] strategy document would appear in a beautifully bound copy, full color, and it was a great read first time through. But then it landed on a shelf and barely was ever pulled out again."

6. It contained a commitment from the senior leadership. "The back of the book had a commitment from the leadership team that said, 'We're signing up for this. Please join us.' And everyone signed it, including both the families, both Pete Coors and Eric Molson."

The handbook was a success. "People had a lot of fun with it! They found it highly engaging, they could go through it on their own, they could take it home and go through it with their family. A lot of the managers took it onto the brewery floor, dropped it on top of a keg [or] on a desk, and used the images, text, and exercises to stimulate a conversation."

That was exactly what the leadership wanted. "The idea was that this thing should not collect dust, that it should be attractive enough that people would want to put it on their desk, where they can refer to it regularly. I certainly found myself doing that, and I saw it everywhere I went, on everyone's desk. It was, I think, successful to the greatest extent a static communication tool like that can be."

Getting Local Managers Onside: "Our Brew in a Box" and Senior Leadership Training

"We didn't just load up books on a truck for delivery, pat ourselves on the back, and say, 'There we go—we got that out of the door.'"

The "static tool," the Our Brew handbook, was only one piece of a bigger jigsaw puzzle, a broader campaign to build and sustain engagement. The rest was informed by the concept of local ownership of the project, in which smaller, regionally specific teams worked together on the exercises and ideas contained within Our Brew. This was not a project disseminated

CASE STUDY

from on high by senior leadership; it evolved through the actions of employees across the organization, at junior and senior levels.

This idea of local ownership was critical to success. "If your goal is to engage people, it's not going to happen top down. It needs to happen at a local level."

So the team provided tools and resources to leaders throughout the organization in the form of "Our Brew in a Box." This package contained videos, presentation slides, stories, and other elements of a toolkit to complement the handbook. Those handbooks were disseminated "only when employees were ready—they'd worked through the exercises, listened to presentations, and understood what was happening."

Considering that the 'last mile of delivery', the briefing and training itself, was being conducted by managers across the organization, the company invested a lot of time and energy in training and engaging those managers first. Senior leadership went out to facilities around the company to conduct the "Our Brew in a Box" training for managers, for those managers to then conduct it with their own teams.

"The one death stroke of a lot of these kinds of engagement campaigns for large organizations is when you drop something off with your managers and then tell them. 'This is what you need to deliver—good luck with that!' You've got to get those managers onside first."

Those managers would see the tools to use for training their own teams in action, they would see senior leadership committed to this, and they'd participate in discussions with that senior leadership about each section of the keg—what it would mean for the company and what it would mean for their individual teams specifically.

"They would get people involved, they would do the exercises in the back of the book, and they would do some storytelling exercises; they would learn how to tell great stories, how to pull great stories out of people. And all of that happened before an employee ever got their hands on a book."

Engaging Employees

The most important point about this final step of engaging the rest of the employee base is the fact it wasn't rushed. Before these employees receive a copy of the handbook, they have undergone training from managers who had their own tailored training, and who received it from senior leadership, who took time out of their own schedules (full days) to visit facilities and

CASE STUDY

conduct that training. Taking time to build each level in a solid way before moving on to the next was fundamental to the Our Brew process.

For this final stage, employees were delivered training and a handbook from their direct manager or supervisor. This was a conscious and important decision. "That made a huge difference because if somebody came in from Corporate, or someone showed up from HR...it would not have engaged these people in the same way. When their own shop floor manager sat down with them and said, 'So, this is important—I'm on board with this, and I want to bring you on board as well,' it has a far deeper impact."

Of course, equally important, those managers were able to point out that the entirety of the topics—the values, the handbook, everything about Our Brew—was borne out of the feedback from those employees and their peers around the organization.

"[Managers] are able to say, 'This is the feedback we hear from you— this whole thing is built around what you said.' And people got it, from the start of the clue hunting exercise, and understood how the thing was built before they ever turned the handbook's first page."

Did It Work?

In 2008, the "engagement score"—a metric run by Towers Perrin against a calculation of how many people within the company are "engaged"—stood at 80%. At that point, the highest-performing companies using this metric were getting a score of 84%.

So when Molson Coors launched this engagement process, the goal was to get to 84% in the first three-year cycle, by 2012. As Lewis told me, this was a long-term effort, and the company gave itself time—a full three years—to get it right.

Yet in 2009, just one year after launching Our Brew, Molson Coors conducted the employee engagement survey again—and achieved an 86% rating. "We had knocked our own target out, and we had actually exceeded the baseline target for high-performing companies. The result coming out of the blocks was immense."

People were deeply engaged. The company had hit a whole set of key metrics, succeeding against employee judgment on how leadership was communicating with employees, employees' beliefs on the company's future, and employees' confidence in leadership.

CASE STUDY

Sustaining Success

"We were obviously enormously pleased [with our 2009 scores], but then the challenge shifts to how you sustain that very high level."

In 2008, when launching Our Brew, Molson Coors was in a privileged position: It was able to assign time, effort, and focus to build and run a comprehensive employee engagement process while under no real internal or external pressures to do so.

Of course, as time goes on, situations tend to change.

New Acquisitions

For Molson Coors, that began to happen in 2012. The company made a large acquisition in central Europe, adding 11 new markets, 7,000 employees, and several very different cultures to the company. "It was an enormous test of Our Brew because it would be the first time that we tried to take it to a completely new culture."

Of course, the initial clue-hunting exercise conducted to build the engagement tool—the hops in Molson Coors' brew, if you will—had not been conducted with any of these new employees.

That collaborative approach that had been so important to the initial success of the program was impossible to replicate with this new group. The company couldn't completely change its corporate culture whenever a new group of employees was hired.

"The people we were taking Our Brew to now had not participated in any clue hunting and [had not been] involved in the process of building Our Brew. And so that was an enormous challenge, but [it] also ended up being a great opportunity."

The company decided to use a similar but less extensive process with these new employees. They told these new employees that they were not prepared to change the fundamentals of Our Brew as seen on the keg, but they would make adjustments. "[We said,] 'We're very interested in hearing your feedback on how we should talk about these things, how we bring them to life in the business, and any thoughts for us that would make us better at what we're trying to do.'"

Based on that feedback—a mini version of clue hunting—the company made several tweaks to Our Brew. That process was completed between 2012 and 2014, and success has been equivalently barnstorming as the original Our Brew rollout.

CASE STUDY

"[These employees] are actually our most highly engaged workforce at this point—they're very excited, and there's a lot of enthusiasm."

Continuing Evolution

At the end of 2014, Peter Swinburn, the CEO who ran Molson Coors while Our Brew was developed and launched, retired.

Mark Hunter, previously the European CEO, took on the role of global CEO. He felt that the early stages of his tenure was the best possible opportunity to make any changes to such a successful project.

During the six years in which Our Brew ran, the company had continued to gather feedback on Our Brew and refine the ambition and purpose of the company. In late 2014, the early days of Hunter's tenure, the company took the opportunity to evolve and augment the program. With this feedback in mind, Hunter edited down the purpose of the company from "Challenging expectations to create extraordinary brands that delight the world's beer drinkers" to the more succinct "Delight the World's Beer Drinkers."

The previous iteration of "Our Ambition"—to become a top 4 global brewer—was found via continuous feedback not to engage employees well enough. They didn't understand how it directly related to their role, and they could not apply it to their everyday work. So this, too, has evolved, into "Become first choice for consumers and customers."

The overarching message from this new process? Keep evolving.

Lewis told me that "My takeaway from the work since 2008 is that you have to keep evolving. You don't change your fundamentals—your values can't be changed with each strategic planning cycle—but you have to stay open and flexible, you have to be listening, and you have to keep programs like Our Brew highly relevant to the workforce, or else you'll lose touch and it won't matter to people."

How Does Internal Engagement Influence External Brand and Marketing?

"Times have certainly changed since 2008, but I think we tapped into something early on that has become a much bigger part of brand building and a much bigger part of a company like ours that wants to stay close to its consumers and stay connected to the market."

CASE STUDY

The biggest thing Molson Coors learned from the internal clue hunting process, and the creation of Our Brew as a whole, was unexpected. And something that gave the company valuable insight on what it takes to flourish in today's more collaborative, social, and consumer-controlled world.

Building a culture focused on engagement—on staying connected to a brand purpose and story, having people pulling in the same direction, and giving them a voice in the process—gains extra importance in the new world of customer expectations we're operating in. As Lewis told me, "What we know is that brands don't belong to companies anymore; they belong to the people who choose to buy them."

As we see throughout the feedback that has built this book, it's no longer possible to simply "market" to potential customers. You've got to meet them where they are and speak to them about things they're really interested in. You've got to tell them a story that they can believe in. And, as Lewis told me, "You can't just shout about your products."

To be successful, your company must be authentic. And to be authentic, you must harness your entire organization—getting everyone aligned behind the same consistent brand story and then encouraging them to tell that story.

"Your people give you an authenticity and an outreach and a connectivity, and [they] open the doors to communities that you might never reach if you followed traditional marketing and brand management paths."

How Our Brew Impacted Employee Advocacy

"The brands have learned...that authenticity really matters, and they have really embraced what we're trying to do on the employee side of the house to engage our employees. They've been huge champions of this and are very grateful that we're bringing to them another very authentic, energized, engaged team of people to the job."

The power of a collaborative, employee-led approach (discovered in the process of building Our Brew) has had a deep impact on broader operations within Molson Coors, not least within the marketing department. The employee advocacy program is but one example of an Our Brew descendant.

Marketing content for the company now comes from many more internal groups than previously: brand teams, corporate responsibility teams, the "beer reverence" team, and even the archivist in the company's history

CASE STUDY

center. This content is then made available to all employees, who can make it their own by customizing it and sharing it with their communities.

The uptake for this program has significantly exceeded initial targets. Lewis believes that this is largely due to the high level of engagement imbued by Our Brew. "We were really looking to first get a few hundred people involved in [the employee advocacy program], and I think we actually crossed the thousand mark less than six months into the process. I think this is an extension of Our Brew. It's a belief that 'I am this company, and my voice matters. This is what the company expects of me, and I'm there to help shape the direction and be a spokesperson for the company in many ways.'"

If companies are looking to build the authenticity inherent in an employee advocacy program, they need internal buy-in to the extent that a program like Our Brew generates it.

"We've got people now who, through their social media channels and through the connections that they've built up in their online communities, have the ability to really move the needle in terms of positioning for the company and for brands. They can operate as brand insiders, in many cases, and share stories and insights about the company in a very authentic way that we wouldn't get by just following a more traditional path."

What Did You Learn, and What Can Other People Learn from Our Brew?

Throughout the ongoing Our Brew journey, Lewis and the team learned a few important things. First, you shouldn't—and can't—effectively market to employees, nor can you use brand building techniques to build a corporate culture. You must engage them. Our Brew simply told the story of the company—it wasn't an attempt to brand internal culture, implemented in a top-down manner by senior management. As Lewis pointed out:

"I don't believe in branding your culture. These are exercises that feel good to management but mean very little to people. You've got to tap into and guide what's already there.... You have to collaborate with [your] stakeholders to build something together. The unique thing about Our Brew is that it is of, for, and by the people. They were very much involved in creating it."

CASE STUDY

How You Get There Is Often More Important Than Where You End Up

The last word goes to Lewis, who told me that the journey itself was actually more important than the destination:

"It was the process for getting there that had a lot to do with where we ended up. I think that that's probably the piece that we lowballed, that we didn't really expect. The process to getting to Our Brew ended up being so important and so powerful that it had this...ability to engage, far beyond what we had actually originally intended. And now that we know that, we've adopted that approach to engaging our people more broadly in lots of other areas.

"[The process of collaboration] has actually changed the culture, really changed the culture in terms of the way we make decisions and engage our people. It was a watershed moment, but it was definitely an 'Aha' moment—it wasn't something we expected."

6

How an Evolved Internal Structure Drives Authentic, Relevant, and Transparent Marketing

"[T]he ability to cross lines and connect the various parts of the organization in a way we've never worried about histori- cally is much more of an imperative."

—Barry Wolfish, Chief Marketing Officer, Land O'Lakes

Let's say that you want to evolve a marketing department into one that's capable of flourishing in the years ahead. You want a depart- ment that's able to meet customer expectations for authentic, rele- vant, and transparent marketing campaigns. It's essential, then, that employees are buying into a longer-term strategy and that the com- pany is giving those employees the environment and resources they'll need to flourish. Your strategy to evolve and improve internal organi- zation models is thus critical to the success of your marketing.

In this chapter, we look at the core elements of this strategy. The chapter consists of four parts.

First, we look at how the role of the CMO is evolving. As we've seen, the role of the marketer within a business is expanding to cover other aspects of the customer experience. The chief marketing officer is often at the vanguard of this shift.

Second, we investigate the importance of a centralized "market- ing execution" team. Although this sounds more like a tactical devel- opment than a strategic one, a team like this is essential to the success of a more modern, "ART" based approach to marketing. Not only is it set to better share insight and learnings internally, but its presence frees up the rest of the department to focus better on longer-term, strategic goals.

Third, we look into one of the banes of any attempt to make marketing more nimble, agile, and transparent: silos. We look at why they spring up, why they're a problem, and how you can begin to eradicate them within your business.

Fourth, we look at agility. As businesses face pressure to "increase the speed" on many levels (because of customer expectation, fragmenting of marketing platforms, new types of competition, and more), it's essential that companies reformat themselves to become more agile and nimble. In this chapter, we look at how some leading companies are beginning to do exactly that.

The Chief Marketing Officer's Evolution

Sixty-nine percent of senior marketers are "trusted, strategic members of the C-suite" and/or are "increasing their stature and credibility with key business leaders in their organization."[1]

If a company wants a coordinated response to customer experience and seeks the capacity to generate marketing that is relevant, engaging, valuable, and relatively seamlessly delivered from the customer's point of view, then it's essential to actively build a strategy and structural framework to deliver that. The CMO role is critical.

As David Court at McKinsey points out: "What's now required of CMOs is a broader role that realigns marketing with the current realities of consumer decision making, intensifies efforts to shape the public profiles of companies, and builds new marketing capabilities.

"Companies need an integrated, organization-wide 'voice of the customer,' with skills from advertising to public relations, product development, market research, and data management. It's hard but necessary to unify these activities, and the CMO is the natural candidate to do so."[2]

After all, marketing is currently at the center of coordination for customer service, communication, and data analysis (see Part II, "How Are Companies Coping?"). The marketer is largely responsible for initiating and developing relationships with customers. The marketer knows more about the customer than anyone else. And when customer-centricity is a critical step on the road to ART, the marketing department should be leading the charge.

CMOs themselves certainly realize this fact: 59% of them are saying that they "aim to expand their leadership and influence in general business strategy."[3] Indeed, the extensive Marketing 2020 survey conducted by Millward Brown Vermeer found that, "from 2006 to 2013...marketing's influence on strategy development increased by 20 percentage points."[4]

From Part of the Matrix to a Leadership Role

Of course, it's not quite that simple. Customer experience is multifaceted. Customer touchpoints are found across an organization, and are often the responsibility of several different departments. Therefore, the marketing department itself will have to evolve. The department will become responsible for understanding the customer's overall experience when interacting with the company, and improving all elements of that experience. That will necessitate collaboration with—or even control over—several more business departments than traditionally the case.

Marketing is already one of the most matrixed groups within a company because it sits at the intersection of product development and product sales. Yet, as Pravin Nath reports in *Harvard Business Review*, research shows "marketing organizations [are already taking] command of sales, public relations/communications, product development, and major parts of information technology management, and many have advocated for more expansions of marketing's scope."[5]

As we move from a situation of reacting to the increasing power of the customer, and with customer experience responsibilities fragmented across a business, toward one in which that experience is unified and consistent, it's logical to assume that marketing will take increased responsibility for all those touchpoints.

That leadership role means that the CMO's responsibilities will span all the way from how products are created, to how they're discovered, bought, used, and even serviced and supported.

This increased set of responsibilities is echoed in the raised profile for the CMO at the board level and a corresponding increase in CMO tenure to 45 months as of 2014, double the previous average duration.[6]

Not only is the CMO role changing and expanding across the business, but also the role of the entire marketing department.

"It's clear that 'marketing' is no longer a discrete entity (and woe betide the company whose marketing is still siloed), but now extends throughout the firm, tapping virtually every function."[7]

As the influence of marketing continues to spread within a business, performance has already been shown to improve. Even simple extensions to customer experience coordination via an expansion of the CMO role has had a positive effect on broader company results. Research conducted by Pravin Nath and reported in the *Harvard Business Review* concludes that "when CMOs have the additional responsibility of sales, firms deliver superior growth."[8]

To conclude, the marketing department is well placed to manage the entirety of an increasingly complicated customer lifecycle, and manage an increasingly fragmented customer experience. Indeed, it is already beginning to do so. Social media, which was often launched as a tool for marketers to extend the reach of product messaging, quickly became a customer service channel for customers and a risk mitigation issue for brands. As it did so, the role of the social media department therefore expanded—and took a core role in customer service delivery. In short, social media has sped the spread of marketing's influence across a business. Although social media teams now have a core role in customer service delivery, 69.8% of those social media teams sit within the marketing department.[9] Although the job might be customer service, the direct report is still the CMO. Social media extends the responsibilities of the marketing department, and the CMO's role expands accordingly.

Why a Centralized Marketing Community Is Critical

As Barry Wolfish, Chief Marketing Officer at dairy producer Land O'Lakes, told me:

"[T]he ability to cross lines and connect the various parts of the organization in a way we've never worried about historically is much more of an imperative. Marketers need to think much more about the supply chain than they did historically—how things get made, where they get made, what the various options are—because...you just can't have handoffs anymore. There's much more of a matrixed way of thinking about the strategy."

As seen in Figure 6.1, about a quarter of marketing departments restructure once a year, but it's rarely as extensive a restructuring as has been laid out in this chapter thus far.[10]

How often does your marketing department undergo some sort of reorganization?

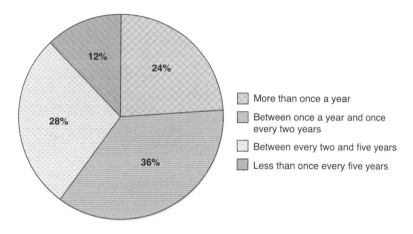

Figure 6.1 Marketing departments restructure often.

If you're fortunate enough to be planning for your own department's restructuring, take the opportunity to make changes to operational structure to ensure that the resulting organizational model is more conducive to the delivery of ART. By shifting roles and responsibilities, you're making the ground more fertile for the seeds of change you're hoping will take root.

Should Marketing Expand Itself Out of Existence?

Across many departments, an expansion of responsibilities is akin to spreading a single pat of butter across an ever-expanding slice of toast. The farther one spreads, the thinner the butter gets stretched, until it's hard to make out at all.

For many different functions within a business, this "spreading out of existence" (and being subsumed into pre-existing departmental structures) is not only inevitable, but actually sought.

Consider corporate responsibility. The goal for a corporate responsibility and sustainability team is to reduce its own role to something akin to a coordinator—and doing so as the rest of the company builds responsible business practices and strategies into its daily routine.

Social media is somewhat similar. Social marketing shouldn't be treated as a separate department from the rest of marketing—it's more of a channel and a tool for others to do their jobs better. The same is true for digital more broadly.

As marketing spreads and evolves to become something broader than it is currently, and as responsibilities are broadened and customer experience becomes the core focus, then it's inevitable that the dividing line between marketing and other departments will blur.

Splitting the Marketing Department

That most emphatically does not mean that marketing, as a distinct community within a company, should go the way of CSR, digital, and social media—where overall success can be defined by the redundancy of the discrete department.

Instead, many CMOs advocate *adding* new departmental structures, by splitting the marketing department into two. The first group would focus on strategy. It would look at brand equity, brand sentiment, and be tasked with understanding how marketing and external communication can add value to the company as a whole.

The second, rather less glamorous, department would be the previously mentioned "marketing execution" team focus on implementation, experimentation, and shared expertise on the functional aspects of marketing around the company.

This last point of shared expertise is critical. It's essential that your centralized marketing hub be able to collate best practice examples and then redistribute them to the relevant areas of the business. As such, it's critical to incorporate an internal communications responsibility into the marketing execution team.

According to Dominic Collins, Chief Marketing Officer, Legal & General, "I've brought in the team that looks at the internal brand and the internal culture and the employee value proposition [into the marketing execution team]. If you're going to take the business on a journey, then you need to move the business forward both internally and externally. We've brought them together so we can align internal brand activity and external brand activity so that moves forward as a whole."

Another company that has experienced a split between marketing strategy and marketing operations is Land O'Lakes. It now has two marketing structures: marketers within business units who own the profit and loss figures and set strategy, and a centralized marketing services team that is responsible for tactics and execution more than strategy.

That second group, according to Barry Wolfish, Chief Marketing Officer at Land O'Lakes, is actually beginning to merge with another internal department—IT. As Wolfish recounts, the marketing operations team is "slowly but surely becoming seamless with the corporate IT function around the aggregation of data that informs better decision making and the selection of the tools and the systems that will drive better analytics that allow us to make better decisions."

Another CMO I spoke to has also adopted this approach and this collaboration with IT—building a "center of excellence" that is responsible for working closely with IT and CRM teams to build platforms, services, and insight for marketers with a more strategic function to leverage. This team plays an essential role in providing a workable alternative to the silos that bedevil many attempts to foster transparency and agility, and is an important factor in encouraging more flexibility and sharing of insight across the business.

The CMO established a new marketing operations department that has a responsibility to build the data structures needed to find and then leverage data from across the company. Historically, significant amounts of data resided with the customer service team, or within the supply chain, or within sales, for instance. Although the marketing operations team doesn't have the power to actually "own" those data sources, the establishment of a centralized marketing operations department means that the information can all be pulled into marketing. This unified pool of customer data is then able to contribute more effectively to a fuller, more extensive picture of the businesses success, the customer, and future strategy.

As the CMO points out, this is an absolutely critical development in becoming an agile marketing function and, more broadly, a company that can deliver relevant and valuable marketing and products to customers: "The biggest area of investment I've made across marketing in organizational competencies is in the marketing operations group. That name is perhaps an under service of the role—it sounds very engine room, back room driven. But it's really the tip of the iceberg in terms of our ability to scale and our ability to turn insight into action."

New Roles and Responsibilities

According to a McKinsey survey, "9/10 of executives say their companies have some pressing need for digital talent in the next year, especially in analytics."[11]

As the responsibilities of the marketing department spread, the diversity of roles within it increases. The most popular new positions that marketing departments are looking to fill are in the following areas:

1. **Product marketing support (33%):** The executives working in the marketing operations department outlined earlier—responsible for collecting and sharing insight and processes for increased agility and efficiency.

2. **Customer analytics (33%):** Turning the data collected from around the company into usable insight on the customer—and using it to define future marketing strategy. Many CMOs told me that this was a critical new position. As marketers increasingly find themselves working with data scientists to build

insight and learn more about customers, it's becoming vital to hire in "translators"—who are responsible for ensuring both sides understand each other and work well together.

3. **Content development (33%):** Reflecting a drive to build content in-house to ensure a closer alignment with brand voice and produce content at the rapid pace expected of today's marketers

4. **Social media (32%)**[12]**:** Handling engagement and outreach across the rapidly changing social landscape.

Focus on Agility

Agility—the ability for companies to react quickly to customer feedback, market insight, and other new sources of data—is essential in a new world in which customers hold the power and where communications are almost instantaneous. As Barry Wolfish of Land O'Lakes told me, "Things happen faster, and theories are more measurable—it's much more competitive. Capital is precious, and I don't think organizations can afford to be overly structured and didactic about how they respond to things the way that maybe they once were, when things fit into neat compartments."

This agility is essential to success in such a fast-paced new world for four main reasons:

1. As we've seen, marketers are finding competition springing up everywhere.

2. New marketing channels and platforms are emerging all the time.

3. Companies have new potential for success by inserting themselves into organic conversations happening in social media—if they can move fast enough.

4. Companies can increase efficiency and reduce risk if they can collect and process data quickly enough to impact a campaign as it is still happening.

To leverage these opportunities, companies need to loosen up. Organizations can no longer afford to maintain a complex and rigid structure or set of internal processes for customer engagement.

The structure of a marketing department, the subgroups within it, the collaboration between it and other departments around the company, and the skills required for it to be successful are changing and becoming more fluid.

Why IT, Data, and Marketing Departments Need to Work Together

"When I was a young marketer, I thought IT was something that kept track of an inventory, and we used [it] to bill our customers and collect money. But other than that, I never thought about it."

—Barry Wolfish at Land O'Lakes.

Marketing departments still need good creative thinking. They need people who can manage and establish processes, lead teams, and attract people to their ideas. But they also need people who can implement new technologies—and do so at speed.

In the past, for instance, marketers didn't spend much time thinking about IT—but as Figure 6.2 makes clear, it's now essential that they collaborate together effectively.[13]

A good marketing department now needs technologists embedded within it. Failing that, the department needs to work incredibly closely with technologists in other departments. Fifty-three percent of marketing executives say that a key alliance to form for future success is with the CIO.[14] Yet only 41% say that the marketing and IT departments have a common vision on what that alliance should look like.[15] There's evidently some work still to do to build this most important of relationships.

As highlighted in the list of areas in which CMOs are hiring (see the earlier section "New Roles and Responsibilities"), as data becomes a more important source of insight, it becomes a more pressing concern for business leaders to find and utilize people who are able to translate often indecipherable datasets into actionable insight that marketers can use to do their job better.

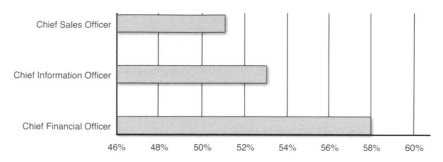

Figure 6.2 Marketers must collaborate with Sales, IT, and Finance more than ever before.

Source: Maddox, "81% of CMOs are Confident They'll Meet Revenue Goals."http://adage.com/ article/cmo-strategy/study-81-cmos-confident-meet-revenue-goals/294614/

Therefore, a centralized data analysis function that reports quickly and directly to marketing becomes a competitive advantage. In many organizations, analytics capability is still split across many different pockets of the business. When information is siloed like this, it's hard to spot trends and journeys across an entire business. That information isn't distributed to where it's needed the most at the time it's needed. However, as Marc Speichert, formerly Chief Marketing Officer at L'Oreal makes clear, getting this right generates real opportunity:

"Moving toward a centralized insights function means that we're now really able to follow our consumers, whichever channel they move in—wherever he or she goes from a shopping perspective. Before we centralized our market research teams, we had a lot of depth in understanding channel by channel. So we had a few dedicated to the mass market channel (and they knew everything inside out for that channel), but not so much the others.

"And yet, the reality is that the percentage of consumers that are only shopping in one channel of distribution is very small. So being able to track that consumer across all of our distribution channels has been very valuable. It helps us to better position our portfolio of brands and also have more productive conversations with the retail organizations across these channels."[16]

When Victoria Burwell began in her position as CMO for educational publisher McGraw-Hill, she had that same problem—being unable to accurately track all customers across the business and leverage the opportunity that better data analysis presented. So she hired a vice president who was responsible for strategy and analytics and brought in a team underneath him of people responsible for segmentation, market research, and pricing. Why?

"They're all making sure that we are starting at the very beginning of our product development process with data, with the voice of the customer's data," she says.

Giving a discrete team the responsibility for this—to talk to the customer and to coordinate, collect, and translate data—to build actionable insights based on proven figures facilitates far better decision making and strategy moving forward.

The presence of this group at McGraw-Hill means someone is going out to talk to the customers and understand their needs, what their products should look like, and how those products can be better than anything else out there to benefit their lives.

It turns the typical product development process (roughly akin to "I know a chemistry professor—let's put out a chemistry book") on its head and ensures that products come from the customer's need. No longer are products created and then marketers look for an audience for them.

Breaking Down Silos for a More Comprehensive Customer Picture

As we've seen, it's absolutely essential for customer data to be put into the hands of one unified, centralized group. Only then can a marketing department (or a company as a whole) claim to have true 20/20 vision—and be confident they're acting on the best available information. Yet as it stands, only 18% of marketers feel they do have this sort of view.[17] As Frans Cornelis, Chief Marketing Officer at Randstadt, points out, there is unfortunately "a natural tendency as a business grows to form silos." These silos stop the quick and complete flow of relevant insight around a business.

And getting rid of those silos is easier said than done. Since humans began to organize themselves into groups, there have been power struggles, attempts to gain influence, and build "private kingdoms."

Within companies, the problem is as prevalent as ever. When asked "how effectively does your company integrate customer information across purchasing, communication, and social media channels?" on a scale from 1 to 7 (where 1 was the worst performance), the average ranking was 3.6.[18]

That weakness has a significant negative impact on opportunities for marketing success. It prevents two essential things:

1. The unification of information
2. The unification of response

Unification of Information

One of the three pillars of the marketing moving forward is the successful provision of relevance. It's becoming increasingly important to customers that interactions with brands convey information or content that they will find insightful, useful, or engaging. Otherwise, you're just one of those hundreds of other marketing messages those customers receive every day. Noise, not signal.

For a number of years, marketers have made the best attempts they can to be as relevant as they can. Perhaps you've received mail congratulating you on moving into a new home and offering a credit card to make those new furniture purchases you've been thinking about. Perhaps you've just been in a car accident and are inundated with information on new insurance policies. Perhaps your purchase of diapers has prompted a plethora of information on where you can get a good babysitter.

Customer data has been gathered, parceled up, and sold to companies for decades. Somewhat terrifyingly, the sheer amount of data one can gather on an individual simply by paying for access is unsettling, to say the least. Companies have been keen to avail themselves of the massive amounts of demographic and behavioral data newly available as so much of our world moves online, and use it to target audiences in more precise and targeted ways than ever.

Yet in one area the appetite for data is equally voracious but significantly further from being sated.

Internal Data

It is simply too common for marketers to bemoan the state of their internal data sharing. All too often, the left arm does not know what the right arm is doing. This leads to dissatisfied customers, impaired brand sentiment, and, fundamentally, missed opportunities and lost profits.

The reason for this persistent failure is a lack of sufficient structures, processes, and will to share data better internally.

Brandy from the customer service department does not share the complaint she just got from Customer X with the marketing team, who merrily emailed Customer X later that same day with a request to "take his relationship to the next level" with the company. Had Marketing known about his experience with Customer Service hours earlier, they probably would have changed the tone and content of the message—and thus wouldn't be facing a Twitter storm of complaints from hundreds of Customer X's colleagues, friends, and followers right now.

Of course, the marketing team is none the wiser, since the Twitter feed is handled by a combination of the external agency partner and the communication team. Monica from the communications team is really proud of having grown the company's follower numbers by 3,000 over the last quarter and doesn't want to share much about the Twitter storm, considering that her review is coming up and she's angling for a raise.

But then Shaun, the CEO, jumps on Twitter at the behest of his teenage son, who wants him to check out a Vine clip from a recent soccer game. He sees that his company is trending and, intrigued, clicks on the hashtag to see an outpouring of bile from countries he didn't even know his companies had operations in.

Yes, it's a somewhat exaggerated example, but the point still stands. Silos of information—and the broader lack of communication and collaboration they signify—act as blinders and stop allowing a company to react in the way it would if all the facts were visible.

Uniformity of Response

According to Frans Cornelis, Chief Marketing Officer of Randstad, "The most efficient way to build a brand is with consistent messaging. Those messages need to be integrated because people will now pick up on inconsistencies that much faster via social media. You can very quickly become a laughing stock if your message is out of sync."

We've already talked about how transparency has changed marketing, how consistency is critical, and how companies are struggling to deliver both. A collection of data silos around a company is a main reason for that struggle.

Previously, a chemical firm, for example, could advertise and sell products in one part of the world quite happily while misbehaving and alienating a local community in another part. The latter would have no real impact on the former. To put it mildly, that is no longer the case. Now a social media storm can brew quicker than the corporate communications department realizes it even has a crisis.

Silos stop opportunities being leveraged, ensure that unnoticed risks are taken, and frustrate teams looking to do good work. They make companies look backward, inauthentic, and out of sync with their customers. They're one of the most common issues marketers talk about today, and if eradicating internal data silos isn't near the top of your priority list, it should get there fast.

But how? What follows is a case study on exactly that.

CASE STUDY

How Randstad Avoids Silos and Collaborates Better Through Proximity and Serendipity

According to Frans Cornelis, chief marketing officer for human resources and employment firm Randstad, the first step on the road to a world without silos is for the boss to say, "Hey guys, no silos, please."

Cutting silos means eradicating little kingdoms. If a change will cause someone to lose power or change what they're doing, it is not likely to elicit a positive response. Cutting silos is exactly that sort of change. Therefore, a company must have an internal authority conveying the message and get buy-in from senior executives.

This is one area in which even the CMO struggles to be an appropriate voice. The CMO's role is more helpfully to engage the CEO to begin a charm offensive with customer service, sales, communications, and all the many other departments that are responsible for specific customer touchpoints.

Another reason it's worth getting the CEO on board early? This is a big, long-term job, and it's going to cost a lot of money.

Global Companies Have Bigger Problems

It's appropriate that I write this section while on a plane over Greenland on a flight between London and San Francisco. It's more common than ever for companies to have operations and marketing departments spread across the world. However, in an attempt to deliver relevant and appropriate marketing for localized markets, the cost tends to stem from a lack of global coordination. Every new region where a company operates is another opportunity for another cluster of siloed learning, insight, best practices, skills, and data.

Silos get harder to manage as companies grow. For FTSE 100 multinationals with thousands of employees spread over the globe, they're almost impossible.

It doesn't help that, typically, more marketers report to geographical regional workflows and reporting than to a centralized, global marketing hub. That means lost opportunities for collaboration, shared insight, quicker learning, and a more consistent global message.

CASE STUDY

Although it would be impossible (or, at least, flawed) to attempt to run a global marketing operation out of one office, someone needs to "guard the whole."[19] A single executive (or team) needs to have oversight on a globalized marketing operation, to ensure that specialists in different cities work together—and work in the same direction.

Otherwise, as Frans Cornelis points out, "You get artwork on the web that doesn't resemble or match the impression of artwork in the paper or in-store."

A rich roster of technology solutions is designed to help internal collaboration, from CRM systems such as Salesforce as the home of all customer data, to chat apps such as HipChat and Silicon Valley's latest darling, Slack. These are designed to foster a more collaborative, closer-knit company that can share insight and information across geographic boundaries.

Get Your Team Closer Together

Coordination is critical, not only on a geographical level, but also across departments.

Marissa Meyer was roundly mocked as a dinosaur for cutting back on work-from-home hours for employees at Yahoo! Yet, she has allies in many of the senior marketing executives I've spoken to. The most important aim—and it sounds corny—is to get the main deciders in each other's vicinity.[20]

Frans Cornelis highlighted the enormous value to be gained through designing office space for serendipitous meetings, a concept Steve Jobs followed closely when designing Apple's giant new space-ship-like campus in Cupertino.

Thinking about location and team placement within an office building can encourage this serendipity, and that can work as a replacement for more formal structures that are harder to launch and harder to stick to.

It's not necessary to build open-plan offices, nor does a company need to gather the entire C-suite around a rich mahogany table in the center of an office. If you want to use proximity as a tool for collaboration, you simply need to ensure that important, relevant people to that collaborative effort are together most of the time. Proximity encourages enough in terms of ideas and creativity.

For Cornelis and Randstad, that means designing so that the marketing and communication chiefs all sit on the ninth and tenth floors. The idea

CASE STUDY

is that they "all meet each other at lunch, they don't have to book meetings, [and] they can simply meet each other at the coffee machine."

That's a neat example of proximity engendering serendipity. The initial move to the ninth and tenth floors was mandated, but from there, Cornelis could afford to simply let those two powerful forces do their work.

The corporate communications chief and the international marketing chief work together naturally now because they're confronted with each other on a daily basis. That's great for Cornelis: "If they were in different offices, I'd have a rather more difficult job."

This is an increasingly popular strategy. Susan Lintonsmith, the CMO of fast food chain Quiznos, has a similar approach. She ensures that the entire executive team travels together to "operationalize strategy" with franchise operators and then works together to debate how effective that strategy has been.[21]

"Light Touch" Has Limits

To this point, we've advocated a relatively light-touch, low-contact approach to de-siloization and collaboration. Management guidelines and proximate working operations are the limit thus far. Of course, companies have more to mandate and a deeper structure to implement.

At Randstad, social media channels are seen for what they are: channels on which people can communicate. As such, the company has no specific social media team. Platforms such as Twitter and Facebook "are basically for all participants and are usually run by whoever is best placed," says Cornelis.

However, if a company gives access to networks like this to multiple groups, it must ensure uniformity and consistency of message. Randstad does this through a clear "house style." If more people are communicating with customers, independently both reaching out and scheduling messaging, it's essential to have harmony and clarity, as well as a clear brand voice in any and all messaging.

Think About What Silos to Open

When talking about internal silos, it's easy to assume that we're simply referring to those silos of customer insight and touchpoint data, squirreled away by the relevant business units responsible for them. But that would

CASE STUDY

be missing another significant area where silos are prevalent: internal marketing performance data. That means a lack of visibility on who and which team is performing well, and which teams need additional work. Without visibility here, companies will struggle to deliver efficiency, agility, and lean teams and projects.

Visibility is essential. A successful approach goes hand in hand with the centralized marketing operations team we advocate for earlier in the book. That team can also run and maintain a common market research system. Such a system is in place at Randstad, where all countries are able to measure themselves and their top 20 competitors in exactly the same way. This offers enhanced ability to benchmark.

In addition, visibility of those numbers across the business incites debate. Teams actively reach out to each other to question particularly high scores against key metrics. They're confident that the research isn't skewed because it's exactly the same, wherever the team is in the world.

Endnotes

1. Kate Maddox, "81% of CMOs Are Confident They'll Meet Revenue Goals," *Ad Age* (18 August 2014). www.adage.com/article/cmo-strategy/study-81-cmos-confident-meet-revenue-goals/294614/.

2. David Court, et al., "The Consumer Decision Journey," *McKinsey Quarterly* (June 2009).

3. Sheryl Pattek, with David M. Cooperstein and Alexandra Hayes, "The Evolved CMO in 2014," *Forrester* (March 2014).

4. Marc de Swaan Arons, Frank van den Driest, and Keith Weed, "The Ultimate Marketing Machine," *Harvard Business Review* (July 2014).

5. Pravin Nath, "What Makes a CMO Powerful," *Harvard Business Review* (July 2014). https://hbr.org/2014/07/what-makes-a-cmo-powerful/.

6. Peter Dahlstrom, et al., "The Rebirth of the CMO," *Harvard Business Review* (5 August 2014). https://hbr.org/2014/08/the-rebirth-of-the-cmo/.

7. Arons, van den Driest, and Weed, "The Ultimate Marketing Machine." https://hbr.org/2014/07/the-ultimate-marketing-machine/ar/1.

8. Nath, "What Makes a CMO Powerful."

9. The CMO Survey, "CMO Survey Report: Topline Results" (August 2014). http://cmosurvey.org/files/2014/09/The_CMO_Survey-Topline_Report-Aug-2014.pdf.

10. Future of Marketing Survey.

11. McKinsey and Company, "The Digital Tipping Point: McKinsey Global Survey Results" (June 2014). www.mckinsey.com/insights/business_technology/the_digital_tipping_point_mckinsey_global_survey_results).

12. Maddox, "81% of CMOs Are Confident They'll Meet Revenue Goals."

13. Maddox, "81% of CMOs are Confident They'll Meet Revenue Goals."

14. Maddox, "81% of CMOs are Confident They'll Meet Revenue Goals."

15. Pattek, Cooperstein, and Hayes, "The Evolved CMO in 2014."

16. Nick Johnson, "Marc Speichert on How He Has Evolved L'Oreal's Marketing Focus," Incite Marketing and Communications (14 June 2013). http://incitemc.com/marc-speichert-on-how-he-has-evolved-loreals-marketing-focus/.

17. Pattek, Cooperstein, and Hayes, "The Evolved CMO in 2014."

18. The CMO Survey, "CMO Survey Report: Topline Results."

19. Frans Cornelis, Chief Marketing Officer, Randstad.

20. Frans Cornelis, Chief Marketing Officer, Randstad.

21. Pattek, Cooperstein, and Hayes, "The Evolved CMO in 2014."

7

Data for Relevance and Agility

*"People [have] said for as long as I can remember that mar-
keting is a blend of art and science. I still think [that]'s true
today. But when I started my career, it was more art than
science. And I think the big difference is that that has shifted."*

—Russ Findlay, Head of Marketing, Hiscox Insurance
North America

Importance of Data and Science

In this chapter, we look at the impact that the huge influx of customer data has had on marketing. First, let's review *why* data and
science have become such fundamental pillars of any cutting edge
marketing team, There are four main reasons, discussed in the sections that follow.

1: The Scale Is Incredible

Because of a broad shift in how people communicate, spend time,
and interact to the digital world, suddenly, everything leaves a trace.
Opportunistic people, being acquisitive sorts, began to collect those
traces. Now with computing power, patterns in those traces can be
spotted, correlations can be found, and optimizations can be made.

Data is a huge opportunity for many large companies. The scale
of the change that the proliferation of data has engendered is equally
huge. Many CMOs I've spoken to tell me that the prevalence and volume of data is one of the biggest shifts in marketing for decades. As a

result of that shift, analytics and data management have become core competencies for marketers.

Marketers were once brushed off as creatives who happened to work in-house instead of at an agency. They might have been seen as working on fluffy, broad topics with little accountability, able to laugh about knowing that 50% of their advertising worked, but not knowing which half.

That's no longer the case. Marketing is increasingly a numbers game. ROI is the essential metric. The capacity to track and improve campaigns and strategies is huge. The opportunities are major.

"Yet many, many organizations have way more data than they have insight," according to Barry Wolfish, Chief Marketing Officer at Land O'Lakes. And that's leading to major changes in investment and resource allocation throughout an organization, particularly within marketing departments. As Michael Zuna, Chief Marketing Officer for insurance giant Aflac told me:

"Where are we focused in marketing most aggressively? You've got it—data and technology."

Science, then, seems to be winning the war with art. And plenty of angst is permeating marketing departments around the world as marketers ponder the extent of science's dominance: how much potential does data have to replace creativity? What's the role of the creative moving forward? Will marketers eventually be replaced by algorithms?

2: The Opportunity Is Enormous—and the Imperative Is Unavoidable

Better analysis of customer insights "can improve marketing return on investment by 10–20% and drive average profit growth of 14%.[1]

72% "of overperforming marketing teams were making decisions off the back of data insights, compared to 45% of underperformers."[2] And as De Swaan Arons, van den Driest, and Weed have found, "Companies that are sophisticated in their use of data grow faster."[3]

Given those findings, it seems obvious that companies should continue to pour resource into improving the "science" of marketing.

Especially given there's so far still to go—"only 30% of companies believe they understand their customers' needs well enough to identify what initiatives will drive growth."[4]

As Russ Findlay, chief marketing officer of insurance firm Hiscox, says, "People are sitting on terabytes of data but don't know what the hell to do with it." It's in every marketer's interest to ensure that changes.

3: You're Now Competing with Digital Natives

"Digital homogenizes expectation."

—Dominic Collins, Chief Marketing Officer, Legal & General

The imperative to improve isn't simply one of opportunity cost or losing ground to more data-savvy competitors. The ubiquity of data, and the agility of those companies well-set to deal with it, has meaningfully changed the expectations that customers have of their interactions with *all* businesses.

Those expectations are already being met by companies birthed in a new world where data, digital, and social all loom large: the digital native. These companies tend to be more agile, more nimble, and better able to deliver tailored customer experience than older companies. Those businesses have been brought up living and breathing data as a fundamental element of operational strategy.

Growing used to the personalization that the Amazons and AirBnBs of this world deliver, customers are beginning to demand an equivalent level of service from any business they interact with. So fundamentally, if a company buried its head in the sand, it wouldn't be stationary. It would fall rapidly behind. As Chris Lindner, President of footwear brand Keds, told me,

"Is [good data management] an opportunity or a necessity? I think it's both."

Large, established brands find it hard to compete with smaller, nimbler players. These players are often able to use customer data to provide better, more relevant, and more engaging online experiences because they're built from the ground up in this new world; they're not furiously trying to augment or replace huge, complex legacy CRM systems that hinder any attempts at progress.

Michael Zuna of Aflac said to me that "The insurance industry was a leader in technological innovation, and because of that there are a lot of legacy systems that are not as functional today as when they were created. Like many of my colleagues in the industry I think we would like to blow out our legacy systems and start with the latest technology in and around today's customers." Unfortunately, that's easier said than done.

Yet that makes the imperative no less pressing. In a world of more and more marketing messages, directed to a customer base tired of receiving them, marketers must take every chance they get to stand out from the crowd. Data's ability to help with personalization, agility, and better customer insight is a chance that should not—and cannot—be passed up.

4: Data Helps You Spot Problems

Data enables insight. And that insight won't necessarily simply spot improvements and opportunities. Many companies have found that a stronger focus on data analysis and insight has revealed fundamental problems in the business that they had missed previously.

Without a better approach to data analysis, these same mistakes would have kept happening and would have lain unresolved, impairing progress, for any number of years.

At Randstad, when the first big data efforts began to bear fruit and drive insight from the vast datasets the company is building, the company decided to run a report showing the correlation between the price of its services and the volume sold. The aim was to determine whether it was possible to discover the extent to which average prices deviated from the company's stated approach to pricing its services.

Frans Cornelis, Chief Marketing Officer at Randstad, called his first sight of the results an "Oh, horror" moment.

The most logical explanation for the chart he saw was that the prices were utterly random. Almost no rhyme or reason seemed to have been employed in deciding upon prices. Looking at the prices against their transactions, it seemed impossible to tell what the pricing policy even was. The figures were such a shock that, at first, no one internally believed them. Another team was asked to run the numbers and came back with a more troubling response: If anything, the first group had underestimated the size of the problem.

On a broad scale, the company was able to spot and then address an issue through data. Previously, that issue would have been significantly harder to spot. "Twenty years ago, [had we noticed that we weren't] getting the average margin that we deserve, [we would have started to ask the wrong question, like] who do we focus more on in the value message in our advertising?" Cornelis says.

Gordon and Perrey highlight another example in the February 2015 edition of the *McKinsey Quarterly*, in which an industrial products company was struggling with a fragmented portfolio of products and a diverse customer base spanning several industries. The problem had grown such that prices varied significantly with no real explanation, which impacted efforts to manage margins. The purchase of a new analytical tool able to scan through millions of transactions quickly "helped the company redraw customer segments, identify products with opportunities for pricing flexibility, and recommend new prices. Ultimately, it reset about 100,000 price points."[5]

Setting Up for Data

According to Barry Wolfish, Chief Marketing Officer at Land O'Lakes "[O]ne of the challenges of big data [is that] many, many organizations have way more data than they have insights—because the first challenge is, 'How do you connect the wiring and even recognize just how much data you have?'"

We've already spoken about the need for a coordinated effort to manage and collate data from around a business. Now that digital media is increasingly the first place customers engage with brands, the sheer number of customer touchpoints building datasets is increasing exponentially.

It's important, therefore, to set up for success. There are four core elements of this process:

1: Hiring the Right People and Evolving the Marketer's Role

Perhaps the most obvious challenge of building data into marketing is that, as Chris Linder, President of Keds, pointed out, data management was simply "not the skill set that we all learned growing up."

In the first instance, it's important to note that, for the majority of marketers at work today, the importance of data was simply not evident when they began their roles, and they do not have the appropriate skill sets.

Many CMOs mentioned one particular new job as a hiring focus: a "data translator," who can act as the intersection between marketers and data analysts, translating numbers into observations and turning data into actionable insight. As Russ Findlay of Hiscox Insurance says, "I think that the skill sets of people are going to change significantly."

All marketers must have a somewhat analytical brain, to extract insights from data and turn those insights into an improved strategy, an improved campaign, or some form of story for internal or external distribution. As Findlay points out, the marketer must "understand and be able to extract the stories that the numbers are telling you."

One marketer's role, therefore, will often not actually *be* that of data scientist, but a translator, turning a data scientist's feedback into insights and activities to understand customers better, optimize activity, and spot and leverage new marketing opportunities.

As marketers face increasing pressure to act more effectively as the "voice of the customer" within a business, it's going to become ever more critical that they're able to leverage the significant insights to be gleaned from a good handle on data management and analysis.

2: Build the Right Organizational Model

As the marketing role changes, so does the marketing department.

We've already highlighted the need for **a centralized hub for the collection and analysis of customer data**—a "Marketing Operations and Execution" department. We've also seen that CMOs are desperately looking to hire translators able to decipher the language of data scientists and turn it into something that marketers can understand and use.

The next step, if a company is looking to move from product-centricity to customer-centricity, is to ensure that all data is housed in one place—not split over several silos controlled by several different departments. This unification of customer data means that instead of collating details on all the people who, for instance, buy a particular kind of shampoo in isolation, one can collect data on *all* customers in one place. Recall Marc Speichert, previously CMO of L'Oreal, comments on how useful it was for the company to centralize disparate market research teams into one centralized insights function. The company was able to make several significant findings, which simply wouldn't have been possible without this centralization of *all* customer data in one place. Without it, the unexpected overlap between premium face wash customers and budget shampoo customers would never have been noticed.

So it seems sensible that a marketing organization brings together data sets, and brings together the teams responsible for those data sets to the greatest extent possible. To facilitate this, companies should attempt to build an organizational model that incorporates collaboration between groups responsible for those data sets at the highest levels.

As Michael Zuna, chief marketing officer for Aflac says of the situation at his own company, "Nothing from a marketing standpoint could happen without an incredible partnership and friendship with the chief administrative officer and the chief information officer."

That's an important first step: building an incredibly close working relationship between the chief marketing officer and the people who own and control customer touchpoints.

3: Set Clear Goals Aligned to Overall Corporate Goals

Also essential in preparing the ground for marketing's increasingly data-centric role (indeed, an increasingly data-centric world) is ensuring that the activity and resources expended on developing new models and processes to leverage data better are closely aligned to pre-existing overarching corporate goals.

It's critical to build a clear picture of what you're doing and what's working. Then you can begin to focus on what is possible and build out the next stage in your data-centric strategy for delivering better marketing and customer experience.

At this point, the partnerships established with IT and other departments will come to fruition. It's critical for the marketer to understand the legacy IT systems, how they work, and how they need to interact with any new state-of-the-art mobile app, technology, or other piece of software.

4: Find the Signal in the Noise

A veritable flood of data has been made available to the savvy marketer. The challenge, as Nate Silver so eloquently puts it, is to find "the signal in the noise."[6]

It's essential for marketers to avoid "analysis paralysis" and to build a system and process to ensure that the right, relevant, actionable data is surfaced and disseminated.

Think of the cockpit of an airplane. Pilots need to know an enormous amount of data, whether at takeoff, when landing, or in flight. It means that a plane's cockpit is a pretty complicated place.

Yet the system works to put the most important and relevant information in front of those pilots at the time they need it and in a visible, straightforward, easily processable way. They see the information most related to and most helpful in maintaining the safety of that airplane.

The goal for marketers should be to build their own version of a cockpit. You've got to surface and disseminate the most important data to "fly your business" as effectively and efficiently as possible. Focus on the simple, as Michael Zuna of Aflac says: "Think about Occam's razor, where in a complex situation, the simplest solution is often the best."

As a marketer, a lot of data will find its way to you. The goal is to ignore the irrelevant and focus on the things that matter. A fantastic introductory resource for finding the metrics and data sets you should be paying attention to is is *The Lean Startup* by Eric Ries.[7]

The Benefits One Can Expect from a Comprehensive, Forward-Looking Approach to Data Management and Analysis

So you have a centralized data and analytics team. You've removed silos. You've built your "data cockpit," and you've hired in the relevant people to ensure that data analyzed by the data team is transitioned effectively into insight.

Becoming a more data-led business offers many benefits, the most obvious being the ability to be more relevant to your customers when communicating with them.

When marketing began as a distinct discipline, delivery mechanisms were quite broad. Marketers working for large brands could access a market via newspapers, TV advertising, billboards, and radio advertising.

Yes, the demographics for *I Love Lucy* might have been different than those for the evening news. The billboard in Times Square probably drew a slightly different audience than the one at the intersection of 6th Avenue and 10th Street. But fundamentally, marketing was like using a sledgehammer to crack a nut. A massive ad buy would certainly lead to a reasonable confidence that you were broadly reaching the right customers. But unfortunately, you were also reaching many other people, too.

Equally, "the right customer" was a pretty amorphous concept. You could not target with any real clarity or precision, nor understand customers with the granularity possible now.

As Victoria Burwell, CMO at educational publisher McGraw-Hill, points out, "In the olden days, when there's potentially TV advertising and print for a large segment of your audience, you don't know if people read it, you have no idea. It's hard to segment. ... It was much more spray and pay."

As technology progressed, segmentation became more feasible. Marketers began to create "personas"—composite characters designed to represent a particular type of customer. Those personas developed in complexity and precision from "mother" to "teen mom earning $100,000 a year" over time.

A Note on B2B/B2C Differences

As you might have noticed, this book attempts to deal with marketing as a universal discipline, beyond the distinctions of B2B and B2C, Fast Moving Consumer Goods and energy, and so on.

However, this attempt to provide universal insight is unhelpful at certain points. We have reached one. As John Kennedy, CMO at Xerox, points out, personalization in marketing is somewhere B2C and B2B companies differ widely.

Kennedy raises the valid point that although B2C marketers began to introduce personas (defining groups as teens, moms, blue-collar workers, and so on), B2B companies had a different drive. Instead of marketing to the individual or a segment of similar individuals, B2B marketers were more focused on marketing to an entire company. Their approach was therefore more basic than that of their B2C counterparts.

However, that has now changed. The buyer in the B2B space has far more access to information and an awful lot more capacity to research (in short, more of the transparency we've introduced as a core concept), so the B2B marketer has become far more obsessive about that buyer, in the same way the B2C counterparts are.

"It's very analogous now, and that's a big change," Kennedy says. "This need to know the buyer is something equally important to both B2B and B2C marketers because digitization has given full transparency in both directions. The buyer can know the company, but the company can also know the buyer with far more clarity than before.

"Indeed, it's absolutely possible that, given the typically smaller audience sizes for B2B companies, we can be a little more relevant, detailed, and direct to our consumers. In the B2C space, one may never really know one's end users—you'd still, to an extent, be pushing to a persona. For the B2B company there's an inherent advantage, considering [that] they have fewer and easier to target customers. So B2B companies perhaps have the capacity to really push an approach to personalization ahead of their B2C counterparts."

This shift to segmentation and personas was a great step forward. In my own experiences running a startup business (and, I think, in the experience of anyone producing any marketing ever), it's obvious that whatever you can do to target messaging to specific groups results in a better response.

Thus, marketers were thrilled with the advent of digital marketing and the ability to segment audiences with more precision than ever. Google's business model is predicated on just this observation: being able to present ads to people based on their search queries, thus defining audiences by their behavior rather than broad demographic data.

So technology has allowed marketers to take long strides to understand target audience groups with more depth and clarity than before—and as Barry Wolfish, Land O'Lakes said to me:

"If we are listening well, using our social platforms, we should be able to learn a lot more about what...is driving the satisfaction or lack thereof with a particular product, but we should also be able to learn a lot about consumer behaviors or consumer need states, and be able to leverage those.

"There is a greater degree of accessibility and visibility of feedback, whether it's very narrowly about your own products and brands, or whether it's about the business spaces that you're operating in—it's a tremendous opportunity to leverage it and capitalize on it."

Yet many marketers still struggle to build new personalization and segmentation opportunities into their operations. Thirty-two percent of marketers do not personalize their website at all. Of those that do, 45% simply make different product recommendations and 32% just insert the customer's name into the website copy.

Eighty-one percent personalize email content, but 60% of the respondents mean "inserting a first name into the email's subject line," which is hardly maximizing available opportunities.[8]

Those struggles are having a meaningful negative impact on business performance. Sixty-seven percent of businesses that personalize some element of their customer experience see a much higher retention rate than those that don't.[9]

Better Understanding for More Relevance

Of course, as well as more precisely targeted marketing campaigns, data allows marketers to build a far more comprehensive and useful picture of their customers. With a sensible approach to data management and collection, you can build a high-definition picture of a customer where once you had only grainy standard definition.

Considering the imperative for brands to deliver on the "R" in "ART" (more relevance), this more detailed and nuanced view of the customer will enable you to flourish in an increasingly challenging environment against a backdrop of rapidly heightening customer expectations.

It's essential that marketers are able to understand what's going on in a market, what the opportunities are, and how to target and take advantage of them.

Before big data, this was largely done by manually evaluating existing data sources, having conversations with customers, and attempting to spot patterns. Now, given the ubiquity of data, marketers have many more automated and scalable ways to create and deliver that insight.

Yet presently, too many marketing departments base decisions on a picture of their customer that is vague, lacking in nuance, or simply incorrect.

As Professor Jean-Claude Larreche, A.H. Heineken Chair of marketing at INSEAD, told me, "Marketing people too often don't know their consumers and their customers. They know how to spend money. They know how to talk to agencies. They know how to spend resource. They know how to do a lot of things. But very often, they don't know their consumers. They're too busy to do so, too arrogant. The very good marketers start with a humble attitude and a thirst to discover the consumers in depth."

Yet when a company begins to collect and analyze data sets on customers, it's hard to avoid the fact that a customer is not, in fact, X, but is more Y. There's no longer an excuse to sell the wrong benefit or tailor a product to a nonexistent customer. Indeed, this more accurate and more detailed picture of the customer enables an unprecedented relevance, in terms of both marketing strategy and outreach, and even with product development.

Finally, a Replacement for Focus Groups

The fundamental principles of how to derive insights for marketing have remained fundamentally the same for decades: Companies are still gathering qualitative data in engagement with customers and have been doing so for years. But until the maturity of data analysis technology and "social listening" (combing social media comments and feedback for insights) the only real option to do this was to set up a focus group. Insight was flawed because it was small scale and because, in a focus group, customers are somewhat influenced by their surroundings: they often tone down criticism to avoid offending the company they're focused on. As Dan Lewis of Molson Coors told me, the change engendered by the prevalence of customer data and better data management has been a major one:

"Nowadays, all you have to do is go in—you can do this off your own website if you've got the right way to engage people, and they will tell you, right there, without dragging them off the shopping mall floor into a dark room somewhere to give you their insights."

Things have taken a leap forward. You get a tremendous amount of insight and perspective if you've opened a channel of communication and you're listening. Social media gives access to a customer base and a target audience that would have been nearly impossible to reach a decade ago.

Through social media sentiment analysis and unstructured data processing, it's possible to glean insight from the organic conversations happening over social media, which are less likely to be influenced by people's worry about capacity to take offense.

The nuance and detail marketers can access through qualitative research can be combined with the scale and reach usually reserved for quantitative analysis. Social media listening, as one small part of this broader development, allows a brand to access and learn from, within 24 hours, tens of thousands of customers meeting a particular segment. This accelerates a process that previously took months and cost incredible sums of money.

For a good example of how a company utlilized social listening, see the case study "How One Medical Group Conducts Social Listening—and Turned What It Learned into Better Performance" on page 164 near the end of this chapter.

Enhanced Relevance: Building Better Campaigns— and Better Products

"We're really able to do some incredible one-to-one personalization at a mass level."

—Michael Zuna, Aflac

And this granular personalization has been proven to work. Sixty-seven percent of businesses that do some sort of personalization for customers find that customer retention rates increase to a greater extent than for companies that do not personalize messages.[10]

As Victoria Burwell of McGraw-Hill said to me, "You used to put up one ad that you hope gets folks across the nation. Now I can send not only distinct messages to distinct people, but using a vehicle I know they'd prefer. While they're searching, I can catch them. While they're on social media, I can engage them. We just have so much more data to actually personalize the message because we understand the customer so much more."

Personalization can begin with first name; progress through geography; touch on family unit makeup; cover job role, seniority, and company size; refer back to products previously purchased; link to social media comments made; and touch on location (both at one time, as when you're hovering at a particular display in a store, or based on patterns, as with a message to pick up a cup of coffee as you pass the shop you always pass on the way to work).

As Xerox's John Kennedy points out, "Digitization has created the ability to deliver personalization that was never possible before—personally, through ecommerce and media channels. [That's] a whole new transparency for the buyer and prospect. Now marketers can actually identify a person. It's not as much about knowing a market as knowing an individual and the person."

Marketing success in the future will be defined and impacted by a marketer's capacity to deliver relevance. Data and analysis give those marketers the tools they need to deliver this relevance, through precision targeting, personalized messages and experiences, and even products more closely aligned with customer need.

Data and data science have allowed marketers to become much more specific in the targeting they're able to do, in tying together information on a person from a wide range of data sources (from customer care to delivery).

If a brand wants a customer to care, then reaching out in a more personalized way, armed with a comprehensive history of the pre-existing relationship, and using that information to inform the approach and continuing relationship is a far better strategy than "spray and pay."

The case study "How KidZania's Loyalty Scheme Drives Deeper Consumer Engagement and Loyalty" on page 170 at the end of this chapter is a good example of how one company uses its loyalty scheme to deliver personalized experiences to its customers.

Examples of Brands Using Data for Better Marketing

University of Phoenix and Try Before You Buy

The more advanced companies today are also using this data to directly influence product development. Arra Yerganian, CMO of One Medical Group, told me about a new product feature at the University of Phoenix, where he was previously Chief Marketing Officer. It came into existence directly from customer feedback surfaced through a comprehensive social listening approach. He noted that a high proportion of students kept talking about a desire to "try before you buy" with different courses the institution offered. The company began to not only offer a free trial, but also make that benefit a core plank of its marketing outreach. As Yerganian told me,

"That would have never existed five years ago because we wouldn't have had our finger on the pulse, we wouldn't have had that feedback loop. [M]aybe we would have done it in focus groups, and through interacting, nine months later, but we can now do it [in] real time and get immediate gratification."

L'Oreal and Wild Ombre

Companies that work in fashion and style might have trouble separating a long-term trend (a lucrative opportunity to leverage) from a flash-in-the-pan fad. No one wants to invest time and resources building up a unit able to leverage the opportunities inherent in shiny silver trousers if they were seen on one catwalk and then laughed at for eternity.

L'Oreal had that problem. It was doing business as usual: social media listening, following blogs, and so on. At this point, "ombre" hair—dark roots, light tips—was having a bit of a moment in high-end salons.

Through L'Oreal's social listening, the company noticed that people with less money, those unlikely to spend top dollar in an exclusive salon, were ingeniously attempting to re-create the look themselves. They were using chemical products and dying their hair with toothbrushes—then passing on how they did it over YouTube and other websites.

L'Oreal realized it could produce a product for this very market and launched Wild Ombre, a hair dye under the popular and affordable Feria brand.

Molson Coors and Thanksgiving Beers

Dan Lewis, Chief Public Affairs Officer at Molson Coors, gives a relevant example from the beer industry. Lewis points out that increased customer understanding about "need states" has given the brand more capacity to reach out with relevant messages that mesh with customers' priorities at a given time:

"We can now think about customer interactions as more like an occasion-based experience. We can drill down into what's happening on that occasion, the emotional connection, and what the consumer [is] trying to convey by their brand choice, as opposed to simply trying to be the #1 pick at all times."

That allows for a certain number of efficiency savings. The company can spend its marketing budget in a more targeted way, to drive better bang for the buck.

During Thanksgiving dinner, most people drink wine. As Lewis found, beer brands struggle to insert themselves into that setting. But better customer understanding at Molson Coors has led to the identification of other opportunities, and an attempt to find its way into the Thanksgiving gathering in a more appropriate way:

"Perhaps [we can focus on] the pre-dinner occasion, where they would have a beer. While we'd love to be part of the dinner occasion, we have to find a way to get ourselves into that part of their portfolio, which is a real challenge for us because that's not something that beer has been great at."

Aflac and Storytelling on the Fly

More than using better customer insight to drive more appropriate messaging at certain times, marketers can now begin to personalize all elements of customer interaction with a brand.

For instance, it is now possible to tailor all customer touchpoints based on previous interactions. Michael Zuna, the chief marketing officer at Aflac, the American insurance giant, told me about his company's capability to "literally tell a story and stop, and have the consumer self-select which path they go down."

Zuna and the team attempt to elicit a useful response from the target customer to determine demographic information, number of children, and so on. Then they use that information to impact the communication that customer gets as part of the experience. As Zuna said,

"Depending on what a customer inputs into that digital experience, the story that comes out in relation to my brand is entirely different. We never had the opportunity to do that in a pre-digital age."

Zuna also highlights a problem with what initially can look like an opportunity: "If we're not on the 'pointy tip of the spear' on all things technologically possible, [our] creativity will suffer."

If a brand isn't leveraging new opportunities to personalize and send relevant messaging, the capacity to be creative—and thus engage with a customer base—will suffer.

Chris Lindner, President of footwear brand Keds, agrees with Zuna: "We're not personalizing every step of a customer's journey with us—directly or through our partners—right now. Ultimately, that is the future. How do you connect with somebody if they're buying a Keds Champion at Nordstrom and still maintain a relationship with that consumer if in the future they're buying at keds.com? How should we interact if they're just looking for a set of fashion tips and advice, or if they want something else from our brand? We're definitely not there yet, but we're pushing to get there—but that's something that, for sure, is a demand of our consumers long term."

Data for More Agility: Insight at Speed for On-the-Fly Campaign Evolution

David Court, et al., have found that the best-performing brands are able to reallocate up to 80% of their budget for digital marketing while a campaign is ongoing.[11]

A proven correlation exists, then, between success and speed. Forward-looking companies work to process and disseminate data-driven insight at speed, allowing them to be more agile than ever.

Aflac is able to connect qualitative, broader customer data with its own primary data on customers on a real-time basis. When a customer calls Aflac or interacts with the brand's website, we've seen that that person is now served a personalized experience, based on data such as whether the individual is a policy holder or looks like an ideal policy holder, among other metrics.

In sufficiently agile organizations, the feedback loop regarding the success of a campaign or product to change future strategy can be almost instantaneous. Digital marketing insights can guide traditional campaigns, and vice versa. Mei Lee, previously senior director of digital marketing at clothing brand J.Crew, wrote in an article for *Harvard Business Review* that "At J.Crew, I would determine my paid search marketing investments and choose which clothing product categories to drive online demand based on in-store sales data. For example, if the mint green cashmere sweater is a top category seller at stores in New York City, I would shift my paid search advertising to concentrate on relevant keywords, and target by geography and remarketing lists to customers in similar zip codes as they shop through search engines."[12]

Marketing is no longer about brands simply pushing messages at customers and hoping they get it right. Now, a savvy brand can get real-time feedback about what resonates in a campaign and what doesn't—and react accordingly.

See the case study "How Land O'Lakes Uses Data to Make Better Decisions" on page 180 at the end of this chapter to see how Land O'Lakes uses data to make better decisions

Data is not a miracle cure. There are limits to its utility.

As Professor Jean-Claude Larreche, A.H. Heineken Chair of Marketing of INSEAD told me, "People in marketing use market research more for confirmation than for discovering something new. Very seldom has market research been a tool for discovery. It has been a tool for confirmation."

Several risks are inherent in an over-reliance on data within a marketing department and, more broadly, a company. Russ Findlay of Hiscox warns that "You can't drive your brand through the rear view mirror ... I think that's really foolish."

As Steve Jobs said, "Some people say, 'Give the customers what they want.' But that's not my approach. Our job is to figure out what they're going to want before they do. I think Henry Ford once said, 'If I'd asked customers what they wanted, they would have told me, "A faster horse!"' People don't know what they want until you show it to them. That's why I never rely on market research. Our task is to read things that are not yet on the page."[13]

First is the danger of falling into the trap of driving the brand through the rear-view mirror. That means beginning to rely on past information to guide future strategy, attempting to replicate next year's strategy based on last year's analytics.

It's dangerous because you're never looking ahead—you're looking backward. You're also assuming that things will remain the same—your competition, your products, the marketing landscape you use. As we know all too well, that just won't happen.

Allowing Data to Replace Creativity

"I don't imagine a day [when] there will not be a strong level of human interaction and judgment that goes with winning decisions in the marketplace."

—Barry Wolfish, Chief Marketing Officer, Land O'Lakes

Building on Wolfish's comments, it's too easy to allow data to have too much impact and lose original thought as a result. Data can take you only so far when building marketing strategy and creative. You've got to retain a creative approach and keep a strong brand voice and proposition in mind at all times. Otherwise, you run the real risk that granular insights begin to incite granular responses and lead to a fragmentation of your message and a loss of clarity.

Are We Headed for a Data Drought?

In 2010, Mark Zuckerberg said that privacy was no longer considered a "social norm." The outcry over NSA "snooping" into the call records and metadata of the population of the U.S. (and beyond) might have given him pause and has certainly led to an increased wariness from customers about the data they share online.

Combined with an increasing savviness about online tracking (witness the momentum behind Do Not Track and privacy-focused apps such as YikYak and Secret), it's reasonable to posit that customers might not always be so free and easy with the data they share. Equally, other risks begin to increase. As companies begin to rely more on the collection and analysis of vast stores of customer data, those stores increase. As they increase, they become more attractive targets for hackers and other criminal elements in society.

We're in a transitional time: Collecting customer data is frighteningly easy, and companies have not put the requisite resources into protecting it when they have it.

The results of this lackadaisical policy have been splashed over newspaper front pages for years now. From Target, whose share price dropped to $1.20–$1.30 per share from a previously expected $1.50–$1.60 after a hack exposed the data of as many as 70 million of its customers[14]; to Sony, embarrassingly crippled by an attack from North Korea; and even to Silicon Valley darling Uber, which exposed 50,000 driver names and license plate numbers in a 2014 data breach,[15] it seems a new crisis happens every day.

It's likely that this lack of data security is in part driving customers' increasing focus on privacy. Those customers are becoming more discerning in choosing which brands they share data with and the extent of the data they share: Eighty-six percent of Internet users have taken some kind of steps to avoid being identified or tracked online.[16] Thirty-eight percent of Millennials have deleted apps because of privacy concerns.[17]

Brands often are disconcertingly arrogant and *laissez faire* about this growing customer skepticism surrounding sharing personal data and the need for companies to secure that data strongly against hackers and other criminal organizations. A panel put together by McKinsey is a good example—blasé about the trust that customers will have in the "fundamental goodness" of major global corporations: "Our panelists [CIOs, chief risk officers, CMOs from brand-name companies] presume that, in the data-collection arena, the motives of companies are good and organizations will act responsibly."[18]

When asked to rank, on a scale of 1–7, how worried companies were that customer data use for targeting could raise questions about privacy, a huge 71.8% answered with a 1–4 rank (where 1 is not at all worried).[19]

This presumption that all is generally well and that there isn't much of a problem is echoed in our own research (see Figures 7.1 and 7.2).[20]

It seems there is a real disconnect between the brand expectation of this possible risk and the very real action customers have already begun to take. Given the major shift most companies are making toward a data-driven marketing plan and a corporate-wide strategy, this is an alarming position for brands to be in.

How will customers' approach to personal data change over the next five years?

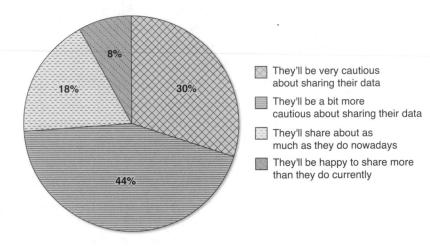

They'll be very cautious about sharing their data

They'll be a bit more cautious about sharing their data

They'll share about as much as they do nowadays

They'll be happy to share more than they do currently

Figure 7.1 Companies can see that customers will become more wary about sharing personal data...

Will that be a problem for your business?

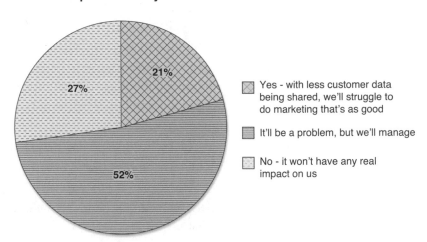

Yes - with less customer data being shared, we'll struggle to do marketing that's as good

It'll be a problem, but we'll manage

No - it won't have any real impact on us

Figure 7.2 ...but don't seem to anticipate this causing them any problems.

Avoiding Creepiness

Data stewardship and a more privacy-conscious customer base are perhaps the most obvious risks presented by an increasing reliance on customer data within large brands, but they're most certainly not the only ones. Another is navigating the "creepiness factor." Customers expect a certain level of personalization in the messages they receive, but companies can (and do) go too far.

I don't know about you, but I don't want Duane Reade to know how much I weigh and congratulate me when I lose weight by offering me a chocolate bar. However, it's entirely within the realms of possibility, given that I now own a Withings Wifi-connected scale.

Customers are almost certainly unaware of the sheer volume of data you hold on them, and sometimes it pays to keep it that way. Don't assume customers will be comfortable with you using every single thing you know about them in your marketing to them. It has the capacity to get "creepy" fast.

Golden rule: Keep being valuable. If you're using data to provide value, then chances are, your customers will remain okay with it—at least, that's the prevailing wisdom in marketing departments around the world. But take some time to pause and consider that rule before pressing Send on your next email campaign.

Conclusions

Relevance will be an increasingly important facet of any marketing campaign moving forward. Data facilitates that relevance.

The advent of digital marketing has allowed for more understanding of one's customer base—what customers like, what they don't, how they interact with you, and simply who they are. That presents a greater marketing opportunity than has been possible to leverage before now. But it's not simply an opportunity.

Customers, particularly Millennials, have been brought up to expect a level of personalization that was alien just 20 years ago. Amazon was the harbinger, and the other "digital native" companies have sprung up since the millennium. The enhanced, more personalized and relevant experience they've offered has dragged their competitors either up (into a similar level of personalization) or out (into the realms of ex-companies).

Noise is also a factor. The opportunity generated by the creation of more niche and specific marketing channels and venues for individuals to gather both on- and offline (particularly influenced by the massive impact on the price of distribution in a post-digital age) has another side to the coin. Customer numbers haven't increased at the same pace as channels have exploded. And that means the John Smith of 1960, who maybe saw a couple billboards and a newspaper ad on his way home from work, is very different in his experience than the John Smith of 2020, who gets ads over the radio, ads on digital billboards, ads on his iPad, ads on his Apple Watch, and ads on his phone.

There's an awful lot more marketing out there, an awful lot more companies scrambling for consumer attention. You have to work harder to grab that attention for yourself. A personalized, relevant message is one way to do just that.

Endnotes

1. Peter Dahlstrom, et al., "The Rebirth of the CMO," *Harvard Business Review* (5 August 2014). https://hbr.org/2014/08/the-rebirth-of-the-cmo/.

2. Nadia Cameron, "Forbes: CMOs Are the New Transformers of Business," CMO.com.au (30 July 2014). www.cmo.com.au/article/551212/forbes_cmos_new_transformers_business/

3. Marc de Swaan Arons, Frank van den Driest, and Keith Weed, "The Ultimate Marketing Machine," *Harvard Business Review* (July 2014). https://hbr.org/2014/07/the-ultimate-marketing-machine/ar/1.

4. Peter Dahlstrom, et al., "The Rebirth of the CMO," *Harvard Business Review* (5 August 2014).

5. Jonathan Gordon and Jesko Perrey, "The Dawn of Marketing's New Golden Age," *McKinsey Quarterly* (February 2015).

6. Nate Silver, *The Signal in the Noise: Why Most Predictions Fail—but Some Don't*, Penguin (27 September 2012).

7. Eric Ries, *The Lean Startup*. (Crown Business: New York 2011).

8. Jerry Jao, "Marketers Still Rely on Intuition over Data," CMO.com (29 October 2014). www.cmo.com/articles/2014/10/29/study_shows_marketer.html

9. Tatiana Mejia, "The Luxury of Choice and Personalization," CMO. com (7 July 2014). www.cmo.com/articles/2014/7/6/the_luxury_of_ choice.html

10. Tatiana Meijia, "The Luxury of Choice and Personalization," CMO. com (7 July 2014). www.cmo.com/articles/2014/7/6/the_luxury_of_ choice.html)

11. David Court, et al., "Winning the Consumer Decision Journey," McKinsey on Marketing and Sales (December 2011).

12. Mei Lee, "Too Many Marketing Teams Are Stuck in the Past," *Harvard Business Review* (September 2014). https://hbr. org/2014/09/too-many-marketing-teams-are-stuck-in-the-past/.

13. Walter Isaacson, *Steve Jobs* (Simon & Schuster, 2011).

14. Maggie McGrath, "Target Data Breach Spilled Info on as Many as 70 Million Customers," *Forbes* (10 January 2014). www.forbes.com/sites/maggiemcgrath/2014/01/10/ target-data-breach-spilled-info-on-as-many-as-70-million-customers/

15. Megan Geuss, "50,000 Uber Driver Names, License Plate Numbers Exposed in a Data Breach," *Ars Technica* (28 February 2015). http:// arstechnica.com/business/2015/02/50000-uber-driver-names-license- plate-numbers-exposed-in-a-data-breach/

16. Molly Wood, "Facebook Generation Rekindles Expectation of Privacy Online," *The New York Times* (7 September 2014). http://bits.blogs.nytimes.com/2014/09/07/ rethinking-privacy-on-the-internet/?_r=0)

17. Kashmir Hill, "9 Surprising Things We Learned about How Millennials Are Using Technology," *Fusion* (10 February 2015). http://fusion.net/listicle/42529/9-surprising-things-we-learned-about- how-millennials-are-using-technology

18. Brad Brown, David Court, and Tim McGuire, "Views from the Front Lines of the Data-Analytics Revolution," *McKinsey Quarterly* (March 2014).

19. The CMO Survey, "CMO Survey Report: Topline Results" (August 2014). http://cmosurvey.org/files/2014/09/The_CMO_Survey- Topline_Report-Aug-2014.pdf)

20. Future of Marketing Survey.

CASE STUDY 1

How One Medical Group Conducts Social Listening—and Turns What It Learns into Better Performance

About One Medical Group

According to the One Medical Group website, the company offers a "new model for primary care." Its goal is to improve the patient-doctor relationship and disrupt the $125 billion primary care industry through a focus on customer experience and innovative digital technologies.

The company has 27 facilities across the United States, in major cities such as New York, San Francisco, Los Angeles, Chicago, and Washington, D.C. New locations are opening all the time.

Arra Yerganian is the company's chief marketing officer and was my main source for this case study. He has been with the company since May 2014 and was previously the CMO for the University of Phoenix.

What Is Social Listening?

A common refrain across the rest of the book is the importance of understanding one's customer better and taking advantage of the various new opportunities a company has for doing so.

Social listening is one such opportunity. TrackMaven.com defines social listening as "the process of *monitoring* digital media channels to devise a strategy that will better influence consumers. Taking information from places that consumers participate in online can be invaluable."[21]

Essentially, social listening is as simple as it sounds: using social media to listen to customer feedback.

How Does One Medical Group Do Social Listening?

As CMO, Arra Yerganian reads every single piece of feedback One Medical Group receives via social media—and the rest of the executive leadership team for the company is not far behind. He says:

---

[21] http://trackmaven.com/marketing-dictionary/social-listening/

CASE STUDY 1

"We're all very engaged. We want to know what our members are saying about us, and most importantly, when we receive feedback, we don't want to come across as some sort of robot in our response."

Yerganian and One Medical Group are mindful of the fact that feedback takes time to give and that it tends to come from the most engaged cohort of customers. His goal is therefore to ensure that One Medical Group comes across as genuinely engaged in its response.

The action of response is an important element for the company; social listening, in Yerganian's eyes, is not simply about using one's ears. It's an active process, and the simple act of response can get across messages one would struggle to transmit over traditional marketing channels.

One Medical Group's approach to response focuses on these three aspects:

1. Driving authenticity with a customized response
2. Attempting to take the conversation offline quickly
3. Avoiding self-aggrandizement

As Yerganian said, "I see so many organizations that respond in a way that just doesn't seem as if they've taken time to customize the response for the provider of feedback. At One Medical Group, we take a slightly different approach. We try to take the discussion offline so it doesn't become public banter back and forth. We don't celebrate wins publicly, either—because I don't think it's great to self-aggrandize...and we know that on occasion things don't go well. And when you have to take withdrawals from that emotional piggy bank, you want to make sure that the piggy bank is full."

Localized Listening

While senior executives attempt to read every bit of feedback One Medical receives, they do not have the main responsibility for understanding and acting on customer feedback.

The company has a decentralized structure, with different facilities in different cities enjoying significant amounts of autonomy. Each of those local primary healthcare providers has a Provider Captain who is essentially the owner of the local market and leader of that facility. That person shoulders the majority of the responsibility to listen to customers and engage in dialogue with them. The Provider Captain has an integral role in leading the entire business, but the social media engagement is a facet of that role. Yerganian told me that:

CASE STUDY 1

"The Provider Captains are responsible for actually engaging in the dialogue, so it's not relegated to the social media content specialist or the community manager. We have those people—and they're there to provide guidance—but we really want the local market owner to engage in that discussion with the member."

Giving real accountability to local markets helps the company scale this social listening provision as it grows. Because social listening is a relatively labor-intensive task, scaling issues bedevil many startups as they become more successful and begin delivering to a broader and more populous customer base.

"If you think about the local teams having ownership for the discussion, it makes them so much more accountable. Even as we double and quadruple in size, if we have a structure in place that allows local teams with a manageable number of responsibilities to take action [on customer feedback], then I don't think we lose our efficacy."

Avoiding Silos through Communication

A risk of decentralization is the propensity to turn these local areas into silos of insight and information. Without a comprehensive and well-thought-out approach to sharing data and expertise beyond the walls of the local facility, this often tends to happen.

One Medical has this comprehensive approach:

1. **Regular meetings:** According to Yerganian, it all starts at the top. The company's leadership team meets for three hours every week to ensure inter-company transparency, the dissemination of insight, and the surfacing of issues. The facilities in each market (New York, L.A., and so on) also meet weekly.

2. **Market reviews:** On a monthly basis, each region submits a market review directly to the leadership team, in which key operational challenges are reviewed and insights are collected.

3. **HQ as a center of excellence in a decentralized model:** In the One Medical Group model, the "product is the Providers." The essential resource and differentiator is the quality of the physician treating the customer. That realization is what led to a somewhat decentralized structure at One Medical. In this environment, the head office acts as a center of excellence, focused on customers and responsible for gathering and then disseminating insight about them to those autonomous facilities.

CASE STUDY 1

Yerganian uses Headquarters' involvement to enhance consistency of message—something that would be at risk in such a decentralized organization normally: "We at headquarters are responsible for supporting [our Providers]. As we view what's happening market by market, we focus on the customer—that's what ensures we can disseminate a consistency in terms of tone and voice. We spend so much time thinking about, responding to, and normalizing feedback around the company."

Top Down Means Things Get Done

From the chief executive and founder, Tom X. Lee, down, the company is always on the lookout for ideas to improve its customer experience. That level of engagement from the senior executives first sends a signal about how seriously the company takes customer feedback. Second, it lends weight and authority to any subsequent attempt to change things based on said feedback.

Just Do It

Of course, feedback can be either a relatively simple change or something more fundamental that requires more consideration and resource.

"If it's what we call a 'just do it' and it doesn't require a long engineering process, we try to implement something quickly."

To ensure that the company is agile enough to implement quickly, the company keeps a portion of its product and engineering team freed up enough to execute quick-turnaround projects as soon as they come in.

"That's the nimble nature of a company that's always listening."

Integrating Qualitative with Quantitative

Social listening tends to provide more qualitative than quantitative data. Integrating these two types of data is essential for a more comprehensive customer view.

One Medical has a robust business intelligence team that provides the central executive with data on metrics such as appointment availability, scheduling, the time it takes to see a provider, and other areas that are often particular pain points for customers. The goal is to ensure that qualitative insights from social listening are either supported or debunked by hard numbers.

CASE STUDY 1

"We were smart early on to ensure that it wasn't just us basing decisions on 'feeling'—it was us backing those hypotheses with real facts, based on numbers and trends and data that we can report on.

"Every two weeks, we review KPIs, and the business intelligence team reports on those to get a real sense of where we are. We're not just in this la-la-land where we base decisions exclusively on what we feel or think or hear."

How Has Social Listening Informed One Medical's Performance?

Engaging in social listening and understanding the customer better has led to a multitude of impacts on the One Medical business.

Streamlining Membership

The company received multiple comments suggesting that the sign-up process of becoming a member of One Medical was somewhat cumbersome. As Yerganian said,

"We'd actually gotten in our own way. So we're in the process of transitioning now to what I would describe as Quick Registration, as opposed to having to fill out many pages and dozens of fields. And by ensuring that we don't overburden the person who wants to join up front...I think we can ease the process of onboarding to our member base."

Negative Feedback to Define Brand Proposition

Negative feedback is, of course, valuable to companies seeking to spot problems and improve themselves. But it can also be useful in terms of brand positioning. Certainly, One Medical appreciates the nuance that negative reviews can bring to an understanding of who the company is. Yerganian pointed out that negative feedback helps to define the One Medical Group offering with more clarity:

"On occasion, we'll get a review that says 'I can't believe One Medical doesn't have doctors with lab coats and name badges—what kind of doctor's office is that?' We're thrilled because it tells the world exactly who we are, and who we're not, and who we serve, and who's best suited to become a member.

CASE STUDY 1

"And that speaks volumes. We don't have to go out there and say, blasting from the balconies, that we're unique. Our members and those who experience One Medical do it for us."

Better Recruitment for Better Providers

Considering the importance of quality doctors for One Medical Group's model, the process of recruitment is a critical one. The company accepts only 2.3% of applicants who try to become providers. The recruitment process is thus an important element in driving success in the future.

The company has made meaningful changes based on customer feedback to ensure that the recruitment process highlights candidates who fit the culture of the company. Yerganian concludes:

"We're hearing a lot of feedback on the recruitment, hiring, and culture side of the business. That helps us to formulate how we should present ourselves [in this process], what elements of the business to prioritize, how we communicate about ourselves in interviews. This is all important for us to take into account because we're hiring, of course, not only for great skill, but also for this cultural fit."

CASE STUDY 2

How KidZania's Loyalty Scheme Drives Deeper Consumer Engagement and Loyalty

"As the story goes, we believe KidZania exists because kids were fed up with how adults were running the world.

"These kids were inspired to declare their independence from adults and create their own special place where they could train and experiment as part of exercising their rights to Be, to Know, to Care, to Play, to Create, and to Share."

—Sarah Marsh, Vice President of Customer Loyalty, KidZania

KidZania is a chain of interactive family edutainment centers where children can role-play real-life experiences—like adult jobs—and earn KidZos, a form of currency, doing so.

When children come to KidZania, they can role-play 120 different experiences. The center introduces them to careers and relevant adult life experiences in an engaging way, in a naturalistic setting.

KidZania currently operates 18 locations around the world, from Jakarta to Sao Paulo, Tokyo to Cairo. The centers have welcomed 35 million visitors since the first location opened in Mexico City in 1999.

For this case study, I spoke with Sarah Marsh, Vice President of Customer Loyalty. Marsh joined KidZania in September 2011; before that, she worked at Virgin America, Merkle, and Metzner-Schneider Associates, among other companies.

B-KidZanian: Citizenship, Passports, and Personalization

A fundamental part of the KidZania experience is for children to be able to explore careers or experience activities the adults in their life discuss, such as getting a university degree, having a bank account, or knowing what to do in case of a fire or flood.

The team wanted to recognize the choices those children made and use that information to personalize both their experiences at KidZania and the communication that parents receive in the run-up to their visit and

CASE STUDY 2

afterward. As a result, the company launched its first loyalty program, B-KidZanian, in 2011. The central element of the program was the metaphor of citizenship, of children choosing to become CitiZens of the global Kid-Zania community. Sarah Marsh points out, "Citizenship is something every human being on the planet can relate to."

After KidZania receives parental consent for children to participate, the counter signs up kids as CitiZens in the'"PaZZport" Office. In the process, the children receive their first KidZania PaZZport, personalized with their details much like the real-world equivalent.

From that point on, the team at KidZania can personalize a child's experience in real time, to drive deeper engagement and offer new experiences to the most engaged customers: "That, to me, is the ultimate: We can recognize the children within a household and celebrate their achievements through their level in B-KidZanian. We can personally reinforce the benefits they're getting at that particular moment and give the parent a window into their child's experience of KidZania."

The PaZZport

The PaZZport itself has stamps to show where the children have been. The first stamp a child receives is a holographic sticker marking where the passport was issued. Future stickers are added when children visit other cities, and specially designed stamps are added when children experience different roles and jobs while at KidZania. Marsh explains:

"The PaZZport mirrors to these children what they've accomplished and achieved at KidZania, and it's a personalized piece of that experience that they can show their friends while within the facility and then take home with them. Our hope and expectation is that they'll bring back that PaZZport on future visits and continue to collect stamps for the program."

Playing on the rewards mentality inherent in any gamified model and common across loyalty schemes (witness "gold members" of airline frequent flier services), children can earn three levels within B-KidZanian, based on their activity.

1. **Naturalized. CitiZen:** This is the entry point to B-KidZanian.
2. **Distinguished CitiZen:** As children acquire more skills and participate in more activities (whether as doctors, firefighters, chefs, or airline pilots, for example), they collect more stamps. When they reach 30 stamps, they move up a level to become a Distinguished CitiZen and earn a new orange PaZZport.

CASE STUDY 2

3. **Honorable CitiZen:** Children reach this level when they have earned 60 stamps.

KidZania was cognizant of the challenge inherent in designing these tiers without inadvertently creating an elite program that would run counter to the brand values of the company and the goal of the facilities. According to Marsh, "[The positioning] thus stresses working toward goals and being recognized for one's pursuit of knowledge and experience. The levels are called 'Distinguished' and 'Honorable' to imply the title of a statesman rather than the more typical approach of Silver, Gold, and Platinum levels. The words *status* and *elite* are simply not used."

When Children Are Consumers but Parents Are Customers

KidZania's loyalty program—indeed, its entire marketing operation—has added complexity. The children who experience Kid-Zania and are the actors in the loyalty mechanic are not necessarily the direct purchasers of the products KidZania is selling.

Therefore, the loyalty scheme needed to perform in the same way as all KidZania's customer experiences: It needed to appeal to both the children who were interacting with KidZania experiences and the adults who were choosing to pay for those experiences.

What Was the Goal?

The B-KidZanian loyalty scheme was launched out of a recognition that personalized, relevant experiences would create more value for customers, build preference, and thus engender more repeat visits to KidZania facilities. The ultimate goal for the program was to increase revisitation, to encourage a situation in which, if children and parents were given a choice, they would choose to come back.

Beyond that, the company recognized the benefits of delivering a richer digital experience to accompany the on-site experience, one that encouraged continuing engagement post-visit and thus contributed to increased revisitation.

On a more practical level, a loyalty program gives a reason for parents to opt into ongoing communication from the company and for allowing the activities of their children to be tracked across visits. Building addressable

CASE STUDY 2

leads was a goal, as was generating insight and customer understanding to deliver better marketing campaigns and creating a better experience for customers as a whole.

"It's about being able to deliver a relevant experience for both parents and children, and understanding that [what that means] constantly changes—and that's really hard."

How Did B-KidZanian Launch?

KidZania had recognized the potential of a loyalty scheme for years. Driven by Chief Marketing Officer Cammie Dunaway, the company had been working on opportunities to drive repeat visitation, to deliver personalized customer experiences and build preference among consumers.

The use of a PaZZport as the tangible emblem of the program, playing on the desire to be part of something bigger than oneself and a CitiZen of the KidZania world, was one of the first elements of the campaign to be established. Using stamps as recognition of achievement had been defined when Marsh joined the company in 2011 to drive the program to launch.

Buy-In from the Top—From the Start

"If you don't have a loyalty champion at the top, it will never, never work," according to Marsh.

As is echoed so often by marketers around any large-scale project, having a champion high up in the organization is critical to success. Happily, the B-KidZanian scheme had two: CMO Dunaway and founder/CEO Xavier Lopez Ancona.

"As much as we try to minimize risk, [a project like this] is still a leap of faith. [Often] the economics may not prove itself from day one, and it's quite a major investment on the technology front, the creative front, and the legal front. And I give a lot of credit to the company for making that bet—because it's absolutely the right choice to be made."

Planning

In 2011, the company began to move forward on the practicalities. It conducted a Request for Proposal for a marketing automation partner (which was won by Neolane, subsequently acquired by Adobe) and began to consider some of the practical questions that needed to be answered:

CASE STUDY 2

1. What training of staff will need to be conducted?
2. What does the physical property look like? Should it be a Passport Office within each KidZania?
3. How do we coordinate with legal and IT on data management, governance, and IT infrastructure?

The data management strategy was key. "When I walked in, there was an idea and a concept of the data that would be a core part of the program, but there wasn't actually a data management strategy. And now we were asking to operationalize sophisticated house-holding logic [That was critical to establish because a loyalty program is cross-functionally very intensive]. What we're trying to do is integrate every possible guest touch point—not just at the KidZania facility itself, but beyond that, in the home. And that was truly new for the organization as a whole."

Organizational Structures

"Loyalty programs naturally intersect with every guest touch point. That means virtually every department, known as Ministries at KidZania, became involved in the program launch."

A loyalty scheme is an enormously cross-functional, matrixed project. A lot of time was spent working out the employees who would be impacted by the rollout, those who had a role to play initially and longer term, and how the project would be run on an ongoing basis.

The original launch involved 30 to 40 people. Post-launch, this was scaled back to a core team of five, who reported to Marsh, as Vice President of Loyalty. This central team was augmented by loyalty managers in each market who function as single points of contact at the assorted global facilities and who are responsible for rolling out projects within those distinct locations.

The five-person central team now functions much like a marketing service provider to the individual facilities. Within that team are a campaign manager and specialist, an analyst, a programmer, and an IT project manager who has been specifically assigned to the loyalty team.

The Functionality and Benefits of B-KidZanian

Marsh and the team found two major benefits from the B-KidZanian launch: driving deeper engagement, and building more comprehensive customer understanding.

CASE STUDY 2

Tying Rewards to Action—in Real Time—to Drive Deeper Engagement

A fundamental precept of KidZania is to give the children visiting the chance to earn a form of currency for their "work": kidZos.

The loyalty scheme evolves this concept. Children who gather more KidZania experience are, like their real-world counterparts, rewarded with more kidZos per activity as they move up the PaZZport scheme. It's a scenario akin to AirMiles services: the more loyalty customers show, the more rewards they get.

Children with deeper engagement and more experience at KidZania get new or improved opportunities over typical "tourists" (KidZania term for visitors who haven't signed up for the loyalty scheme). For instance, a child with more experience may get the opportunity to take the lead role in a theater production, or create a different kind of perfume bottle from the other participants. Those experiences are localized, and different in every market—from Mexico to Dubai.

Not only that, but the technology and systems in place at KidZania have given the team the ability to personalize children's experiences in real time: "If they have a passport, we can actually greet them by name when they come to be a Firefighter. And we can say, 'Congratulations, Bobby! You've achieved enough activities to become a Distinguished CitiZen today, so you're going to earn an extra 4 kidZos and you'll have an opportunity to ring the bell on the firefighting truck.'"

Equally, personalization happens when children travel from one city to another. Children can bring their passports with them wherever they travel and get tailored experiences based on previous visits.

If a KidZanian passport was issued in Mexico and a child visits KidZania Dubai, he or she can be personally greeted as a CitiZen of KidZania. That child then gets a special city hologram sticker in his or her PaZZport to commemorate the visit.

"To do that, it does require a solid thoughtful infrastructure, a lot of coordination between databases, and a diverse group of point-of-sale systems in different time zones. That is part of the complexity of the program, being able to deliver a real-time, localized experience within a global framework."

CASE STUDY 2

Deeper Customer Understanding for More Targeted Marketing and More Engaging Experiences

Through their programs, KidZania can now discover who is visiting a center for the first or the tenth time. Having the ability to connect those visits over time has been a major advantage of B-KidZanian. The company then knows who visits on a regular basis and who might need an incentive to visit again, allowing a more targeted and efficient marketing spend.

Knowing guests on an individual level means that the company "no longer has to operate on the basis of averages." For instance, the company knows that, in Mexico, it's not unusual to see clicks on email campaigns as many as four to five weeks after initial delivery. In Malaysia, on the other hand, the majority of clicks happen in the first two to three days. The company also knows that, in some locations, families are larger and have less time elapsed between visits.

Granular insights such as these promote deeper understanding and, consequently, more targeted and relevant campaigns. The examples are perhaps simple ones, but the company can adjust the lead time for communicating an event to parents, customize the duration of promotions, and predict the likelihood of multiple family members using an offer, depending on the location being targeted.

Integrating Online and Offline Experience for Deeper Engagement

"When we were formulating this program, a key focus was to think about how we [could] take the excitement and engagement that happens at KidZania and translate that into something that parents and children could enjoy at home or on the go," said Marsh.

A fundamental goal for B-KidZanian was to encourage continuing engagement between customers and KidZania between visits, in the hope of increasing return visitation.

The program itself gave a broader swathe of parents an incentive to engage more actively. Consequently, the addressable and permissioned audience on the database expanded from a few hundred names to hundreds of thousands in just a few months.

This gave the delivery of an exceptional online experience, via email or the KidZania web properties, extra importance. Of course, the company also has more data and insight to do so from children enrolling as CitiZens

---

CASE STUDY 2

---

and through their engagement at facilities. The company can build campaigns for parents that are both relevant and valuable.

Alongside classic loyalty program lifecycle offers ("One more visit and your child will become a Distinguished CitiZen"), new tailored promotions have higher response rates than previous untargeted efforts.

Consider two examples of personalization KidZania implemented.

Birthday Email 2.0

Marketers working across many different industries are likely familiar with the birthday email, to recognize and celebrate a birthday within a target household. This sort of message tends to be one of the best-performing campaigns across a multitude of product types and customer groups. People seem to be more receptive to marketing on their birthday.

Yet very few of these marketers are able to actually personalize the content in that message to the individual having the birthday. KidZania has been able to do so by making the birthday email personalized by both the parent and the specific child within a larger household. The campaign is now consistently among the company's top performers.

Crayola at KidZania Cuicuilco

KidZania often enters into partnerships with brands to better create realistic experiences that enliven a guest's experience at KidZania. One such sponsor was Crayola, the children's art supply brand. The company approached KidZania with an idea to sponsor an event focused on creativity at the Cuicuilco center in Mexico City.

KidZania and Crayola built a targeted campaign to raise awareness of the event and sent invitations to households in the Mexico City area with children ages 3 to 7. Thirty-nine thousand messages were sent, with 8,000 registrations generated. Two thousand children and parents attended on the day of the event. That resulted in a 20.5% lead generation rate and a 5.2% registration rate, a significant positive result.

Indeed, the campaign was a win on three fronts: "First, the guests who were invited actually had a complimentary admission to KidZania. We knew it was an experience they would enjoy, it was free, and not only that, it was an experience they would not ordinarily have at KidZania.

"For Crayola, it was great: These were 8,000 new permissioned contacts. For KidZania, ultimately, it was great: We were able to schedule the

CASE STUDY 2

event during an off-peak time of day, so it was great for capacity utilization and, again, [was a] value-enhancing experience for our guests."

Online Web Experience Optimization

The B-KidZanian program will also enable KidZania to optimize and personalize the online web experience for citizens. The new experience, launching in 2015, will allow parents and children to log into the KidZania site and view a history of the activities they've completed at KidZania, the experiences they've had, and the progress they've made, all published in a form of online resume.

"A child will be able to say that they went to the university and earned a degree in tourism. They'll see that they gained experience as a chef in the culinary school, or that they scaled a climbing wall using the latest safety techniques."

Children will also see all the experiences they have not yet participated in, which will encourage a visit to another KidZania center. "It's a very simple technique, and it allows them to see their achievements over time, but also to set some very discrete goals for them to accomplish."

How Do They Measure Success?

On a daily basis, the loyalty team is looking at three key KPIs, which are then published to the loyalty managers in each KidZania location running the B-KidZanian scheme:

- **Enrollment Conversion**—This metric measures the potential pool of guests (KidZania calls them tourists) who could join the program and then tracks how many are actually converted into new CitiZens.

  "That's looking within the operations—how good of a job did we do on capturing that audience and converting them into members of our program?"

- **Daily Program Penetration**—This metric measures the percentage of all visitors to KidZania in a day who were new CitiZens and returning CitiZens. "Once again, it's about driving the highest enrollment conversion, but also making sure that we're doing the best we can on the marketing front, to encourage the CitiZens to come back."

CASE STUDY 2

- **Email Penetration Rate**—This metric tracks the success with which KidZania captures accurate and actionable email addresses at the time customers enroll in the B-KidZanian scheme. Beyond that, the team looks at the marketing opt-ins, to see what percentage of the population can actually be marketed to.

Has It Worked?

As for success against these metrics, Marsh says the impact has been huge. The loyalty scheme creates a reasonable context in which to ask parents to be recontacted. Any company working with products for children knows that parents are understandably picky about providing information about their children unless there's a clear and immediate benefit. That increased addressable leads from hundreds to hundreds of thousands, but it also increased the quality of those leads.

"[That], of course, dramatically improved our ability to reach the parents' inbox so that deliverability rates are in the high 90% range and response rates exceed industry standards."

The impact of the scheme of course goes beyond email campaign metrics. KidZania now has a wealth of actionable data that has been put into practice to improve efficiency and experience. The company has built a mechanism by which it can personalize customer experience, both online and offline, based on customers' previous engagement with KidZania and the potential of what they can achieve.

KidZania also has built a program in which parents and children are clearly motivated to continue to engage with the company.

Fundamentally, the goal was to build a program in which guests could experience the brand in deeper and more personalized ways, no matter where they are. This has worked: The company sees that households that have engaged with the loyalty scheme have a higher propensity to come back to KidZania.

CASE STUDY 3

How Land O'Lakes Uses Data to Make Better Decisions

Barry Wolfish, the chief marketing officer for dairy brand Land O'Lakes, took me through how the company uses social interaction and conversation data to inform future strategy.

Potential opportunities for better performance are found at "the inter-section between judgment and quantitative analysis," he says. For example, perhaps a marketing manager who receives reports on social activity begins to see that many people are talking about the amount of gluten in recipes Land O'Lakes distributes via its content strategy. The manager can then use that insight to inform future marketing, to perhaps build content in the form of gluten-free recipe ideas. That level of insight can be addressed fast—often even overnight.

The challenge, as Wolfish sees it, is with the broader, deeper changes that are spotted. As he points out, the people at the "coalface" who are listening to and conducting conversations with customers tend to be relatively junior. They are relatively tightly focused in their role and thus less likely to even notice those broader, wider-ranging issues arising.

Equally, they don't (and should not) have the capacity to talk directly to the company president, lobbying for a new formula for butter that's not hard when it comes out of the refrigerator. Therefore, at Land O'Lakes, senior management at the company is proactive. They ensure that they're asking the right questions of their team and building internal forums where these types of topics and issues surface routinely. Alongside that model is a reporting and data-collection function to create broader visibility around topics and areas that are trending.

Back to the hard butter example: Changing the formula for the product is a big job. Addressing it takes science, technology, perhaps a new manufacturing process, and maybe even an entirely new factory. That's a major investment and a long-term project.

Nevertheless, it's essential that these issues be spotted and addressed. The challenge comes in deciding which of them are worth responding to, especially when the response necessitates breaking ground on a new butter factory.

If an issue surfaces routinely at Land O'Lakes, the "focal point" junior employee passes it to the manager. That manager is responsible for escalating the issue to a broader group of decision makers. The "bigger dollar"

CASE STUDY 3

decisions at the company have broader levels of visibility around the company and more senior people involved in the yes/no decision.

A natural escalation of topics is driven by the magnitude of the spend and the potential impact (positive or negative) on the business. It's a ground-up model in which the company does rely on people who are in focal point roles as managers, whether a manager of research trends or a manager of a brand, to move these issues through a decision-making funnel.

8

Why Multichannel Matters

"When I became CMO of Yahoo!, I think it was at almost the height of chaos. [T]he rules for how you succeeded with consumers had completely been disrupted by the digital transformation. And then there was an explosion of new channels.... You still had the same goals, but all of a sudden, all of the traditional wisdom that [you'd] relied on was not necessarily serving you in the same way."

—Cammie Dunaway, Chief Marketing Officer, KidZania

Cammie Dunaway has held senior marketing positions in multiple industries in a career that spans over twenty years. As such, she is well-placed to discuss the changes that have impacted on all marketers over the last couple of decades. One of the most significant developments? The explosion of new marketing channels.

Seventy-six percent of marketers feel their multichannel strategy is not as developed as it should be,[1] while 85% of marketers say that traditional marketing channels (TV, radio, and so on) are going to get progressively less useful over the next five years.[2]

That goes some way to explaining why 80% of marketers will spend a smaller portion of their marketing budget on traditional channels in the years ahead.[3]

Like fishermen standing in a fast-moving stream, if marketers want to simply stay in the same place nowadays, they're going to have to work hard. The marketing channel landscape is evolving quickly and shows no sign of slowing down. To keep up, one thing is clear: Multichannel marketing is only getting more diverse, and marketers have to use a more extensive roster of channels than they did five years ago.

The rapidity with which things are changing is getting increasingly difficult to keep up with. As Linda Rutherford, Vice-President of Communications and Strategic Outreach at Southwest Airlines told me a couple of years ago, "[N]ew ways to engage your audience with your brand...are popping up every day—the speed with which things are moving means we are constantly going to be learning about these new opportunities to connect. It's the biggest challenge right now.... The pace of change in the technology of communications is obviously an overwhelming influence on everything that we, as executives, do."[4]

The majority of new channels that marketers are being forced to consider come from the world of social media. Among American adults of age 18 and up, no less than five social media platforms are used routinely by 18% or more of the population, as you can see in Figure 8.1.[5]

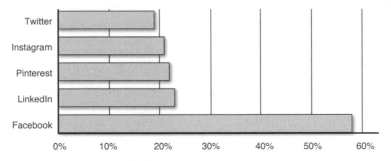

Proportion of American adults that use social networks

Source: "Social Media Update 2014," Pew Research Center.

Figure 8.1 Facebook dominates, but all five major social networks are used by about 20% of the population or more. That's hard to ignore.

When 18% of the entire U.S. population is using a channel, any marketer will have to incorporate it into their thinking. New channels and platforms are constantly being incorporated into Millennial media consumption and communication behaviors, thus forcing marketers to consider them if they strive to "be where their customers are."

Russ Findlay, Chief Marketing Officer for the U.S. arm of the insurance firm Hiscox, says, "Who knows what's around the corner in the next five years? You've got to follow your consumer, and so if all a sudden they start to communicate on a particular media that we're not on, I'd be foolish not to take that pretty seriously and consider it."

For further insight into Hiscox's creation of a new brand platform, see the case study "Bringing 'Encourage Courage' to Life Via Multichannel Brand Marketing" on page 192 at the end of this chapter.

You've Got to Spread Yourself Thin

"There is no silver bullet answer to how you're going to reach millennials and your target audience."

—Dan Lewis, Chief Corporate Affairs Officer, Molson Coors

New marketing and social media platforms that marketers are forced to consider tend to be in addition to, not a replacement for, existing channels. That only adds to the problem, and means that modern marketing campaigns tend to be run across many more channels and platforms than was previously the case. For instance, as you can see in Figure 8.2, no less than eight channels are used routinely by more than 50% of marketers. Ten years ago, this was more like two or three.

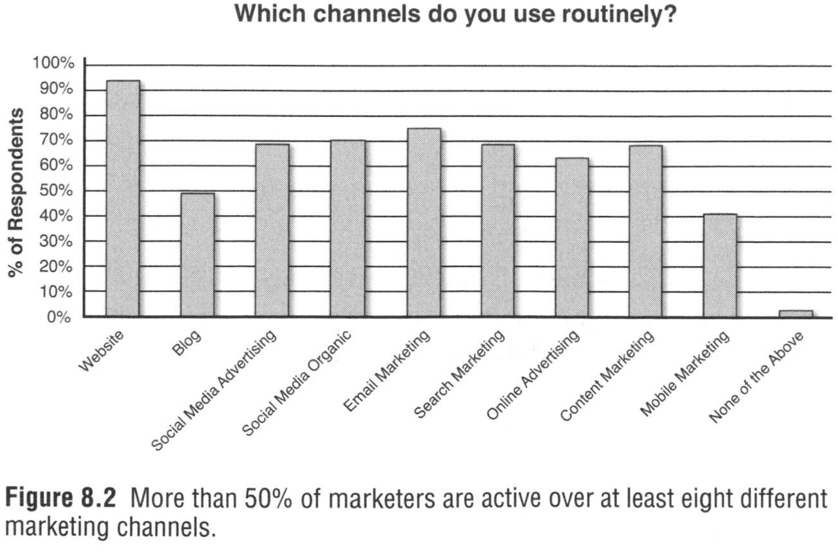

Which channels do you use routinely?

Figure 8.2 More than 50% of marketers are active over at least eight different marketing channels.

The spreading of marketing campaigns across more channels means complex decisions must be made on budget allocation and resource spend. In addition, given the changing media consumption habits that have engendered this spreading across multiple channels, it's far more difficult to achieve "blanket coverage" than it was in the days when you had to cover only relevant TV channels and radio stations. Nowadays, customers spend some time on Facebook, a little time watching TV, then jump on Twitter to live tweet a sporting event, and tune into the latest YouTube series on their laptop. To get the same level of market penetration, or channel dominance, as you did by buying up ad space on Channel A in 1990, you'd now need to be either a) as rich as Croesus or b) committed to a strategy akin to putting all your money on lucky 13 at the blackjack table. Instead, sensible marketers are striving to know their customers, and their media consumption habits, better. They have to target campaigns more specifically, to more well-defined customer groups—and they have to build campaigns that work across many channels.

It all adds complexity, stress, and confusion for the marketer at work today. To help navigate the challenge, marketers must bear in mind three key elements:

1. Work out which channels are worth the money to you.
2. Define how to use channels appropriately.
3. Make sure channels work in some form of harmony.

Work out Which Channels Are Worth the Money to You

One thing is for sure—it's essential to make the right bets on where to spend your marketing budget and time. The challenge is that each channel has different metrics—which means comparisons between multiple channels is that much harder. It's difficult to ignore the suspicion that the channel owners (the Facebooks, Twitters, and Instagrams of this world) have a vested interest in ensuring that the metrics they promote to measure engagement can't be easily comparable to those of their competitors.

Twitter highlights "engagements" and "conversions"; Facebook focuses on "reach" and "clicks." As a result of these competing metrics, it's essential that as marketers, you keep your own internal KPIs and metrics at front of mind and do not allow yourself to be swayed by a social network's pronouncements on how important "Tweet Engagement" is to tracking marketing success. Your goal should be to move the needle against your own metrics, not those of Twitter, Facebook, or Google.

Define How to Use Channels Appropriately

Of course, multichannel campaigns are made harder because these aren't simply new TV channels launching; they're entirely new mechanisms to connect with an audience: Facebook public likes, sharing on Twitter, creative photography on Instagram, and Snapchat's temporary image-based private communication. What this means is that marketers need to get comfortable quickly with entirely new marketing formats and delivery mechanisms. What works in an email campaign won't work on Facebook, and what works on Facebook won't work on Snapchat.

Jennifer Dominiquini was Chief Marketing Officer for fitness, sporting goods, and toys at Sears and Kmart when I spoke with her back in 2013. She pointed out:

"There is an increasing need to balance emerging marketing techniques with more tried and tested techniques. The challenge is to experiment sensibly to find value.[6] Using a new technique simply because it's new does not necessarily make sense. But likewise, not trying something new because it's not proven also does not make sense. You've got to think through the marketing mix and find bang for your buck, a proven ROI."

The ways one interacts on social channels are markedly different than with previous, more traditional channel marketing strategies. John Kennedy, Chief Marketing Officer at Xerox, told me:

"I like to think of social as the customer's channel. It's not just a free channel for the marketer to jump on to. We're guests on the customer's channel. Marketers have to become much more savvy in

terms of participation. Using social is less about promoting themselves, more about education, teaching, entertaining, and providing
value."

Kennedy is right. Social media requires a conversational approach,
as covered in Chapter 10, "The Imperative—and Opportunity—of
Conversation." We're not doing marketing here—or, at least, we're
not doing the 'Buy Now/Sale Ends' style of marketing. We're doing
something softer, slower, less scary, and more useful.

You've Got to Make Sure That Channels Work in Some Form of Harmony

First, an important note. Be careful not to labor under the mis-
conception that the plethora of new channels has reduced traditional
channels to irrelevancy. That's not the case, as is clear from Figure
8.3. As is pointed out earlier, new channels are being *added* to the
marketer's To Do List—they're not entirely replacing what came
before. Although budgets for those channels are expected to continue
to decline, traditional channels will still have a role to play in future
campaigns. And that's entirely justified, given the fact that more traditional marketing channels still seem to be driving more ROI than
newer opportunities:

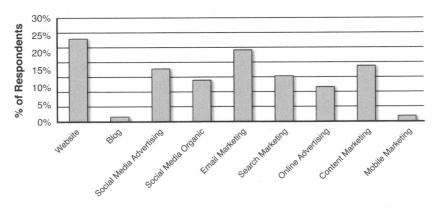

Which channel delivers the best ROI?

Figure 8.3 Email and website marketing still deliver the best results, but
content and social media are catching up fast.

Remember those rising Super Bowl ad prices we covered a few chapters ago? We've already seen how important live events are to big, brand-led marketing campaigns. Few other places get you millions of people watching one thing, at one time, in one place.

TV, radio, and other traditional channels will continue to exert a particular influence and play a role that newer channels can't hope to match, as Arra Yerganian points out:

"For brands that have the budget, I think that media like television and radio can serve as a great messaging platform."

Yerganian was previously the CMO at the University of Phoenix. The company spent the vast majority of its budget on online, digital campaigns. But toward the end of his tenure at the company, he began, with significant success, to work radio into his budget.

He did so, however, as part of an integrated, consistent campaign. Yerganian used social channels to listen to and engage with his customers. From engaging in this conversation, he realized that customers wanted a way to try the University of Phoenix offering before buying. Armed with that information, he made a commitment to broad-scale radio advertising to get the message out that free trials were now on offer:

"That would have never existed five years ago, because we wouldn't have had our finger on the pulse, we wouldn't have had that feedback loop," he says. "You know, maybe we would have done it in focus groups, and through interacting, nine months later, but we can now do it real time and get immediate gratification.

"I think smart brands will use a bunch of different media to evaluate how to reach consumers with authentic voice. Those that are myopic will lose."

Frans Cornelis, CMO of Dutch human resources consultancy firm Randstad, agrees with Yerganian's observation and faith in the continued relevance of more traditional channels. Cornelis also points out that although new channels come online with alarming speed, it takes longer for outmoded ones to die out. Thus, TV and radio will probably be around for a number of years yet:

"I don't think TV is beaten yet—that's the one that is still standing," Cornelis says. "In fact, you could argue that it's quite likely that people will later conclude that web marketing and TV actually reinforce each other (and radio, to a limited degree). You must remember that it took ten years from people saying faxes [would] disappear for them to really go."

Multichannel As a Foundation

Campaigns must be built with this multichannel approach incorporated from the ground up if they are to flourish. Marketing messages are no longer consumed in one place; they're consumed across several fragmented platforms, at different times, and in different locations. It's why storytelling has become so important. Look at Coca-Cola's broad "delivering happiness" campaign, pushing the same overall message across viral videos, social media sites, TV ads, and more. Those TV and radio ads—the broad, traditional channels—still very much have a role to play in raising awareness, while social campaigns then build engagement and a more human, personal connection.

Dan Lewis, Chief Corporate Affairs Officer at Molson Coors, told me: "We have to remove some of the conventions of engagement with consumers that still dominate the thinking in marketing in many ways. So a television advertisement is going to be the way we engage at one level, and then we're going to look for other tools beneath that, instead of driving a campaign that way."

Multichannel marketing is complicated and challenging. But by determining where your customers *are*, finding the right message for the right channel, and ensuring a consistent, harmonious approach in what is often a pretty fragmented environment, marketers can not only survive, but thrive—with more engaging, relevant, and pervasive campaigns.

Endnotes

1. Nick Johnson, "Peacekeeper, Navigator, Student: The Marketer to 2015," Incite Marketing and Communications (2014).

2. Future of Marketing Survey.

3. Future of Marketing Survey.

4. Linda Rutherford, Vice President of Communications and Strategic Outreach, Southwest Airlines, quoted in "Peacekeeper, Navigator, Student: The Marketer to 2015," Incite Marketing and Communications (2014).

5. Maeve Duggan, et al., "Social Media Update 2014," Pew Research Center (9 January 2015). www.pewinternet.org/2015/01/09/social-media-update-2014/

6. Jennifer Dominiquini, former Chief Marketing Officer, Sears/Kmart, quoted in "Peacekeeper, Navigator, Student: The Marketer to 2015," Incite Marketing and Communications (2014).

CASE STUDY

Hiscox: Bringing "Encourage Courage" to Life Via Multichannel Brand Marketing

About Hiscox

Hiscox is an insurance provider listed on the London Stock Exchange and a member of the FTSE 250. The company was founded in 1901. In 2013, it had revenues of 1.7 billion and a workforce of 1,400 employees across the world.

Russ Findlay is the Chief Marketing Officer for Hiscox in the United States; offices were set up in that country in 2008. He previously held senior marketing roles with PepsiCo and IHOP, and he was the CMO for Major League Soccer. In addition to contributing to the book as a whole, Findlay allowed me to interview him for this more in-depth case study. Quotations throughout this case study are from him.

The U.S. arm of Hiscox runs a slightly modified business compared to the rest of the company: It runs both a classic B2B brokered business and a direct-to-consumer B2C platform that focuses on small business insurance.

In October 2014, the company launched a new brand platform, "Encourage Courage." This case study focuses on how Findlay and Hiscox launched this platform through a comprehensive multichannel marketing strategy.

Encourage Courage

"Encourage Courage" is the name and tagline for Hiscox's new brand positioning platform. Launched in fall 2014, it was designed as the antithesis of the current insurance industry's positioning: focused on an aversion to risk.

"The insurance world trades on mitigating risk. Some people will almost say it's borderline fear-mongering—essentially, 'If you don't do this, bad things will happen.'"

Encourage Courage attempts to differentiate from that position, pointing out that nothing really great happens in the world without embracing some sort of risk. People shouldn't fear risk, the platform asserts—they shouldn't be stupid or irrational, of course, but they also shouldn't shy away from risk.

When the planning was done for launching this new brand platform, the goal was to bring it to life in a variety of ways across several different marketing platforms and channels.

CASE STUDY

Bringing a Brand to Life

Findlay launched Sierra Mist, Sierra Mist Free, and PepsiMax while working for PepsiCo, and he drew on those experiences when he began the brand launch work for Encourage Courage at Hiscox.

At launch, Sierra Mist was due to compete with well-known brands such as 7Up and Sprite. What's more, Sierra Mist was coming from a standing start: "This was a brand that came out of thin air. It had zero brand awareness because the brand literally did not exist previously."

Therefore, in his first year with Sierra Mist, Findlay did little more than drive brand awareness, focusing on ensuring that America knew this was a lemon-lime soft drink from Pepsi, not a piece of furniture or a clothing brand. "You can't take anything for granted. You don't assume people know what you're talking about."

In the second year, the focus shifted to activation. Once brand awareness scores reached a certain point, the challenge was to position Sierra Mist in the right way. "So now I've [got] a pretty good sense that America knows what the brand is. Now I want to tell them how they should think about it."

At that point, Findlay focused on bringing the brand to life through sponsoring soccer and comedy, attempting to associate Sierra Mist with *refreshment*.

At Hiscox, the company is still focused on making people aware of the brand (which is a relatively small player in the U.S., particularly for the direct-to-consumer business). The company as a whole has been in operation for 115 years, but no one outside the insurance business really knew who the company was in the U.S. "We hadn't really done much small business marketing, so the small business owners in the U.S. really had no awareness of us whatsoever."

What They're Doing at Hiscox

For the small-business, direct-to-consumer business at Hiscox, marketing is characterized by a multichannel approach. Social channels are an important element of any campaign, and this is no less the case with the brand launch work for Encourage Courage. Traditional print and advertising are also involved, as is a brand website at www.EncourageCourage.com.

CASE STUDY

Internal Buy-in

Before any external outreach, however, the company focused on getting the internal house in order. A big brand launch is an "all hands on deck" exercise. Everybody across marketing needs to play a part in something as broad and large as a brand launch. A company must inform, inspire, and excite both internally and externally to ensure the success of this approach.

At Hiscox, that meant talking to human resources personnel about the potential impact on company culture, to facilities personnel about changing the look and feel of offices, and taking now-traditional rebranding steps such as changing corporate screensavers and business cards.

Perhaps more important is the training conducted to ensure that staff are knowledgeable enough about the project when customers ask. "Our claims people, those people working in our call centers, need to be knowledgeable about what we're doing because they're the ones at the front line receiving lots of phone calls from our Existing Insureds and potential customers."

Fundamentally, the approach recognizes that responsibility for delivering a consistent brand message does not (and should not) fall solely on the shoulders of the marketing department: "It's not just the marketing team. It's way too important to be left to the marketeers."

To encourage buy-in from a broad swathe of the company like this, the Hiscox approach echoes the Molson Coors approach in building "Our Brew": Fundamentally, you bring everyone along on a journey from the start, requesting feedback, sharing long-term goals, and giving everyone impacted a sense of ownership of this large scale-project.

"It wasn't just me going away for six months and coming back and saying, 'Here, we've got the answer.' That would have been disastrous."

Incorporating Social Channels into a Broader Campaign

On the B2C side of the business, Hiscox used both Twitter and Facebook as elements of its broader brand launch. Considering the very low awareness ratings for Hiscox among small businesses in the U.S., the choice of Facebook and Twitter was largely based on their scale. "Because we have very little awareness, there was really little science needed to decide which [social channels to use]. We went for the biggest and most broad and relevant."

Hiscox did not segment out the budget and assign a certain amount of money to Facebook and a certain amount to Twitter. The company instead

CASE STUDY

looked at the overarching goals of the launch project (driving awareness, increasing reach, driving brand affinity) and then developed a broad media plan around that.

"Within that conversation came, 'Okay, so how do we want to do that? Where do our customers spend a lot of their time?' and then the plan unfolded from that. So I didn't go into it with, 'Here's how much money I have to spend on social—let's split that across Facebook, LinkedIn, and Twitter.' I looked at it more from the point of view of, 'Here are our overall objectives. Let's develop a plan across different media types and then budget accordingly.'"

Before this brand launch, Hiscox already had a social media manager in place. Regardless of any brand launch work, an employee was already involved in that public conversation. The company didn't have to hire someone specifically to focus on social engagement around the brand launch; this executive was simply refocused to spend a sizable amount of time on the launch as and when required.

With Facebook, Hiscox added rich content to the Engage Courage launch, in an attempt to bring some of the backstory to the traditional campaign to life. On Twitter, the company focused on becoming part of a far larger conversation than it would otherwise have access to.

"It was harder—much harder—to bring Encourage Courage to life in full, in a robust way, on Twitter. So we had to look for conversations that were happening out in the ether that were somewhat courageous. Then [we tapped] into that support, that attempt to become part of the conversation and so forth, while also tweeting about what was happening with the Encourage Courage launch across other channels."

Tracking Success

The ultimate goal for the brand launch was to drive awareness and affinity for the new branding for Hiscox.

Regardless of the fact that this was a multichannel project, before diving into specific platform and channel metrics, the company took a broad view. "We looked across all these different channels, to see if the whole campaign is working to drive brand affinity. We hoovered up all the different elements of the campaign to assess the success of the thing—which should ultimately be born out in overall brand awareness.

"You can get engagement on Facebook—you can get followers on Facebook, some interaction and engagement on LinkedIn. But if all that doesn't ladder up to awareness and brand affinity, then you've failed."

CASE STUDY

The core KPIs, therefore, were as follows:

1. Brand awareness
2. Brand affinity
3. Purchase consideration
4. Purchase decision

From there, the company began to focus on the specific channels—traditional print's metrics on reach and frequency, digital on engagement and velocity. To track brand health, the company also looked at its Net Promoter Score (NPS) and used social listening.

"[You] look at the conversation happening out in the wide world of social media, and you get a sense [of] whether the sentiment score is going up or down. [You collate] that insight with customer service scores to build a more holistic picture."

Fundamentally, Hiscox's emphasis was on incorporating many different metrics together to build a detailed, holistic picture of performance, in large part to avoid the risk that "if all you have is a hammer, then everything's a nail." Had the company used a more limited set of metrics, those metrics would have taken on outsize importance and been misleading. As Findlay points out:

"If all you measure is NPS all the time, then you're probably blind to a lot of different things that you need to be knowing and measuring. Just as a good carpenter knows how to use a lot of different tools to build a house, a good marketer knows how to use the right marketing tool at the right time."

Happily for Hiscox and Findlay, the multichannel, social-focused campaign performed strongly. Unaided awareness of the Hiscox brand in the U.S. jumped 5x, while aided awareness jumped 2x.

9

Content Marketing to Drive Engagement

"One must require more marketers to develop content capabilities so there's a way to engage other than selling and pushing. Marketers must be looking to stay relevant when people aren't in a place to buy."

—John Kennedy, CMO of Xerox

As we've seen, "content marketing" is an increasingly popular and important term in the world of marketing in 2015. Before going into detail on what is a broad and somewhat amorphous topic, it's worth trying to define the term. Content marketing is simply about using engaging, relevant content to attract an audience.

It's about finding valuable, shareable insights to engage—not sell—to an audience.

It's a concession that customers have a choice and that you've got to offer more than a shiny sales message to get their buy-in.

And it's a critical pillar in a forward-looking marketing strategy based on authenticity, relevance, and transparency. Content marketing is remarkably powerful in a world in which customers are overwhelmed by sales messages, where social media has given relationship building the capacity to scale enormously, and where brands are starved of customer attention.

That's why 64% of marketers say that content marketing is "definitely" important and "working really well" for them, with an additional 30% saying that's "probably" the case, as you can see in Figure 9.1.

Is content marketing important?

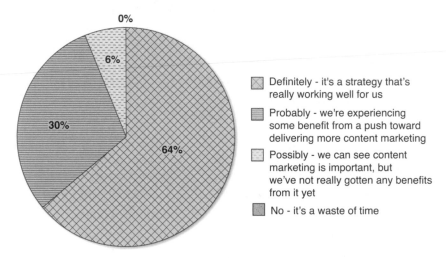

Figure 9.1 The majority of marketers see content marketing as important for future success.

Given all that, it's entirely unsurprising that a huge seventy-four percent of marketers will "definitely" do more content marketing over the next five years, and an additional 19% will "probably" do so, as you can see in Figure 9.2

The popularity of content as a marketing strategy is perhaps the most obvious manifestation of a broader shift in marketing to reflect customer power. Marketing is no longer about positioning your product and then pushing people down a funnel. It's about attempting to engage a bored population that is skeptical of sales messages and almost omnipresent advertising.

In an age when customers hold the power, the marketer's job is to position the brand as part of a conversation on increasingly powerful social networks. Content—stories, videos, audio, and more—is a powerful tool to do just that while also building a longer-lasting relationship at the same time. If we treat marketing over social media as

Do you plan on doing more content marketing over the next five years?

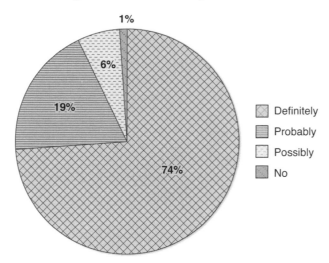

Figure 9.2 There's going to be a whole lot more content marketing over the next five years.

similar to creating a good impression at a dinner party (for more on this, see Chapter 10, "The Opportunity—and Imperative—of Conversation"), then *content* is the stories you use to reel people in and entertain them around the canapés.

Fundamentally, content allows brands to be more worthy of a customer's time than the competition.

Of course, it's rather difficult. As brands become authors and publishers, they effectively have to enter an entirely new industry. Consider the four key challenges in scaling a content strategy highlighted in Figure 9.3:

1. Creating content of the requisite quality
2. Ensuring produced content is relevant to your target audience
3. Disseminating content in the right way
4. Measuring the impact of content strategy

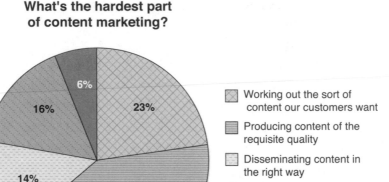

**What's the hardest part
of content marketing?**

Working out the sort of
content our customers want

Producing content of the
requisite quality

Disseminating content in
the right way

Measuring the impact of
our content strategy

Other

Figure 9.3 Quality is the biggest challenge for marketers looking to do content marketing.

Create Content of the Requisite Quality

Companies must compete for the attention of customers via the creation of engaging content, so quality is a core consideration.

I remember discussing how this might end up. I joked with several CMOs that if things continue at this rate, with a rapid increase in the quality of, and budget for, content marketing, we'll end up with brands rivaling Hollywood. Companies will plough more money into content in an increasingly essential attempt to grab customers' attention and put that brand front of mind.

Then in February 2014, *The Lego Movie* launched. Brands are already rivaling Hollywood. It's somewhat unsurprising, therefore, that 41% of marketers say that producing content of the right quality is the biggest challenge they're facing right now.

Relevance: Appealing Directly and Engagingly to Your Customers

Twenty-seven percent of marketers say the most challenging part of building a content marketing strategy revolves around working out what the customer wants—determining what content will appeal to and engage them.

It's another manifestation of the "relevance" pillar of marketing as ART. The content you disseminate must be engaging, useful, and valuable in some way to the target audience you're attempting to appeal to. Again, we can revisit the social media dinner party: The stories you tell your grandparent are somewhat different to those you tell your best friend. It's the same with content marketing. As with traditional marketing campaigns, picking the right message for your customer is essential. What's more, particular target audiences want their content delivered via a particular medium, or via a particular platform.

When striving for relevance, companies tend to focus on either content that aims to be useful or content that aims to be entertaining.

Content That Is Useful

A great example of useful content comes from HubSpot, the marketing software provider. Hubspot is a business to business (B2B) company—companies in the B2B space have been leaders in content marketing for some time, largely because of the way marketing works in the B2B space. Customers and products tend to be of higher value. The purchase cycle is longer, and more is spent on individual customer acquisition. Therefore, the value proposition offered by content marketing is more obvious.

HubSpot sells a marketing technology. The goal of its content campaign is to make its owned media a valuable destination for the target audience to spend time at. The company thus spends an awful lot of time generating white papers and other insights to share with its community.

Not only does this content position HubSpot as an authoritative voice on marketing best practice (thus increasing loyalty, trust, and the likelihood of a longer-term customer relationship), but it's also designed to highlight that HubSpot does the job these customers are looking to do better than any of their competitors. The use cases and step-by-step guides that the white papers cover all use HubSpot as the tool for getting the job done.

Content That Is Entertaining

The video opens in a close-up on Jean-Claude Van Damme's face. His voiceover begins to tell us that his life has been made up of his fair share of bumpy roads and buffeting winds. Through focus and a relentless drive for perfection, he's overcome all challenges. He points out that the precision engineering of his body has allowed him to master "the most epic of splits."

As he solemnly intones an inspirational version of his life story, staring directly into the camera, that camera pans out. First, we realize that he is standing on the wing mirrors of two Volvo Globetrotter articulated trucks.

Next, it becomes apparent that the trucks are moving. Backward. Fast. Finally, as the voiceover reaches "the most epic of splits," the trucks begin to part, forcing Van Damme to do the splits—12 feet up, fast, and in reverse. As the camera swings around him and the rapidly reversing trucks, some text is superimposed onto the screen:

> This test was set up to demonstrate the stability and precision of Volvo Dynamic Steering[1]

Seventy-seven million people saw that video on Volvo's own YouTube channel alone. When they finished with it, they saw links to other "Volvo Live Test" videos, including one featuring a gerbil driving a truck using some sort of mechanical contraption that converts the rodent's scurrying around an exercise wheel into steering a several-ton truck. Another shows a ballerina performing on the roof of a truck as it speeds down a highway.

The Volvo video campaign is a high water mark for entertaining content. The company managed to broadly entertain and engage a huge audience, considerably raising the general population's awareness of the Volvo brand and products. What's more, for the core target audience of truck drivers and fleet owners, there's a "dog whistle" that only they can hear—a series of specific references to the truck's attributes that will further engage this core audience.

This group can, for example, appreciate the difficulty inherent in driving two trucks with such precision that Jean-Claude Van Damme doesn't end up in a crumpled heap on an airport runway. They can appreciate a ride so smooth that a ballerina can perform on the roof. They can appreciate steering so precise that a half-pound gerbil can control it.

Volvo commissioned market research firm GFK to survey 2,200 transportation companies (half existing Volvo customers, half customers of the competition) about the impact these "Live Test" videos had on their brand perception.

The results are persuasive. YouTube subscribers for the brand rose from 3,500 to 90,000, and Volvo Trucks website traffic increased from 175,000 to over 300,000. In total, the value of the earned media generated was somewhere around $150 million. More importantly, the highest-performing in the series of videos, *Technician*, convinced 39% of viewers to take action (visit a website or contact a dealer); while another 19% said they intended to take action in the future.[2] Those are strong results from what at first glance looks like a relatively light-hearted brand awareness exercise.

It's worth pointing out the fine balance the overall campaign had to achieve. The Van Damme video (clearly, the most popular of the six videos, with 77 million views) was also the least impactful in terms of influence on brand perception. It seems that, in striving to entertain a broad group, the brand lost out in depth of impact on their actual target market.

Disseminate Content in the Right Way

"It's critical to have really great content—and for it to be flexible. Digital assets really, rather than content—things that you can repurpose across different devices, different resolutions—a version of your story that is quick and seamless to get out, and is rich and engaging. Whether that's user-generated or internally generated, ultimately it's all content."

—Marco Ryan, Chief Digital Officer for Thomas Cook

Fifteen percent of marketers point out that their main challenge in building a content marketing strategy is to disseminate that content in the right way.

For content marketing to augment rather than slow a push toward a more agile, speedy, and nimble marketing campaign, it's essential that content be disseminated quickly and flexibly.

Therefore, you must think deeply about the format and delivery mechanism. As Marco Ryan points out, content must be flexible. You must be able to build up a library of content that you can disseminate across a multitude of new marketing platforms at any one time.

Measure Impact and Track Success

The fourth challenge inherent in the creation of a successful content marketing strategy is to accurately measure the impact of a campaign and activity. Fifteen percent of marketers say this is the main challenge they face (refer to Figure 9.3).

It's essential that at all times a marketer be able to track success appropriately and quickly. Equally, it's important that the marketer be able to use those figures and trends to impact and change marketing campaigns on the fly.

First, marketers must pick sensible metrics, not vanity metrics. As Eric Reis, author of the enormously influential *Lean Startup*, puts it:

"The majority of data available in off-the-shelf analytics packages are what I call vanity metrics. They might make you feel good, but they don't offer clear guidance for what to do.

"When you hear companies doing PR about the billions of messages sent using their product, or the total GDP of their economy, think vanity metrics. But there are examples closer to home. Consider the most basic of all reports: the total number of hits to your website. Let's say you have 10,000. Now what? Do you really know what actions you took in the past that drove those visitors to you, and do you really know which actions to take next? In most cases, I don't think it's very helpful."[3]

Second, marketers must be in a position to change things quickly. The metrics used must report back figures in a quick enough time frame to make changes while a campaign is ongoing. Whether that means using a slightly different version of a video or incorporating a new "snackable" piece of content into a Facebook advertising campaign is up to the numbers.

The vast majority of marketers anticipate doing more content marketing in the immediate future. It works well and drives engagement. But to stand out in an increasingly crowded marketplace, it's going to be essential for quality, relevance, and measurement to improve. If a company is successful in building the right content—getting it out via the right channels and format, and measuring the right KPIs around it—then the impact on marketing's success can be major, as Volvo could tell you.

What's more, in an age where companies are increasingly starved of the attention of their customers, good content marketing grabs that attention and deepens engagement in a way other marketing strategies simply cannot.

Endnotes

1. www.youtube.com/watch?v=M7FIvfx5J10

2. James Swift, "Van Damme Spot Is Least Effective Volvo Ad," *Campaign* (1 April 2014). www.campaignlive.co.uk/news/1288088/

3. Eric Ries, "Vanity Metrics vs. Actionable Metrics," FourHourWorkWeek.com (19 May 2009). http://fourhourworkweek.com/2009/05/19/vanity-metrics-vs-actionable-metrics/

10

The Imperative—and Opportunity— of Conversation

"I think the era of 50-odd years ago, where marketing or advertising happened at you, is over. Now customers expect and demand a conversation."

—Victoria Burwell, Chief Marketing Officer,
McGraw-Hill Education

As we have seen throughout this book, customers want to be part of a brand; they want to be involved in its growth, what it stands for, and how it projects itself. That observation is a fundamental driver of the A (authenticity), R (relevance), and T (transparency) of the ART acronym.

- **Authenticity**—Customers want to help build a brand, and want to engage only with brands they see as authentic, real, and human.

- **Relevance**—Customers want to help define what a brand is, what it stands for, and how it works, to ensure it matches closely with their own values and goals.

- **Transparency**—In an age where information travels fast, customers will be discovering everything about your company quickly—and will be talking about it online whenever *they*, not *you*, want.

In this chapter, we investigate all of this in more detail. It would be fair to say that by not offering customers the ability to collaborate and converse with you, your brand becomes less attractive and engaging to them.

When you look at the best brands in the world, they are ones that are excelling at building a community and making that community a desirable one for outsiders to join. Whether that club is Coca-Cola or Gucci, Google or Apple, customers want to be part of a group of like-minded people that they feel good about being a part of. To be a good marketer in the future, you must care about, facilitate, and learn from that community.

Today, 58% of adults older than 18 in the United States have an active Facebook account.[1] More people visit Twitter than the *New York Times* home page.[2] It's clear that social media channels have grown so huge that they are an unavoidable part of any comprehensive marketing approach. That's why, according to The Incite Group's State of Corporate Social Media briefing, an enormous 90% of companies say that they're using social media for marketing.[3]

Conversation is no longer simply an option for companies. It's not even really an advantage anymore—It's an expectation.

Every social platform, regardless of the minutiae that makes it different from its competition's, is fundamentally about allowing communication and conversation. For marketers to be present on a social network, they must be geared up to take part in that conversation or else run the risk of being seen as irrelevant, inauthentic, or outmoded. As Chris Lindner, President of footwear brand Keds, told me,

"The best brands are thinking about how they're connecting and engaging with their consumers in a true dialogue. ... [I]t has now become a consumer expectation that brands are listening and engaging and ultimately delivering this new level of experience to consumers that [is] involving them in the process or the story in one way, shape, or form."

The Cocktail Party: Dialogue, Not Monologue

When I explain social best practice to new starters at the Incite Group, I use the analogy of a cocktail party.

When one attends a cocktail party, you tend to follow some basic social norms if you want to create a good impression.

First, you don't spend your time waxing lyrically about how incredible you are. Go down that route, and you'll be labeled a rude bore and shepherded toward the exit. Instead, if you're a clever networker, you spend time telling interesting stories of value to your audience, showing them you're worth listening to and being friends with.

Perhaps you want to highlight stories that take place in interesting foreign countries. Or you might talk about the celebrity that popped up when you were spending an evening in the pub with friends. Or you might mention that the Lamborghini was your vehicle of choice when you bought your most recent car.

Second, you tend to listen and respond to comments and questions from the rest of the group. If someone asks you about the particular model of Lamborghini, you tell them—and point out, for extra brownie points, where it can be taken for a test drive. If you're quizzed on where that celebrity usually hangs out, you let them know. And if someone embarks on a tale of their own interesting time in a foreign country, you shut up and let them talk, while acting (or maybe even being) interested.

Third, you don't think of yourself as a performer in the middle of a potential audience—you're one part of a community who, together, are making a party interesting. This is an important distinction, particularly for a marketer whose overarching goal tends normally to be to become the most interesting performer in the room.

A little more subtlety is involved when you're part of a community. You allow other conversations to take place and you jump in where relevant. You listen as well as talk. You smile, nod, and offer color and depth; you don't attempt to constantly dominate the overarching narrative strand. You're friendly and polite, and you don't challenge someone to a fistfight if they start getting aggressive (instead, you'd probably try to come across as nice and understanding, and then ultimately avoid them, if necessary).

How Conversation Drives Authenticity

When striving to build an authentic relationship with customers, it pays to conform to the social norms illustrated in the cocktail party example. It would be somewhat strange—and very much like the large, unfeeling, hundred-thousand-person company you're trying to avoid presenting your brand as—to be rendered mute by a question from an individual. So you've got to be set up to respond, not simply talk. That way, you come across as more human and authentic.

Equally, it would be somewhat strange in this day and age for a conversation around a brand on social networks not to include that brand itself. If you're responsible in some way for shifting perceptions of your company from "corporate behemoth" to "nice, approachable corporate citizen" (critical in the age of ART), then it's incumbent upon you to put your business in a position where it can talk back to customers who are addressing it and looking for a (somewhat realistic) conversation.

Otherwise, the only messages you push out over social media campaigns will look like nothing more than PR fluff. Over the course of this decade, customers have been burned by incidents such as ones involving DiGiorno ("DiGiorno Accidentally Tried to Advertise Their Pizza in a Hashtag about Domestic Violence," *Buzzfeed*[4]), Domino's ("Video Prank at Domino's Taints Brand," *New York Times*[5]), and British Airways ("'Don't Fly @British Airways'? How to Humiliate Brands via Social Media," *The Guardian*[6]). Increasingly, the public has developed a healthy skepticism of brand interactions on social media.

As the customer has begun to hold all the cards in the customer/ brand relationship, those customers' social expectations have become the norm in terms of interactions with business. They expect to deal with companies like they deal with other individuals—holding them to the same high standards as they do their own friends and family. It's challenging, but relatively understandable, given that large businesses have done everything they can to portray themselves as a small group of regular joes—while positioning themselves in the same places their customers see family photos and invitations to weddings.

So now, 81% of your customers not only expect a response from you when they get in touch via Twitter, but expect it within a day.[7] That's a major challenge, given the ease with which a customer can get in touch (and do so publicly). The days when the only way a customer could get in touch with your company to complain or ask questions (and, blessedly, do so in private) have been replaced with a public airing of all issues and complaints. Customers simply have to open their Twitter app.

Conversation Isn't Optional

To be frank, if corporations don't already have a significant social media presence and strategy, they're already behind. Eighty-three percent of Fortune 500 companies have a corporate Twitter account, and 80% of them have a Facebook page.[8]

Your competitors, your industry, and the whole business world see maintaining a corporate social media account as a fundamental part of any holistic marketing and communications strategy. As Victoria Burwell, Chief Marketing Officer at McGraw-Hill, told me, "We all know, with the rise of social media, how quickly something that is heard about you, produced by you, [or] put out by you can immediately get response back from the world-at-large and go viral, get good or bad responses, or engage conversation."

Social media is the new town square. It's where people come together to discuss anything and everything that's important, entertaining, or frustrating to them. If you play your cards right, you'll be in the former two conversations, not the latter.

But as social communication (the one-to-many function inherent in all social media platforms) has become the dominant communication tool of the age, the individual's power to influence has become unrecognizably stronger. London's Speakers Corner used to be where those looking for an audience (to put it charitably) went to talk to large groups. Unless you stood in the background at *Good Morning America* holding up signs, any individual could reach only the few hundred people within earshot when bellowing on a street corner. Nowadays, if your message is interesting, entertaining, or (depressingly) controversial enough, you're able to reach millions around the world. Through consistent and valuable engagement, you're able to build a loyal audience.

In addition, social networks themselves, eager to accelerate this trend and strengthen their own network dynamics, have increased the focus on search and discovery. They now highlight "trending topics" across their site, which means that popular conversations and topics get even bigger and more discoverable.

It's one of the best examples of how the power dynamic in the relationship between company and customer has changed. And it means that the marketer must begin to see customer interactions in an entirely new and more urgent light. Cammie Dunaway, Chief Marketing Officer of KidZania, says that "The view of a single consumer can carry as much weight as the view of an old product authority—and certainly as much weight as a 30-second television spot carries."

That's the terrifying thing about social and conversational marketing. The marketer is no longer in control. No matter how big the budget, how attractive the film star involved in promoting your product, or how many TV ads you buy, you can't stop the chatter online. And without careful management, you can't change it much, either.

The tweets, posts, and shares made by your customers won't be based on a brand message you're trying to propagate. Your customers have no need to follow your brand guidelines or match the campaign goals you're aiming to hit. Just ask the New York Police Department, which was met with a hail of abuse when asking New Yorkers to tag photos of the police with #MyNYPD at a time when tensions between police and the general public were running high.[9]

You don't control the conversation around your brand any more. Your customers do.

Customers will choose for themselves how to discuss your brand. That might be good or bad. You don't have control over whether your customers are crazy (some are, and will beat up on you for no reason other than they can vent—social media provides oxygen for crazies).

The one thing you *can* influence with some certainty is the product and the experience surrounding it. If you're looking for positive sentiment and conversation about your product online, you can influence a conversation through exceptional social media engagement, but the start and end points of any discussion will only ever be the customer experience you provide. That's the first thing to focus on, and that's why we're only talking about social media engagement in this chapter.

That need to focus on customer experience first means that the marketer (as a proxy for the customer) must be involved earlier and more deeply in product innovation and development. Or as Cammie Dunaway of KidZania put it more simply, "Don't work for bad products." It's why marketers find their roles expanding, why collaboration across an entire business is becoming essential, and why the Marketing Department could well end up being more accurately called the Customer Experience Department.

Set Up for Social

You can create a Facebook page or a Twitter account and simply push out a lot of nice product messages. But as we've seen, as soon as you open up what is fundamentally a channel of communication, your customers will expect to communicate back.

They will use the services to ask for support, to complain, and to take the conversation back to you—and do all of that in public. As Dominic Collins—current CMO at Legal & General and previously Director of Digital for British telecommunications firm EE—told me, "You quite quickly will find that you've got 80 people on Twitter who used to be answering the phone—or that's certainly what we found at EE."

And that means internal organization is forced to shift. If the marketing department manages to avoid a wholesale transformation into a customer service team, it has done well. But even if it's the customer service team responding to customer questions and complaints over social media, those team members have been trained in using private phone and email conversations to resolve issues. The challenges of achieving complaint resolution in public, in 140 characters, requires a rather different set of skills

To compound the problem, these people expect the conversation to be conducted as it would be in the real world—that is, in real time. You must be able to respond in a timely manner to their queries, or you risk exacerbating the situation. One study suggests that sixty-seven percent of consumers expect an answer to their question or issue on the same day.[10]

The conversation around your brand, your business, and your customer base will be happening whether you're involved or not. And if you're not, your competitors get a straight shot at your customers. When you link this back to the diminishing power of traditional marketing channels and the ever-increasing importance of social channels for marketing activity, it becomes somewhat of a perfect storm.

Marketers must take social media into account. When looking to be authentic, coming across as being somewhat human helps. To be human, you've got to be responsive. Customers expect that response over social media.

Ergo, authenticity requires conversation.

So how do you build a conversational approach into corporate marketing strategies?

7 Elements of Successful Conversational Marketing from Brands Who've Done It Well

From extensive conversations with multiple CMOs and other marketing leaders, it has become clear that if you want to build conversation into your marketing strategy, it pays to follow the seven pieces of advice provided in the following sections.

1: Strike a Chord That Appeals

"We saw this outpouring of consumers proactively coming back to us and saying, 'This means so much to me, and here's why.'"

—Chris Lindner, President, Keds

To drive authenticity through conversation, you must strike a chord with your audience that appeals to their interests. That way, your campaign isn't limited simply to your current customers, or even to the group that has already followed your brand presence, but to a broader audience of people communicating on a topic.

That's why Coca-Cola tends to talk not about fizzy brown liquid, but "delivering happiness." It's why Dove tweets not about shower gel, but about its "campaign for real beauty." And it's why Red Bull spends considerably less time talking about taurine-infused energy drinks than showing videos of extreme sports.

All are examples of what Andy Gibson, former CMO with Bacardi, calls "passion platforms," a broader area in which a company can talk to customers about their priorities. When looking for that broader conversation, it's essential to ensure that the conversation is closely linked to your brand if you're looking to deliver something somewhat authentic.

2: Be Ready to Listen

"I think it's an incredible world we live in today that, as a marketing person, I can be much more thoughtful and get much more immediate feedback," says Victoria Burwell, Chief Marketing Officer, McGraw-Hill Education.

Social listening is key to a successful conversational approach.

As your schoolteacher or wise grandparent no doubt once told you, we're built with two ears and one mouth, and we should use them in proportion. This is a rule that marketers tend to break on a daily basis. And the rise of social media means the penalties for breaking that rule are more apparent.

Therefore, marketers should spend time preparing the groundwork for a conversational approach. For more on this, see the case study with One Medical Group on social listening, in Chapter 7, "Data for Relevance and Agility."

Remember that you don't have a choice about the listening aspect. According to Dominic Collins, Chief Marketing Officer at Legal and General, corporate social media is "absolutely driven by customer intent." Your customer is in the driver's seat. You might well want to create a Facebook page or a Twitter account, to push out that fascinating branded comment or your latest attempt to jump on some meme-driven bandwagon. But *your* intent is somewhat irrelevant. You need to be interacting in the way your customers expect.

A social media presence is a sign that you're ready for conversation. As soon as you set one up, customers will begin to ask you their questions and interact with you on their terms. They'll tell you what they want from a service, point out issues they need support on, and expect you to respond quickly.

3: *Get Everyone Singing from the Same Hymn Sheet*

We talked previously about buy-in, to drive a unified, authentic voice. Within a conversational approach to marketing, you face the same issue in microcosm.

After launching a conversational, social media-led strategy in earnest, a company must take one of three actions:

1. Hire in or transition an awful lot of people into roles with social media responsibilities.
2. Pass the ability to "speak with your brand's voice" to your agency. Bear in mind the risk that is inherent in that approach: It runs directly counter to the best practice of building authenticity.
3. Give existing employees more freedom and autonomy to speak on your behalf (think of Best Buy's twelpforce initiative).

Any one of these involves cost to your budget. Avoid it having a cost to your brand by picking the right choice. (*Clue:* It's not the second option.)

4: *Ensure That Data Has Been Shared and Silos Have Been Eradicated*

As Victoria Burwell, CMO of McGraw-Hill Education told me, a huge influence on the success of social media marketing is "about how quickly and seamlessly we can be utilizing real-time data and responding quickly to that data."

The challenges inherent in a more authentic, conversational approach to marketing are not limited to the "front end," or picking the right conversational gambits to engage and inspire. Companies must also address significant back-end challenges to make sure that each individual engaged in conversation on your behalf has the relevant backstory and history to call on. We talk about the challenges of silos in more detail in Part III, "Building for the Future."

Suffice it to say, it's incredibly challenging for companies to eradicate those silos and get data flowing as it should. It's almost impossible to do so at the speed the customer demands. That's why only 54% of companies think they're good at de-siloing data internally, and only 34% are confident that they can engage with customers at the speed expected of them.[11]

5: Expose the "Latently Happy"

The number of individuals who are happy about a product but don't talk about it tends to far outweigh those with any sort of grievance. That's because there's a far higher bar set for quality of experience for *happy* posts than there is for *unhappy* posts.

Arra Yerganian, CMO at One Medical Group, focused on getting what he calls the "latently happy" to speak up, too. Highlight the existence and sentiment of that group, and use it to add authenticity to your own messaging.

6: Don't Just Talk about Your Products

It's beyond the scope of this book, but social platforms have more potential than simply encouraging people to buy stuff. Somewhat strangely, the perception of social media within large businesses has come full circle since I set up Useful Social Media, my first company, in 2010. Our job was to investigate the impact of social media on large companies.

In our first conference, the room was full of marketers wanting to discover how social media would allow them to reach customers in the places they were spending time. It was essentially a conference on a marketing channel.

Around the same time, a whole cluster of "social media evangelists" and "ninjas" and "gurus" began to wax poetic about the vast potential of companies going "all in" on social, encouraging them to realize that social media wasn't simply a channel, but an opportunity to fundamentally rework the customer/company relationship. These advocates have always had somewhat of a breathless "fan boy" element to them. If your company exists solely to sell people on the potential of social media and your services around that, then it pays to play up the benefits.

Yet the pitch worked, and marketers began to listen—and make some fairly significant investments in social media resourcing and technology.

So during our second and third conferences, we began to refocus the events on what the customers needed and looked at this broader capacity for social media to impact every area of a business's operations (You can see this spreading of social's influence across many different areas of business in Figure 10.1[12]).

And then, somewhat inevitably, came the cynicism. Over time, as social marketing crested the Gartner hype cycle and fell into the trough of disillusionment[13] people began crying out for numbers. They wanted anything that could speak to a return on their investment, some sort of measurement of their impact.

Those ninjas and gurus were great at PowerPoint presentations, LinkedIn profiles with an overwhelming amount of capital letters and acronyms, and Twitter retweets for each other's "thought leadership." They weren't great at putting hard numbers next to the policies and campaigns they were advocating (apart from an airy proclamation that "if you just focus on measuring the financials, you're missing the point"—when that didn't work, they focused on a somewhat desperate attempt to find alternative metrics to ROI: hello "return on engagement" and "return on relationship").

For many companies, brand social media adoption has thus regressed to focus primarily on social's utility as a marketing and/or customer service channel. That's rather a waste. Social media is a far more powerful ally in the quest for authenticity, relevance, and transparency than many companies currently give it credit for. Incorporating "conversation skills" into customer service delivery, product development, and brand communications will go a long way toward aligning your company with the new expectations of customers.

7: Don't Cause a Scene

Social media campaigns also lend weight to the hypothesis that the correlation between marketing success and marketing budget has been disconnected.

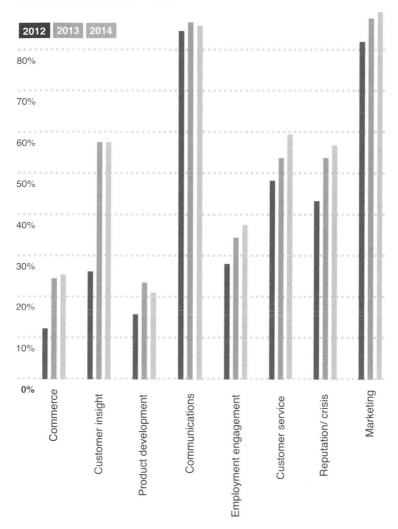

Social media use 2012 - 2014

More than half of all companies now use social media for:

89% Marketing

86% Communications

58% Customer Insight

59% Customer Service

57% Reputation Management & Crisis control

Figure 10.1 Social media has long been far more than simply a marketing tool.

Countless examples arise of brands shooting complex, high-end attempts at viral videos that crash without a trace. Yet for every failure, there's also a low-budget home run. Oreo's "You Can Still Dunk in the Dark" real-time response to a Super Bowl power outage, while necessitating some of the deeper structural (and thus expensive) changes to deliver more agility, was a pretty simple (and cheap) message. That single tweet was retweeted 10,000 times in one hour.

Always keep in mind that the need for authenticity, relevance, and transparency is more pressing in social media than across traditional channels. And that's because *social* engagement is opt-in: Customers must have already chosen to follow you before they'll see your organic social media messages. They (or a friend in their network) must have been convinced of your ability to deliver ART.

The bar is higher than on traditional channels, where your message is going to turn up on that TV screen during an advertisement break unless customers actively skip or turn off the TV. Thus, in many instances, it is better for brands to step into pre-existing conversations, where this bar does not exist, and begin to engage people with valuable contributions that way.

To do this, brands must focus on what Andy Gibson, former Chief Marketing Officer at Bacardi, calls their "passion platforms." Companies must understand their customers well enough to identify broad, unifying core elements of their lives. In Bacardi's case, this is music. From there, brands should focus on delivering relevant and engaging messages around that topic in manufactured and pre-existing social conversations, and linking that activity to a broader, multichannel campaign across several other media.

The challenge is not to manufacture one's own conversation (this is one of the weaknesses of tracking Twitter followers—they're often largely irrelevant to large-scale Twitter campaign success), but instead go where customers already engage each other and become part of the conversation. (Companies still need to attempt some subtlety and sensitivity, though. It's easy for a brand with considerable resources and incentive to become involved in a conversation and, as Gibson says, "stamp all over that conversation with a sledgehammer." Don't do that.)

Against "Humanizing Your Brand": "It's Cool When a Corporation Tweets Like a Teenager. It Makes Me Want to Buy the Corporation's Products"[14]

The importance of authenticity to marketing is a core pillar of this book.

Yet as I advocate its virtues, you can see an obvious backlash growing against brands that attempt to be authentic, real, and human.

Why?

Because too many companies are getting the definition of *authenticity* absolutely wrong.

Essentially—and, one would hope, unsurprisingly—authenticity is about being who you say you are, doing what your marketing says you do, and, in an age of transparency, giving customers the ability to scratch the surface and see that *your* gold bracelet is solid the whole way through.

Yet many companies are too focused on the quick fix, the paint job, and the cheap, gold-plated jewelry. They're attempting a quick fix instead of the broader refocus that authenticity requires.

And what is that quick fix often called? "Humanizing your brand."

"Humanizing the brand" is a shortcut taken by brands that are unwilling or unable to make the more transformative changes that are inextricable from the authentic approach their customers demand.

"Humanizing the brand" is about tugging the heartstrings to attempt to ensure that people can't see the marketing through the tears.

Many companies have attempted to "humanize their brand" so they can more convincingly and engagingly conduct conversations with customers online. It's a sensible reaction, and as part of a broader strategy, it's positive: A corporate press release doesn't really cut it on Twitter, whereas a brand with wit and confidence can be a hit. For customers wanting to build relationships with brands, who are looking for something deeper than another opportunity to read a press release, the beginnings of humanization can be a good move on a brand's part.

Unfortunately, many brands have seen "humanization" (the term itself is even slightly horrifying) as an end in itself, as a fresh coat of paint on a fundamentally unreconstructed company.

Those companies expend a great deal of effort attempting to present themselves as a particularly earnest, passionate (and sometimes, bizarrely, "street") teen rather than a multinational conglomerate headed by a number of 60-year-old white men.

It's a strategy littered with risk and problems—and a poorly thought-out approach to "humanizing" a brand leads to bone-headed, idiotic, sickening, or just downright stupid messages coming out of brands.

Over the Christmas period in the U.K., one particular advertisement was talked about a lot. It depicted a famous event in the long, dark history of World War I. On Christmas Eve 1914, when the British were slumped in their trenches, exhausted and far from home, they heard, drifting over the barbed wire, shell casings, and foxholes of No Man's Land, the famous carol "Silent Night."

The carol was sung in German; the British responded in English. Eventually, the two sides lay down their arms, climbed into No Man's Land, and played a festive game of football on Christmas Day.

It's a famous—and true—story of hope, human kindness, and a shared humanity in the midst of one of the most inhuman and devastating periods in our history.

Sainsbury's, the British supermarket chain, decided this would be a good backdrop for a marketing campaign (which, in fairness, they ran in part as a collaboration to raise funds for the Royal British Legion).

In the supermarket version, this inspirational evening ends not with a game of football, but with a gift from a British squaddie to his German counterpart of an obviously branded Sainsbury's chocolate bar (now available, in vintage packaging, in stores). As the camera pans away, a huge Sainsbury's logo is superimposed onto the scene.

The goal was obvious: tell a heartwarming British story, raise some money for the British Legion, and (win, win, win!) form a generalized link between a British supermarket chain, British history, and warm, fuzzy feelings.

The response was, to put it mildly, mixed.

- "Sainsbury's television advertisement based on the unofficial truce of Christmas 1914 has attracted hundreds of complaints and has been described as inappropriate, historically inaccurate and even "obscene."[15]

- "So why does the advert leave me feeling so unsettled, so uncomfortable, even a touch nauseous? The first answer has to be that, for all the respectful tone, the centennial occasion and the endorsement of the Royal British Legion, the ultimate objective here is to persuade us to buy our tinsel, our crackers and our sprouts from one particular supermarket."[16]

- "It's all very poignant, if you mentally delete the bit where a supermarket logo hovers over the killing fields, which you can't."[17]

A couple months later, the most recent McDonald's ad campaign started running in the United States.

Set over a children's choir, (an increasingly common leitmotif of a "humanize the brand" campaign) singing a several-years-old inspirational pop song (sample lyric: "If you're lost and alone, and you're sinking like a stone, carry on"), the ad shows emotional messages like "We believe in you, Crystal," "Thank you, veterans," "All of us weep for the Columbia Families," "PRAY for the rescue of the MINERS," and "We Remember 9/11."

Eschewing even the subtlety of the branded Sainsbury's chocolate bar, these messages are, somewhat conveniently, displayed on enormous McDonald's signs from across the U.S. (highlighting the active community involvement of the fast food chain, one supposes).

The ad ends in a breathtakingly awkward tonal shift, with the brand tagline "I'm lovin it!" in neon colors and a McDonald's logo popping out of a heart.

In the interests of balance, many people did respond positively to both of these advertising campaigns, and it's important to note that a negative reaction was not universal.

I'm more interested in what seems to be an increasingly obvious undercurrent of cynicism and wariness to "humanized" brand messages like these. Add in the fact that, with the power of social media, a customer's skeptical, doubtful, or downright angry response to a campaign has the ability to grow and spread across a far broader segment of the population than ever before.

In short, the increasing occurrence of responses like these is good evidence of customers' higher expectations. They're evidence that a "coat of paint" won't cut it. Indeed, marketing messages designed to show off a brand's exceptional standing as a corporate citizen can backfire significantly if that company's operations and messaging don't live up to the exceptionally high standard they present themselves as having achieved.

Hence, consider the reaction to the McDonald's campaign on Twitter:

- "McDonald's is presenting itself as the face of corporate kindness? PAY YOUR EMPLOYEES A LIVING WAGE"
- "@McDonald's I just threw up in my mouth watching your commercial. Desperate attempt to rescue your image."
- "That McDonalds' commercial is shameless, vulgar, tasteless, cynical, crass. In other words, as bad as the food"

It's Cool When a Corporation Tweets Like a Teenager

@BrandsSayingBae is a Twitter account with the bio "It's cool when a corporation tweets like a teenager. It makes me want to buy the corporation's products." It has 30,000 followers as of April 2015 and has had countless amused writeups in the advertising and marketing trade press. It retweets instances of particularly cringeworthy attempts at "humanization" from brands, the corporate adoption of street slang:

- Pizza Hut (6,000 restaurants in the U.S., locations in 94 countries, 160,000 employees) now calls people "bruh."
- Sonic (3 million customers per day, $19.2 million in net income in 2011) says its "ice is bae."
- IHOP tells people that they're "always on fleek."

That last term, indecipherable even to a Millennial like myself, was picked up in an article by *Digiday*, who points out that there have been close to 17,000 mentions of the terms *bae* and *fleek* in brand conversations online in 2014.[18]

Shankar Gupta, quoted in the article, is the vice president of strategy at 360i:

"When you see a brand aging down its social channels by tossing in 'bae' and 'on fleek,' it's a warning sign in most cases that the brand is struggling to connect in a meaningful way with its audience....

"If you can't understand your audience well enough to develop a genuine connection, it's an all-too-tempting shortcut to dress up your advertising with youthful slang to create a superficial connection."

You've got to be able to scratch the surface.

Brands are increasingly aware of the benefits of an authentic, story-based approach to their marketing campaigns. It's happening increasingly, and what marks the Sainsbury's and McDonald's examples is the obviously large amount of money spent on the creative linked to the project. It's evident that thought went into developing and implementing this new product line of a vintage chocolate bar, linked to the content itself.

But this also highlights a very real risk. Customers will be able to spot the less genuine and the less authentic. If that happens, the results will be more grating and negative than if you simply focused on a direct-response product message.

Endnotes

1. Maeve Duggan, et al., "Social Media Update 2014," (Pew Research Center, (9 January 2015). www.pewinternet.org/2015/01/09/social-media-update-2014/.

2. Joshua Benton, "The Leaked *New York Times* Innovation Report Is One of the Key Documents of This Media Age," Nieman Lab (15 May 2014); and Craig Smith, "By The Numbers: 150+ Amazing Twitter Statistics," Digital Marketing Ramblings (23 February 2015). http://expandedramblings.com/index.php/march-2013-by-the-numbers-a-few-amazing-twitter-stats/.

3. Nick Johnson, "The State of Corporate Social Media 2014" (Useful Social Media, 2014). http://usefulsocialmedia.com/stateofcsm

4. www.buzzfeed.com/ryanhatesthis/digiorno-whyistayed-you-had-pizza#.rj3p72j7R.

5. www.nytimes.com/2009/04/16/business/media/16dominos.html?_r=0.

6. www.theguardian.com/commentisfree/2013/sep/04/humiliate-global-brands-british-airways.

7. Jeremy Taylor, "Recent research shows that large businesses, including banks, are increasingly using social media for customer service" (OurSocialTimes, 10 July 2012) - http://oursocialtimes.com/new-insights-into-social-customer-service/.

8. Nora Ganim Barnes and Ava M. Lescault, "The 2014 Fortune 500 and Social Media: LinkedIn Dominates As Use of Newer Tools Explodes," University of Massachusetts, Dartmouth (2014). www.umassd.edu/cmr/socialmediaresearch/2014fortune500andsocialmedia/.

9. www.nbcnewyork.com/news/local/NYPD-Twitter-Backlash-myNYPD-Fail-Negative-Photos-Flood-Social-Media-256275661.html.

10. Jay Baer, "42 Percent of Consumers Complaining in Social Media Expect 60 Minute Response Time." Convince and Convert. www.convinceandconvert.com/social-media-research/42-percent-of-consumers-complaining-in-social-media-expect-60-minute-response-time/.

11. Future of Marketing Survey.

12. Nick Johnson, "The State of Corporate Social Media 2014," Useful Social Media. www.usefulsocialmedia.com/stateofcsm.

13. Gartner, www.gartner.com/technology/research/methodologies/hype-cycle.jsp.

14. @brandssayingbae twitter account: https://twitter.com/brandssayingbae

15. Barney Thompson, "Sainsbury's Christmas Truce Advert Defended under Heavy Fire," *The Financial Times* (23 December 2014). www.ft.com/intl/cms/s/0/831453b4-8abd-11e4-be0e-00144feabdc0.html#axzz3OzLZXH1q.

16. Ally Fogg, "Sainsbury's Christmas Ad Is a Dangerous and Disrespectful Masterpiece," *The Guardian* (13 November 2014). www.theguardian.com/commentisfree/2014/nov/13/sainsburys-christmas-ad-first-world-war.

17. Charlie Brooker, "A Trafficked Penguin, a Creepy Talking Doll, and Trench Warfare—Happy Christmas 2014," *The Guardian* (24 November 2014). www.theguardian.com/commentisfree/2014/nov/24/christmas-2014-john-lewis-sainsbury-ads-top-christmas-products.

18. Shareen Pathak, "Bae, Is Your Social Media Strategy on Fleek?" *Digiday* (13 January 2015). http://digiday.com/brands/bae-social-media-strategy-fleek/.

PART IV
A PROPOSED NEW DEPARTMENT

11 The Marketing Department of the Future 231

11

The Marketing Department of the Future

"In our research and work with hundreds of global marketing organizations, we've found that those CMOs are struggling with how to draw the new [organizational] chart."[1]

As discussed throughout this book, marketing has clearly changed at a fundamental level. Indeed, the term *marketing* might now be somewhat limiting to describe the department's role.

In response to unprecedented levels of customer power, groundbreaking fragmentation and evolution of the marketing landscape, and revolutionary levels of data on which one can build a strategy, leading companies are thrusting marketers toward a broader, more strategic role in which they're tasked with facilitating exceptional customer experience to an increasingly demanding group of customers.

Those forward-thinking companies are beginning to refashion their customer outreach to focus on three areas:

1. **Authenticity**—Becoming a company that customers can trust and build a relationship with.

   Companies are focusing on building a brand story that customers, who are increasingly wary and tired of the overwhelming number of marketing messages they receive, can buy into and get engaged by.

   This involves crafting a story that permeates every level of the company, from the CEO to the delivery guy—not as window dressing, but something that the company and its customers want to stand behind.

2. **Relevance**—Delivering value to customers through relevance.

Forward-looking companies have begun to target small, niche groups and are speaking directly to their needs and concerns, delivering value through content and products that are more relevant to them than ever before.

This development is powered by a knowledge of those customers that is significantly more detailed and nuanced than ever and is based on the flood of data managed by the company.

That value is delivered through increasing precision in the use of the channels those customers frequent, and in the places they spend time.

3. **Transparency**—In a world where knowledge is power, the customer now reigns supreme.

Customers are globally engaged—whether they're experiencing inconsistent corporate messaging between Taiwan and Toulouse or seeing a Yelp review from an American tourist about a restaurant in Germany. The flow of information in the digital age reinforces the customer's rightful position at the center of the company.

Marketers no longer have the power to turn a poor product into a successful product with clever marketing. As Cammie Dunaway of KidZania says, marketers can't afford to work for bad products any more. Thus it's incumbent upon them to get involved in the product development process, representing customer viewpoints from the ground up in the hope of delivering something of exceptional value.

Transparency is not only relevant to the relationship between customers and companies; internally, in the relationship between departments, it has become a critical driver. Customers expect relevance, so it's critical for departments to share insights and eradicate silos. Agility, and having the ability to react to data quickly and effectively, matters.

How Will Companies Deliver on ART?

Of course, it is clear that no "one size fits all" response works in the world that corporations now find themselves operating in. A B2B electricity company cannot hope to mimic the successes of a digital-first B2C retailer. Indeed, a German tech company should not mimic the strategies of a Brazilian tech company.

Your approach must be nuanced, must address your own company's strengths and weaknesses, and, most of all, must be aligned directly with the needs and behaviors of your own customer base.

Of course, some common elements will apply to the successful marketing department of the future, and they're outlined below:

1: The Marketing Department Will Put Customer Experience at the Center of Its Operations

To deliver on the heightened customer expectations and altered landscape highlighted earlier, it's critical to deliver a coordinated response. Therefore, one department must "own" the customer, coordinating a smoother and more engaging customer journey while communicating brand and promotional messages in an authentic, relevant, and transparent manner.

The team currently known as the marketing department is best placed to take on this new role. In a reflection of increased customer power and the decreased effectiveness of push marketing over the last decade, it will reformat to be known as the "customer experience department."

This new department will look radically different depending on the industry a company is in, whether a company is global or local to a particular region, the brand story the company has communicated, and, most important, the needs of the customers.

For all companies, however, this new customer experience department will have three pillars:

1. Insight
2. Experience
3. Agility/and Efficiency

Insight

The new customer experience department will be expected to be more of a strategic leader within the business. Marketers will be increasingly responsible for collating all customer data and turning it into actionable insights. Taking on a more prominent role in corporate strategy will be expected.

New insights on a rapidly changing customer journey will lead to changes in Go To Market strategy. A deeper understanding of customer demographics and preferences will significantly contribute to product management and development.

Experience

Consumers expect a consistent and valuable experience, not a series of discrete transactions. Thus, although campaign-based marketing will still have a role to play, it will be challenged by a longer-term, relationship-based marketing strategy. Increasing resources will be given to content provision, and a focus on storytelling will supersede simple product pitches.

Equally, the fact that consumers expect authentic conversations with brands means the one-way loudspeaker approach to marketing will become a thing of the past. A fragmented media landscape means that the traditional TV ad campaign will be usurped by something more complex.

In addition, the relationship with agencies will change as brands bring far more marketing in-house (creative, programmatic media buying, and more).

Agility and Efficiency

Marketers might have more data available to them than they know what to do with, but they still struggle to track their impact on the bottom line.

Marketing budgets are increasing as responsibilities extend (for example, IT spending is increasingly funneled into the marketing department). As this happens, the board will put increasing pressure on marketers to show solid, proveable results.

At the same time, marketers are seeing real opportunities in being more agile and even moving toward 'real-time marketing.' Marketers must get far better at using customer analytics and measurement to do two things:

- **Make sensible choices regarding spending**—Companies must pick the right channels for their message and then evolve their campaigns in real time to promote efficiency.

- **Be more agile**—We look at how companies have eradicated bureaucracy and red tape to ensure that quick movement is possible and ways to ensure that *agile* doesn't mean "cavalier" in the next section of this chapter "2: A Simple Structure to Enhance Agility."

Other responsibilities for the CMO and their team include the following:

- **Align with corporate goals**—As the marketer's role permeates more of the business, from product development to customer insight, to customer service, the chief marketing officer (CMO) will become a more critical member of the executive board. As we've seen, the days when marketers could laugh about which half of their marketing works are long gone. As marketing becomes a more strategic function, performance must be aligned to move the needle against core corporate goals, not simply to collect leads, likes, and page views.

- **Represent the customer in product decisions**—Marketers have always had a role to play in representing the customer's interests in internal decision making. As the customer's power in relation to the company grows, however, the marketer must be more forceful in representing customer views. Products and marketing that are not seen as directly relevant to those customers are more likely to fail.

- **Inform corporate strategy**—Marketing will not simply represent the customer in internal decision making, but will hold the keys to customer insight. As customer data silos are slowly eradicated, all customer data will coalesce in one place, accessible to all relevant teams. In his or her new extended role, the

CMO is best placed to have oversight of this data and ensure that it's getting to the right place. As such, this wealth of knowledge should serve as a fundamental pillar of any data-driven decision-making process throughout the business. The marketer's role as a strategic partner with the rest of the board thus becomes more influential.

2: A Simple Structure to Enhance Agility

"The best companies and management teams have more in common with jazz groups. Jazz is improvisational. The players take their cues from each other. There is freedom to give and take, to be creative and spontaneous."[2]

A common thread in the feedback from the CMOs I spoke with was the need for agility, a lack of rigidity in terms of how a company should look and operate, and a certain autonomy for individuals within a business.

Of course, there will always be structure, and for individuals to flourish, they need structure and direction. But to flourish in a world where authenticity, relevance, and transparency are key, there is no need for a complex new structure to be layered onto existing business practices. Many of the more passionate proponents of a customer-centric approach to business propose doing away with product-centric organizational models and replacing them with a customer-centric version.

This to me seems more idealistic than practical. It's also a project that will take years, and companies simply do not have time to waste. If they don't make a series of more simple changes now, they will be left too far behind their competition, struggling to catch up.

One of those simpler changes is to create one or two centers of excellence within a business, central hubs of insight and responsibility for typically core strategic goals for a marketing department and broader business. This can ensure the sharing of expertise and data in the right way and at the right time. These centers of excellence should go broader than the core marketing department and should have roots in every area of the business, but most obviously in the areas with customer touchpoints (customer service, communications, IT, sales, and the like).

Center 1: Customer Insights for Relevance and Agility

The Customer Insights and Relevance team will be responsible for understanding the customer better, and is most similar to the Marketing Operations team discussed in Chapter 6, "How an Evolved Internal Structure Drives Authentic, Relevant, and Transparent Marketing." This team will use the data gathered across the business and turn it into insights that help make teams more relevant to customers and more agile in their operations.

The team will have several priorities. On a more operational side, these will include building the IT and data management infrastructure within a business, creating marketing automation platforms, and collecting and synthesizing data from multiple sources within the business (customer service, supply chain, CRM, sales forecasting, and so on). The team also will be responsible for pulling together findings from across the company on what marketing and campaigns have worked across what is often a globalized, fragmented business. The team will ensure that other departments and locations get the benefits of success from their peers elsewhere in the business.

On a more strategic side, this team's role will be to feed back into other departments with insights gleaned from the multiple datasets they're responsible for. All marketers have a role to play in representing the voice of the customer, but this team will have that responsibility as an overwhelming priority.

Center 2: Internal and External Brand Building for Authenticity and Consistency

The second center of excellence that companies should build into their business will focus on how authenticity and consistency of message can be encouraged—both externally and internally.

Internal Brand Building

Several CMOs have advocated bringing the internal communications department closer to the rest of the marketing department within a company, to reflect the criticality of delivering an authentic, consistent brand voice at a time when every employee is potentially a brand ambassador.

Of course, a strong internal communications function not only helps with buy-in for the brand story, but also supports the multitude of other changes that the shifting marketing landscape will precipitate.

As we've seen, strong support from the C-suite is critical for the success of any large-scale change in a business. It's a characteristic of the Molson Coors "Our Brew" success and the KidZania "B KidZanian" loyalty scheme.

Equally, when evolution necessitates changing roles, people will naturally be fearful. As we've seen, the eradication of corporate silos and "little kingdoms" is essential to deliver an agile and relevant customer experience. And executives tend to be rather skeptical about the eradication of their power bases.

Therefore, as the customer experience leaders in a business, the marketing department must do an exceptional job of explaining the reasons for and benefits of any proposed shift—both upward into the board, and downward across an entire employee base.

Finally, people are more likely to eat a cake when they know what went into it, regardless of the frosting and decoration on one that turns up ready-made. That somewhat tortured metaphor alludes to the fact that if a company involves broad employee groups from the ground up in defining new structures, responsibilities, and activities, the employees are more likely to go along with it than if they have something dropped on them from the C-suite.

External Brand Building

Content and creative are beginning to be brought back in-house, and out of the remit of agencies, as companies attempt to become more agile and responsive to their customers, and attempt to ensure any brand message is authentically "of the brand" (which is of course more difficult when the brand doesn't write it, but the agency does).

As the same time, content as a marketing strategy is becoming almost omnipresent—with 93% of marketers expecting to make more content in 2015 than in 2014.

This explosion of content—often located on different channels, in different formats—means that there's more capacity for fragmentation of message and brand. That fragmentation will only be exacerbated by the fact that the customer themselves will also have a role to play in building and disseminating that content.

If a company wants a strong brand and strong creative material, it's essential for *one* group to have oversight on all of this, to guide the conversation, shoot the video, and write the story. A strong External Brand Building Team is thus recommended.

Finally, remember that the internal and external brand work is done by two parts of the same team. These are not distinct units. Why? Because it's essential for the internal and external story to match; otherwise, authenticity suffers.

3: New Skill Sets for a New World

As companies come to terms with a flood of data, a need to provide relevance, and a need to do so quickly, several new skill sets are called for, in addition to the new organizational models proposed above. Many CMOs have highlighted the need for companies to hire or develop the following skill sets and roles within their departments:

Creative and Content Leader

Although this book doesn't cover the development to a great extent, it's nevertheless the case that the relationship between brands and agencies is undergoing a fundamental shift.

Companies need to act far more quickly, and thus the inevitable process of engagement with an agency can begin to look onerous. In addition, as companies prioritize transparency and authenticity amid the decline of traditional marketing channels, three things become apparent:

1. It's no longer sensible for agencies to take some of the burden of conversation off brands. In-house employees must conduct social media conversation and outreach if a company is serious about authenticity.

2. As traditional channels decline—or at least jostle for attention with a plethora of new channels and platforms—the creative material and content that was previously successful has had to change meaningfully. Thirty-second ad spots are being replaced by 6-second Vine videos, or are augmented with social campaigns (note that half of the 56 TV ads during the 2015 Super Bowl featured a CTA to Twitter, and even Snapchat was called out by name[3]). Increasingly, the marketing space is too extensive and fragmented for the single "agency of record" model to hold, while having a cluster of agencies working on different platforms is counterproductive when consistency is key. Thus, brands are increasingly bringing the creative function in-house.

3. As channels fragment, agencies have been sluggish in developing deep knowledge of these new platforms and channels (and who can blame them, given the speed with which they spring up?).

Thus, responsibility for creative and content creation will begin to flow back in-house and toward executives within the marketing and customer experience department. At the moment, given the typical marketing role, these skills are not a top priority. This will change.

Data Analyst

Perhaps most unsurprisingly of all, the influx of data into a company will need to be managed. Although data analysis departments currently exist in many major companies, they tend to have a broad role across all elements of a business' operations. As part of the insight center of excellence advocated above, data analysts will be needed. These executives will have a responsibility to gather and analyze a plethora of data sources in an attempt to know more about both their customer and the success of their operations—and they will need to do so quickly.

Data Translator

Depending on the abilities of a data analyst, a translator may or may not be needed. Bringing data analysis within the marketing department will already begin to offset the issue of data teams not understanding the drivers of marketing and the insight those market-ers need. But in many cases, a data analyst will be more comfortable with analysis and less comfortable translating that analysis into some-thing meaningful and actionable for marketing teams.

Given the importance of strong internal buy-in, a position devoted to turning data analysis into usable insight (and engaging relevant individuals and departments on the importance of that insight) will be useful.

IT Specialist

It's a commonly repeated stat, but Gartner predicts that market-ing departments will spend more on IT than the IT department itself by 2017.[4]

That's a reflection of two facts:

1. Only with strong structures can a flood of data be turned into a river of insights.
2. Personalized, relevant experience for the customer, delivered over digital channels, will be a core differentiator.

As such, having an IT specialist on the ground as part of a broader marketing team isn't only desirable—it's expected.

4: The Walls between Employees and Customers Come Down

As we've seen, employee buy-in not only makes internal change easier to facilitate, but it makes for more authentic marketing.

More Authentic Marketing

According to Dan Lewis, Chief Public Affairs Officer at Molson Coors in the case study on "Our Brew" in Chapter 5, "Your people give you an authenticity and an outreach and a connectivity, and open the doors to communities that you might never reach if you followed traditional marketing and brand management paths."

Customers are wary about being marketed to by large monolithic brands. They're searching for a human approach and authenticity. Your employees are uniquely placed to deliver that. Acknowledged experts on beer, or car manufacturing, or clothing design would deliver far more relevant, engaging, and authentic content on those topics than the best agency in the world.

Giving your employees the autonomy to play this role (with certain caveats, policed by the brand center of excellence to mitigate reputational risk and preserve brand consistency) will help you make a meaningful shift toward more relevant, valuable, and engaging content.

Higher-Performing Employees

"A growing body of research shows that end users—customers, clients, patients, and others who benefit from a company's products and services—are surprisingly effective in motivating people to work harder, smarter, and more productively."[5]

Research conducted by Adam M. Grant (detailed in the *Harvard Business Review* article "How Customers Can Rally Your Troops") shows that when a company removes the barriers between customers and employees, that increased exposure has a positive effect on those employees. In one example, a group of telephone fundraisers was given a presentation by a student who had benefited from the group's fundraising efforts. A month after the visit, the fundraisers increased their time on the phone by 142% and raised 171% more money.

In another example, at a restaurant, when cooks and customers were able to both see each other as food was being prepared and consumed, satisfaction increased by 17.3% and service was 13.2% faster.

Companies that are able to mimic the restaurant's actions and remove barriers between customers and employees should benefit in the same way. Look to Best Buy's "twelpforce," a system launched in 2009 in which any employee at the company can sign on to Twitter and respond to customer queries. In the first six months of the service, more than 2,000 employees signed up to use the program.[6] Best Buy saw a 20% drop in customer complaints online in the first year of the service's launch.[7]

Getting employees closer to customers tends to increase satisfaction and performance. In part, this is because those employees can see firsthand what customer pain points and needs are and can work to resolve them personally instead of being told what to do by a manager they might or might not trust.

"Employees generally see end users as more credible than leaders as sources of inspiration. When leaders attempt to deliver inspiring messages, many employees react with skepticism, questioning whether leaders are just trying to get them to work harder. ... End users, however, can deliver convincing testimonials of their experiences with the company's products and services, showing that leaders' messages are more than rhetoric."[8]

Final Conclusions

There has been considerable upheaval in the world of marketing (indeed, in the world of human interaction) over the last decade. The rise of digital communications technologies has given customers a power to both understand and communicate with each other and with large brands far more extensively than ever before.

The best companies have leveraged the potential of these new channels and technologies to build new products and exceptional customer experiences, making their competitors seem like laggards in the eyes of a newly empowered customer base.

A plethora of other influences and developments have led to a point at which marketing, as a department and a concept, is changing fundamentally. Customer interaction that demands authenticity, relevance, and transparency necessitates a different internal organization, a different external outreach approach, and a different corporate strategy. In this new environment, marketers find themselves in an unfamiliar but exciting role. As the proxy for the customer within a business (and at a time when that customer is more powerful than ever), marketers themselves have more power. And with great power, as wise old Uncle Ben in the *Spiderman* films said, comes great responsibility—a responsibility to deliver to that demanding customer an exceptional experience in every interaction they have with the brand.

That means marketers must have ownership of (or at least oversight of) the customer journey in its entirety. They must play a role in building and developing products and in orchestrating customer service approaches, they must accept more of a collaborative approach to brand building, and they must increasingly take on the creative, content-based burden that was previously the domain of major agencies. And they must do all this quickly, in a turbulent landscape where customers stampede from one platform and channel to another at an unprecedented pace.

It's a challenging but exciting time. Marketers have more power, more responsibility, a broader role, and far more potential than ever before.

Endnotes

1. Marc de Swaan Arons, Frank van den Driest, and Keith Weed, "The Ultimate Marketing Machine," *Harvard Business Review* (July 2014): https://hbr.org/2014/07/the-ultimate-marketing-machine.

2. Egon Zehender, "The Dialogues: Wynton Marsalis and Indra K Nooyi." www.egonzehnder.com/marsalis_nooyi.

3. Martin Beck, "Super Bowl Commercials with Hashtags Slipped to 50% in 2015," Marketing Land (1 February 2015). http://marketingland.com/super-bowl-commercials-hashtags-slips-50-2015-116658.

4. www.forbes.com/sites/lisaarthur/2012/02/08/five-years-from-now-cmos-will-spend-more-on-it-than-cios-do/

5. Adam M. Grant, "How Customers Can Rally Your Troops," *Harvard Business Review* (June 2011): 96–103.

6. Pete Blackshaw, "What Best Buy Learned about Service As Marketing and Empowering Employees," *Ad Age* (24 November 2009). http://adage.com/article/digital-columns/digital-marketing-buy-s-customer-service-twelpforce/140708/.

7. Corey Padveen, "Social Media Case Study: Best Buy," T2 Marketing (2 May 2013). http://t2marketinginternational.com/social-media-case-study-best-buy/.

8. Adam M. Grant, "How Customers Can Rally Your Troops."

Index

Numbers

4 P's of marketing, 11-12

A

accountability, impact of data on, 31-32
Aflac example (benefits of data management), 155
agility
    benefits of, 156-157
    centers of excellence, 236-239
    in future of marketing, 48, 234-236
    within organizational structure, 127-130
Amazon, 31
art
    in brand storytelling, 94
    science versus, 30-31
        data insights into problems, 142-143
        data natives, 141-142
        opportunity provided by data, 140-141
        privacy issues, 158-161
        scale of shift to data, 139-140
ART (Authenticity, Relevance, Transparency), 40-41. *See also* authenticity, relevance, transparency
    in conversation, 207
    expanded role of marketers, 62

in future of marketing, 46-48, 231-232
    interlinkage in, 41-42
    internal buy-in and, importance of, 95-96
    storytelling in, 89-93
audience. *See* customers
authenticity
    appealing to customer interests, 214-215
    in conversation, 207, 210-211
    expanded role of marketers, 62
    explained, 42-44, 46-47, 231
    in future of marketing, 241-242
    humanizing the brand, 220-225
    Molson Coors case study (internal buy-in), 114-116
    transparency and, 43
Axel Springer, 101-102

B

B2B companies
    HubSpot example (useful content), 201-202
    personalization, 148
B2C companies, personalization, 148
backstory, brand as, 34
banner ads, history of, 15
Best Buy, 242

brand
  consistent messaging, 77-80
  as conversation, 32-37
    appeal to customer interests,
      214-215
    authenticity in, 210-211
    cocktail party metaphor,
      208-209
    consistent messaging, 216
    importance of, 207-208
    joining pre-existing
      conversations, 219-220
    "latently happy" customers, 217
    listening, 215-216
    as mandatory, 211-213
    organizational structure for,
      213-214
    potential of social media,
      217-219
    silo breakdown, 216-217
  corporate citizenship and, 88-89
  customer experience and, 87-88
  external brand building, 238-239
  humanizing, 220-225
  internal buy-in. *See* internal buy-in
  storytelling in
    art of, 94
    importance of, 89-93
    tips for marketing campaigns,
      93-94
@BrandsSayingBae Twitter account,
  224-225
Burwell, Victoria, 5
  brand as conversation, 35, 37
  channel fragmentation, 29
  collaboration between marketing
    and IT departments, 130
  conversation, 207, 211
  listening, 215
  personalization, 147, 152
  silo breakdown, 216

C

case studies
  Hiscox (multichannel strategy),
    192-196
  KidZania (customer engagement),
    170-179
  Land O'Lakes (data management),
    180
  Molson Coors (internal buy-in),
    104-117
  One Medical Group (social
    listening), 164-169
  Randstad (silo breakdown), 134-
    137
centers of excellence in future of
  marketing, 236-239
channels
  consistent messaging across, 77-80
  fragmentation, 21-29, 70-72, 74-80
  multichannel strategy
    appropriate use of social media,
      187-188
    balancing with traditional
      channels, 188-190
    challenge of, 185-186
    as foundational strategy, 190
    Hiscox case study, 192-196
    importance of, 183-185
    metrics for, 186-187
  speed of change, 39-41, 79-80
CMO (chief marketing officer) in
  organizational structure, 120-122,
  235-236
cocktail party metaphor for
  conversation, 208-209
collaboration within organizations,
  63-68
Collins, Dominic, 5
  data natives,
  impact of data, 30
  listening, 215
  organizational structure, 125, 213

competition
  as data natives, 141-142
  increase from smaller companies,
    18-21
consistent messaging, 77-80, 96-99,
  133, 216
consumers. *See* customers
content development, 127, 239-240
content marketing
  challenge of, 199
  defined, 197
  dissemination platforms, 203-204
  in future of marketing, 238-239
  importance of, 197-199
  metrics for, 204-205
  quality of, 200
  relevance in, 201
    entertaining content, 202-203
    useful content, 201-202
conversation
  authenticity in, 210-211
  brand as, 32-37
  cocktail party metaphor, 208-209
  customer expectations of, 69-70
  in future of marketing, 234
  humanizing the brand, 220-225
  importance of, 207-208
  Land O'Lakes case study (data
    management), 180
  as mandatory, 211-213
  organizational structure for,
    213-214
  tips for success
    appeal to customer interests,
      214-215
    consistent messaging, 216
    joining pre-existing
      conversations, 219-220
    "latently happy" customers, 217
    listening, 215-216
    potential of social media,
      217-219
    silo breakdown, 216-217

Cornelis, Frans, 6
  balancing traditional and
    multichannel strategies, 189
  consistent messaging, 133
  data insights into problems,
    142-143
  impact of data, 30
  Randstad case study (silo
    breakdown), 134-137
  silo breakdown, 130
  transparency and consistent
    messaging, 98
corporate citizenship, brand and,
  88-89
corporate goals, aligning with,
  145-146, 235
Court, David
  agility, 156
  CMO (chief marketing officer)
    role, 120
  customer journey, 53-54
Crayola, KidZania partnership with,
  177-178
creativity. *See* art
"creepiness factor" of
  personalization, 160-161
current state of marketing, 61,
  82-83
  channel fragmentation, 74-80
  collaboration in, 63-68
  customer expectations and
    organizational structure, 62-68
  data insights, 80-82
  expanded role of marketers, 62
  speed of change, 68-74
customer analytics, 126
customer data. *See* data
customer expectations
  of conversation, 69-70
  effect on organizational
    structure, 62-68

customer experience
brand and, 87-88
in future of marketing, 47-48,
233-236
KidZania case study, 170-179
organizational structure and,
120-122
in social media conversations,
212-213
customer journey
consistent messaging in, 96-97
expanded organizational roles in,
56
funnel metaphor versus, 53-55
customer-centric organizational
models, 62-68
customers
appealing to interests, 214-215
brand conversations by, 211-213
"latently happy" customers, 217
listening to, 215-216
personalization
by data natives, 141-142
gaining relevance from,
150-153
shift to, 147-149
power of, 12-14
ART, 41-48
brand as conversation, 32-37
channel fragmentation, 21-29
fundamentals of marketing,
37-40
impact of data, 29-32
increased competition, 18-21
online marketing and social
media, 15-17
removing employee barriers to,
242-243

D

data
collaboration in organizational
structure, 128-130
impact of, 29-32
insight from
current state of marketing,
80-82
in future of marketing, 48, 234
problem realization, 142-143
opportunity provided by, 140-141
scale of shift to, 139-140
silo breakdown, 130-133
consistent messaging, 133
gaining relevance, 131-132
internal data sharing, 132
Randstad case study, 134-137
speed of change, 72-73
translator, 144, 240
data management, 143-146
benefits of, 147-157
Aflac example, 155
agility, 156-157
increased relevance, 150-153
Keds example, 155-156
L'Oreal example, 154
Molson Coors example, 154-155
shift to personalization,
147-149
University of Phoenix example,
153, 189
goal alignment with corporate
goals, 145-146
KidZania case study, 174
Land O'Lakes case study, 180
organizational structure for,
144-145
privacy issues, 158-161
signal in the noise, finding, 146
skills needed for, 144-146, 240-241

data natives, 141-142

digital technologies, channel fragmentation, 20-29. *See also* Internet; social media

dissemination platforms for content marketing, 203-204

Dominiquini, Jennifer, 187

Dove, 91-92

Dunaway, Cammie, 6
  4 P's of marketing, 12
  brand and corporate citizenship, 88-89
  building from ground up, 100
  conversation as mandatory, 212
  Internet's role in transparency, 16
  KidZania case study (customer engagement), 170-179
  multichannel strategy, 183
  product development, 213, 232
  transparency, 45

E

earned channels, 76-77

employee immersion in project for internal buy-in, 101-102

employee involvement. *See* internal buy-in

employee motivation in future of marketing, 242-243

"Encourage Courage" in Hiscox case study (multichannel strategy), 192-196

entertaining content, 202-203

expanding marketing department, 124

experience. *See* customer experience

external brand building in future of marketing, 238-239

F

Findlay, Russ, 6
  art versus science of marketing, 139
  brand as conversation, 35
  data management skills, 144, 145
  Hiscox case study (multichannel strategy), 192-196
  multichannel strategy, 185
  opportunity provided by data, 141
  over-reliance on data, 157

flexibility in content marketing, 203-204

focus groups, social media versus, 151-152

4 P's of marketing, 11-12

fragmentation of channels, 21-29, 70-72, 74-80. *See also* multichannel strategy

fundamentals of marketing, stability of, 37-40

funnel metaphor, customer journey versus, 53-55

future of marketing, 233
  ART (Authenticity, Relevance, Transparency) in, 46-48, 231-232
  authenticity, 241-242
  centers of excellence, 236-239
  customer experience department, 233-236
  employee motivation, 242-243
  responsibilities in, 47-48
  skills needed for, 239-241

Future of Marketing Survey, accessing full results, 5

G

Gibson, Andy, 6
  appeal to customer interests, 215, 220
  authenticity, 42-43
  brand as conversation, 34

consistent messaging, 97
joining pre-existing conversations, 220
storytelling, 91
global financial crisis, effect on brand awareness, 34-35
goals, aligning with corporate goals, 145-146, 235
Gupta, Shankar, 225

H

Hiscox case study (multichannel strategy), 192-196
history
of online marketing, 15-16
of social media, 17
of YouTube, 26
HubSpot, 201-202
humanizing the brand, 221-225
Hunter, Mark, 114

I

individual benefits for internal buy-in, 100-101
insight (from data)
current state of marketing, 80-82
in future of marketing, 48, 234
problem realization, 142-143
internal buy-in. *See also* organizational structure
consistent messaging, 96-99
in future of marketing, 237-238
Hiscox case study, 194
importance of, 95-96
Molson Coors case study, 104-117
steps for achieving, 99-103
build from ground up, 100
employee immersion in project, 101-102
individual benefits, 100-101
long-term focus, 103
internal data sharing, 132

Internet
history in marketing, 15-16
increased competition, 18-21
role in transparency, 16
IT department
collaboration with marketing, 125-126, 128-130
in future of marketing, 241

J

Jobs, Steve, 135, 157

K

Keds example (benefits of data management), 155-156
Kennedy, John, 6
appropriate use of social media, 187
content marketing, 197
personalization, 147, 152
KidZania case study (customer engagement), 170-179

L

Land O'Lakes case study (data management), 180
Larreche, Jean-Claude, 6
customer understanding, 150
market research, 157
"latently happy" customers, 217
The Lean Startup (Ries), 146
Lee, Mei, 156
Lee, Tom X., 167
Lewis, Dan, 6
authenticity, 43, 241
benefits of data management, 154-155
brand as conversation, 33
challenge of multichannel strategy, 185
focus groups versus social media, 151

Molson Coors case study (internal buy-in), 104-117
multichannel strategy as foundational strategy, 190
storytelling, 92, 94
lifecycle metaphor, 55
Linder, Chris, 6
benefits of data management, 155-156
data management skills, 144
data natives, 141
Lintonsmith, Susan, 136
listening
importance of, 73-74, 215-216
Molson Coors case study, 107
One Medical Group case study, 164-169
live broadcasts
of sporting events, 23
Twitter usage during, 25
localized social listening, 165-166
long-term focus for internal buy-in, 103
L'Oreal example (benefits of data management), 154
loyalty programs, KidZania case study, 170-179

M

Marketing2020 study, 62
marketing department. *See also* organizational structure
CMO (chief marketing officer) role evolution, 120-122
collaboration with IT, 125-126, 128-130
data management in, 144-145
expanding, 124
future of, 233
ART in, 46-48, 231-232
centers of excellence, 236-239
customer experience department, 233-236
employee motivation, 242-243
responsibilities in, 47-48
skills needed for, 239-242
restructuring, 65, 122-123
roles in, 126-127
splitting, 124-126
"Marketing's Age of Relevance" (McKinsey on Marketing and Sales), 53
Marsh, Sarah, 170-179
McDonalds example (humanizing the brand), 223-224
McKinsey on Marketing and Sales, 53
media fragmentation. *See* fragmentation of channels
metrics
for content marketing, 204-205
in Hiscox case study (multichannel strategy), 195-196
in KidZania case study (customer engagement), 178-179
for multichannel strategy, 186-187
Meyer, Marissa, 135
Modoc Oil Test example, 13
Molson Coors
benefits of data management, 154-155
internal buy-in, 104-117
Mota, Bethany, 26
multichannel strategy
appropriate use of social media, 187-188
balancing with traditional channels, 188-190
challenge of, 185-186
as foundational strategy, 190
Hiscox case study, 192-196
importance of, 183-185
metrics for, 186-187

N

Nath, Pravin, 121-122
"noise," increase of, 28

O

One Medical Group case study
  (social listening), 164-169
onion metaphor for consistent
  messaging, 98-99
online marketing, history of, 15-16
organizational structure. *See
  also* internal buy-in; marketing
  department
    agility within, 127-130
    CMO (chief marketing officer)
      role in, 120-122, 235-236
    for data management, 144-145
    effect of customer expectations
      on, 62-68
    expanded marketing
      department, 124
    KidZania case study, 174
    restructured marketing
      department, 122-123
    roles within marketing
      department, 126-127
    silo breakdown, 130-133
      consistent messaging, 133
      gaining relevance, 131-132
      internal data sharing, 132
      Randstad case study, 134-137
    for social media conversations,
      213-214
    split marketing department,
      124-126
Our Brew (Molson Coors case
  study), 104-117
owned channels, 76-77

P

pace of change. *See* speed of change
paid channels, 76-77
Pansino, Rosana, 26
personalization
  "creepiness factor," 160-161
  by data natives, 141-142
  gaining relevance from, 150-153
  KidZania case study, 176-178
  shift to, 147-149
Phan, Michelle, 26
Pietzsch, Cavin, 7
podcasts, 23
power of customers, 12-14
  ART (Authenticity, Relevance,
    Transparency), 41-48
  brand as conversation, 32-37
  channel fragmentation, 21-29
  fundamentals of marketing, 37-40
  impact of data, 29-32
  increased competition, 18-21
  online marketing and social
    media, 15-17
print media, decline of, 22
privacy issues, 158-161
problems, revealing via data,
  142-143
product development in future of
  marketing, 235
product marketing support, 126
programmatic advertising, 16
proximity of team members,
  serendipity and, 135-136

Q

quality of content marketing, 200

R

radio, online listening, 23
Randstad case study (silo
  breakdown), 134-137

real-time marketing, 70

relevance. *See also* ART

among increased competition, 18-21

in content marketing, 201

entertaining content, 202-203

useful content, 201-202

in conversation, 207

expanded role of marketers, 62

explained, 44, 47, 232

gaining from data, 131-132, 150-153

research for book, 4-5

responsibilities in future of marketing, 47-48

restructuring marketing department, 122-123

Ries, Eric, 146, 204

Ryan, Marco, 7

dissemination platforms for content marketing, 203

employee immersion in project, 102

onion metaphor for consistent messaging, 98-99

S

Sainsbury's example (humanizing the brand), 222-223

science versus art, 30-31

data insights into problems, 142-143

data natives, 141-142

opportunity provided by data, 140-141

privacy issues, 158-161

scale of shift to data, 139-140

"second screen," increased usage of, 25

segmentation, shift to, 147-149

serendipity, proximity of team members and, 135-136

signal in the noise, finding, 146

silo breakdown, 130-133

consistent messaging, 133

conversational marketing, 216-217

gaining relevance, 131-132

internal data sharing, 132

One Medical Group case study, 166-167

Randstad case study, 134-137

Silver, Nate, 146

small companies, increased competition from, 18-21

social listening, One Medical Group case study, 164-169

social media. *See also* multichannel strategy

appropriate use of, 187-188

conversation via

appeal to customer interests, 214-215

authenticity in, 210-211

brand as, 32-37

cocktail party metaphor, 208-209

consistent messaging, 216

customer expectations of, 69-70

importance of, 207-208

joining pre-existing conversations, 219-220

"latently happy" customers, 217

listening, 215-216

as mandatory, 211-213

organizational structure for, 213-214

potential of social media, 217-219

silo breakdown, 216-217

focus groups versus, 151-152

Hiscox case study, 194-195

history of, 17

humanizing the brand, 220-225

increased competition, 18-21

marketing department roles
in, 127
in organizational structure, 122
speed of change, 70-72
speed of change
in channels, 39-41, 79-80
in marketing, 68-74
in social media, 70-72
Speichert, Marc
collaboration between marketing
and IT departments, 129
customer journey, 55
increased competition, 18
splitting marketing department,
124-126
sporting events, live broadcasts of,
23
storytelling
art of, 94
in future of marketing, 234
importance of, 89-93
tips for marketing campaigns,
93-94
Super Bowl advertising costs, 23
surveys. *See* Future of Marketing
Survey
Swinburn, Peter, 114

T

team involvement. *See* internal
buy-in
television, online viewing, 21-22
traditional channels, balancing with
multichannel strategy, 188-190
transparency. *See also* ART
authenticity and, 43
consistent messaging and, 98
in conversation, 207
expanded role of marketers, 62
explained, 45, 47, 232
Internet's role in, 16
TV, online viewing, 21-22

"twelpforce" (Best Buy), 242
Twitter, usage during live
broadcasts, 25

U

University of Phoenix example
(benefits of data management),
153, 189
useful content, 201-202

V

vanity metrics, 204
Volvo, 202-203

W

West, Jason, 7
brand as conversation, 36
brand positioning statements, 88
fundamentals of marketing, 39
Wolfish, Barry, 7
4 P's of marketing, 11
agility, 127
brand as conversation, 36
channel fragmentation, 28
data management, 143
Land O'Lakes case study (data
management), 180
merging marketing and IT, 125
organizational structure, 119, 122
personalization, 149
scale of shift to data, 140

Y

Yerganian, Arra, 7
balancing traditional and
multichannel strategies, 189
benefits of data management, 153,
189
brand as conversation, 36

individual benefits for internal
   buy-in, 101
internal buy-in, 99
"latently happy" customers, 217
One Medical Group case study
   (social listening), 164-169
YouTube, history of, 26

Z

Zak, Paul, 90
Zuckerberg, Mark, 158
Zuna, Michael, 7
   benefits of data management, 155
   data management and
      organizational structure, 145
   data natives, 142
   "noise," increase of, 28
   personalization, 152
   scale of shift to data, 140
   simple solutions, 146

Acknowledgments

I am grateful to everyone who has ever picked up the phone to answer my questions. This book is the product of your insights and your experiences. I would like to include a special note of thanks to Bill Tolany, who has been picking up that phone for more than five years and is a constant source of advice and insight.

I owe a major debt of thanks to all those who agreed to be interviewed for the book—Andy Gibson, Cavin Pietzsch, Chris Lindner, Dominic Collins, Frans Cornelis, Jason West, Jean-Claude Larreche, John Dragoon, John Kennedy, Marco Ryan, Michael Zuna, and Victoria Burwell. I owe an even more significant debt to Cammie Dunaway, Dan Lewis, Sarah Marsh, Frans Cornelis, Russell Findlay, Arra Yerganian, and Barry Wolfish, who took additional time to help me build case studies around their companies.

I am also very grateful to Charlotte Maiorana, Lori Lyons, Krista Hansing, Nonie Ratcliff, and the team at Pearson. Thanks for guiding a novice like me through this—you made the process painless, and the book a lot better.

I would not have been in a position to write this book without the support and guidance of those at FCBI—in particular, Piers Latimer, Sara Baylis, Mike Setters, Simon Carkeek, Mary Ambler, and Guy Grant. And to the team at the Incite Group—thank you for your drive and your enthusiasm. Your talent and ability has helped build a special company, and has given me the chance to write this book. For that I'm enormously grateful.

Chris Duff, Ruth Pal, Dom Foulkes, Chris Kerrigan—your own terrifyingly impressive achievements in work and life have driven me on to at least be able to say I've written a book. Thank you for being there (even when "there" does mean a Skype chat from across the Atlantic) and for being awesome. New friends in America and old ones in the UK—you're all ace. I'm lucky to have you.

Steve, Frank, and Mary—each of you inspire me. You are my favorite siblings. Mum—I think you would be *anyone's* favourite mum. Without you I would not be here (in both the literal and metaphorical sense). And though Dad is no longer with us, I am still reminded of and guided by him every day.

Finally, and most importantly, to Sabrina, who—through a combination of encouragement, grit, wisdom, humor, love, and Callie—has not only made this book happen, but made me incredibly happy.